PROSPECT PRESS
PORT-OF-SPAIN

Ian Randle Publishers
KINGSTON

First published in Jamaica 2002 by
Ian Randle Publishers Ltd.
11 Cunningham Avenue
Box 686
Kingston 6

ISBN 976-637-050-8 (paperback)
ISBN 976-637-059-1 (hardback)

First published in Trinidad andTobago 2002
by Prospect Press
6 Prospect Avenue
Maraval
Port of Spain

ISBN 976-95057-1-4 (paperback)
ISBN 976-95057-2-2 (hardback)

A catalogue record of this book is available from the National Library of Jamaica

Cover and book design by Illya Furlonge-Walker,
Form and Function, Trinidad and Tobago

Printed in the United States of America

Dedicated to
the loving memory of my dearest Mum, Ivy,
and my sister Grace,
and to my colleague and close friend Ivan Harnanan

CONTENTS

Eric Williams and his father, Henry Williams

PREFACE AND ACKNOWLEDGEMENTS

This book is about the intriguing figure of Trinidad and Tobago's first Prime Minister, Eric Eustace Williams. The first-born in a family of twelve children, he was brought up by stern and demanding parents, and himself, many years later, became a stern and demanding leader. The enigma that he was made him sometimes brutal with his colleagues, yet quite at home playfully balancing a child on his knees. He could be callous in his ability to discard those who at one time or another served him, yet he was caring and generous to his few close friends and to others who sought assistance from him.

It is a book about an individual who almost single-handedly shaped Trinidad and Tobago's society for nearly 25 years but who, toward the end of his rule, was largely out of touch and somewhat isolated from it. It is about an individual who was among the most feared, and the most loved.

The genesis of this book is a series of interviews conducted in Trinidad, in collaboration with the Eric Williams Memorial Collection, to develop an oral history of Trinidad and Tobago's foremost leader. Eventually, five trips to Trinidad were made during 1997 and 1998, funded primarily by my university, Florida International. The result was 60–70 taped interviews, each two to three hours long, with almost everyone who worked or otherwise interacted with Williams. The audio tapes and interview transcripts are on deposit with the Memorial Collection. For the few who were not interviewed, previous videotaped interviews filled in many of the gaps. The dramatic nature of the data, and of the recollections and reminiscences obtained, led to this project.

In another sense, the seeds of this project were planted some 40 years ago, when as a mere teenager the author, like many others in the society at that time, was captivated by the hasty arrival on the political scene of Eric Williams and his People's National Movement (PNM). He can still remember how Roy Joseph, who dominated his home town of San Fernando, and the mighty figure of Albert Gomes, went down to a crushing defeat before the steamrolling PNM in the 1956 general election. The author's first book, *Eric Williams: The Man and the Leader* (1985), was motivated by a fascination with the compelling personality of Eric Williams. The interviews conducted in 1997 and 1998 simply intensified this interest, culminating in the present text.

The book is divided into three sections. The first (chapters 1–7) traces Williams's path from childhood to national leadership. The emphasis here is on the forces that shaped the man, including childhood and family concerns, education at home and abroad, and the years he spent in the United States. The second section (chapters 8–12), in a series of snapshots, shows how the forces that shaped the man were played out in his behaviour as an adult, especially with regard to his attitude to political power, his personal relationships with his wives and children, and his chequered relationship with one of his mentors, C. L. R. James. In the final section (chapters 13–16), the text returns to the final decade of Williams's life, when he was confronted with serious challenges such as the "Black Power" movement and the pressures of isolation, declining health and the indifference of many around him. This, of course, culminated in his tragic death and the resulting controversies.

After a draft of the manuscript was completed, limited access was obtained to study documents in the recently-opened Eric Williams Memorial Collection at the University of the West Indies in Trinidad. However, research was seriously restricted because a bibliography of catalogued items was not yet publicly available. But because Williams preserved so much of his correspondence and documents, some almost 70 years old, the available material nevertheless provided a wealth of information. When fully operational, this Collection will provide enormous data on, and insights into, the Williams years and the history of Trinidad and Tobago.

The primary objective of this book is to unmask the man behind the dark suit, the dark glasses and the hearing aid. It attempts to understand and to explain the forces which shaped Williams's personality: his home, his family, and the environment in which he was nurtured. It explains his thirst for knowledge, and how he sought to instil that thirst in the hearts of his countrymen. For Williams truly believed that education was the instrument of liberation. For many years he sought valiantly to convey this to his people, even though, in the final analysis, he was only partially successful.

For Williams, education promoted liberation of the mind. Consequently, it provided the impetus to transcend the forces of social oppression, especially those promoted by class and colour. In his autobiography he insisted that his father had suffered from a lack of "social qualifications: colour, money and education." Williams believed that he too was the object of this discrimination. He was determined that his countrymen would not suffer as his father, and later he himself, did.

The book places Williams in the context of the colony in which he was born. In 1911, the year of his birth, the British controlled Trinidad. Williams believed that this control impacted on him directly, since both the elementary and secondary schools that he attended were directed by Englishmen. This contributed much, both negatively and positively, to shaping his perspective of the colonizer. It was only shortly before Williams left for university study in England in 1932 that Arthur Cipriani began the campaign for popular participation in the nascent political system. Williams's political consciousness, therefore, was barely developed before he left for England.

When Williams returned to Trinidad permanently in 1948, adult suffrage had just been granted and the colony had begun its final struggle toward self-government and independence. Williams studied, then participated in, and finally led the movement for independence. But a little over a decade later, the social context was so dramatically altered that Williams himself seemed unable to understand the forces reshaping the society, especially their impact on young people. These were the heady days of the "Black Power" movement.

In the final decade of his life, Williams could not accept the transformation in social values that had been unleashed, largely by the oil boom, and had affected his party members as much as anyone else. This, together with his declining health and growing disillusionment, caused him to gradually withdraw, into his home, and ultimately into himself. At the time of his death he was somewhat out of touch with the pulse of a society that he himself had worked for so long to create, surrounded as he was by a group of self-serving assistants and very few who genuinely cared for him.

The wider public saw very little of this. What the public saw was someone whom they believed to be the maximum leader until the end. Someone who stood head and shoulders above everyone; who was gruff, imperious and demanding. For Williams's private life remained shrouded in mystery, and was viewed with a kind of awe. Very few were admitted into it. So that just as this book seeks to explain the forces that shaped Williams's personality and were played out in his life, it also seeks to explain the private Williams.

In uncovering the private Williams, what it finds is an individual who in his private relationships was generally warm, very friendly, hospitable, caring, and even loving. It finds an individual who expressed genuine affection and concern for those who were personally close to him. An individual who, though somewhat preoccupied with the state of his own finances, was willing to provide generous financial assistance to many who sought assistance from him. Indeed, in this context, some considered him a "soft touch". Such was the complex personality of this most complex individual. He was truly an enigma.

For a project of this magnitude, the list of those who contributed in a broad variety of ways is long and their help is very gratefully acknowledged. It includes quite a large number of people in Trinidad, and a smaller but equally important group in the United States.

Entitled to head the list in Trinidad is Patricia (Peggy) Gittens, niece of Eric Williams, who coordinated the five trips to Trinidad during which the interviews were conducted. Simply put, the tight scheduling of relatively large groups of people into concentrated time blocks could not have been accomplished without the meticulous skills of Ms Gittens. She was highly organized, prompt and efficient in a manner that would surely have made her uncle very proud. She accomplished all of this while maintaining her warmth and most pleasant demeanour under stressful conditions. Some of Peggy's relatives, sisters of Williams, in spite of poor health, willingly submitted themselves to lengthy and repeated interviews with amazing candour and courage. To them, especially, I owe a very large debt of gratitude.

Most of the interviews were conducted with close associates of Williams, including a President and a former President, members of Cabinet, other PNM representatives, party officials, Williams's secretaries and family friends. Another small group included those few non-government officials who maintained individual relationships with Williams. Here Dr Halsey McShine stands out. He and Williams first met at elementary school; they both attended the same high school and later studied in England. McShine served as one of Williams's private doctors, and the two men remained friends for about 60 years. Interviews with him were most informative.

When Williams returned to Trinidad in 1948 he drew close to two families: the Dollys of Pointe-à-Pierre and later the Bests, originally of Fyzabad. Williams had first met Ray Dolly in elementary school. The daughters of these families, pre-teens when they first met Williams, looked upon him as a dear and loving uncle, and interacted with him closely as they grew older. Interviews with these daughters provided rare insights into the warm, caring and loving nature of Williams.

Repeated interviews with a small group of close and largely informal associates of Williams, all of whom knew him for over 20 years, were extremely important to an understanding of the essential Williams. This group included Diane Dupres, Carlton Gomes, Ferdie Ferriera, Nicholas Simonette and Ivan Williams. Dr Ibbit Mosaheb should also be included in this group: though now a resident of Canada, this founding member of Williams's party was interviewed twice in Trinidad. We also held numerous telephone conversations and exchanged correspondence. All these individuals were extremely generous with their time, and painstakingly explained, with much candour, their individual relationships with Williams.

Another group in Trinidad, centred at the University of the West Indies, St Augustine, also contributed to this project. I benefited from very lengthy discussions with Professors John La Guerre, Ramesh Ramsaran and Brinsley Samaroo. The staff of the West Indian Collection at the University Library, especially Kim Gransaul, were most diligent in helping me locate source material. The acting Director, Anselm Francis, and the secretarial staff at the Institute of International Relations provided important logistical support. Winston James, librarian at the Trinidad Guardian library, provided important details on the Williams story at very short notice.

Finally, there were close friends and relatives in Trinidad who provided practical and emotional support during the long weeks of interviewing. Among these were Victor and Anabelle Albert, Joanne Albert, Lessy Harnanan, Ramesh and Nadira Ramsaran, Brinsley and Joan Samaroo, Harold, Ruth and Roxanne Sitahal. To all, I wish to express my sincere gratitude.

In the United States, my university, Florida International, supported this project throughout. The College of Arts and Sciences provided several mini-grants that facilitated the transcription of the many interviews. The Latin American and Caribbean Center funded trips to Trinidad. My department, International Relations, provided the support of research assistants for the project, and the assistance of chair Damian Fernandez must be acknowledged. Dr Paul Kowert in my department guided me through the intricacies of political psychology and provided comments on Chapter 10. Taped interviews were transcribed by Yasmin Roman and Jingbin Wang. The manuscript was typed by Julie David, Nicole Rodriguez and Niala Boodhoo, with technical support from Karina Guardia and Jacqueline Kates. Editorial assistance was provided by Gigi Lehman, Carol Robertson and my daughter Kathy Young. I must also acknowledge a great debt to the very professional services provided by my publisher's editor Jeremy Taylor. His meticulous work contributed greatly to enhancing the quality of the text.

In Washington, I benefited from the assistance of Professor Linda Heywood, who introduced me to the archives at Howard University. Extensive interviews there were also conducted with Mr Leo Edwards, who befriended the Williams family in the 1940s.

Sections of the manuscript were read by Drs Ibbit Mosaheb, Simon Ramesar and Ramesh Ramsaran, and by Diane Dupres. While comments from these readers were most helpful, I, of course, remain responsible for the contents. Finally, I must express my gratitude to my wife and family for their support during this lengthy undertaking.

THE ELUSIVE
ERIC WILLIAMS

Thomas Henry Williams and Eliza Williams (née Boissière), Eric's parents

CHAPTER ONE
COLONIAL TRINIDAD
IN 1911

W hen Eric Eustace Williams was born in 1911, Trinidad and Tobago was struggling through the idiosyncrasies of the Crown Colony system of government. It was a system, says Gordon Lewis, "geared to getting things not done rather than done."[1] With its origins in Trinidad, the system was developed just a few years after Britain captured the island in 1797, and would continue for almost 150 years, until the advent of the Gomes government in 1950 (incidentally, Albert Gomes's birth, in March 1911, was a mere six months before Eric's).

Crown Colony government — that "quintessential expression of imperial domination"[2] — had at its core a colonial Governor with almost total power. The so-called Legislative Council consisted of officials and unofficials all nominated by the Governor. A small elected element was not included until 1925. While the officials were drawn from the primary officers in the local government, the unofficials were nominated from among the planter and business class. Ordinary people, therefore, the majority of the colony's population, remained unrepresented in the Council.

However, it was the "great myth of Crown Colony government

that governors and officials were impartial administrators, and at the same time, the special protectors of the poor."[3]

The emerging society of colonial Trinidad and Tobago reflected a particularly complex picture. Its composition was largely different from most of the other British Caribbean colonies. Of primary importance was the fact that until 1797 Trinidad was a colony of Spain, albeit with a very large population of French heritage. At one level, then, there was the challenge to assimilate the Spanish legal system into that of the British. At another level there was the issue of language and culture. Equally significant was the fact that only a few decades after the capture of Trinidad, and with slavery terminated, the British introduced an entirely different group of people into the colony, purely to perpetuate a struggling sugar industry: indentured workers from India. So in a brief period of about 100 years, between 1750 and 1850, Trinidad confronted the challenge of absorbing the Spanish and French, African slaves and people from India, and a British ruling class.

With the broad mass of the Trinidad population illiterate, the British believed that representative government was unworkable. Further, the myth was perpetuated that only the British could protect the interests of this large group, and that the Crown Colony system was the instrument to achieve this. Thus Sir Hilary Blood stated that

> the Queen's Governors were in a position to see to it that the new freemen of the West Indies had equal treatment, fair shares in such social and political benefits as were available . . . Here is a valuable lesson which the West Indies has to teach: namely that at a certain stage in the history of a mixed society it is necessary to limit the political rights of a more advanced section of the community until the less advanced section can catch up.[4]

The limitation of these rights, in two areas where they were exercised towards the end of the 19th century, only served to increase the agitation for reform.

While the Legislative Council included no elected members until 1925, for the period 1862 to 1898 the unofficial representatives actually constituted a majority. They did not represent the interests of the ordinary people, but at least they reflected local interests — those of the planter class. Towards the end of the century, these individuals began to work as a group, to some extent in opposition to the government. The Secretary of State for the Colonies, Joseph

Chamberlain, holding the view that non-Europeans were incapable of administering their affairs, wrote in 1896:

> Local government is the curse of the West Indies. In many islands it means only the rule of a local oligarchy of whites and half-breeds — always incapable and frequently corrupt. In other cases it is the rule of the negroes, totally unfit for representative institutions and the dupes of unscrupulous adventurers.[5]

Chamberlain promptly increased the number of the officials on the Council, thereby assuring them a permanent majority.

He was equally opposed to the elected Port of Spain Borough Council. Established in 1853, this body was an "important forum for local politicians, especially black and coloured radicals and . . . more than ever the only area in which educated Trinidadians not belonging to the capitalist class could participate in political affairs."[6] Even though only a small number of electors participated, as a consequence of high property qualifications, the Borough Council permitted a major voice to be heard in opposition to the political organization of the colony. The clash with the central government, and ultimately with Chamberlain, centred upon finances.

The Borough Council sought to expand its powers; but to do this it needed to increase its funding base. Chamberlain offered financial assistance in exchange for oversight of the budget by the central government. If these terms were unacceptable, the Council would be abolished. Council members clearly recognized that oversight by the central government amounted to a loss of independence. A majority refused to accept Chamberlain's conditions, and in due course the Legislative Council approved an ordinance which abolished the Borough Council in early 1899. This fed the flames of discontent in Trinidad, especially within the French Creole group.

Philip Rostant, a French Creole journalist, was probably the first to lead the movement for reform. Through his paper Public Forum, and in public meetings, he agitated for the introduction of elected members into the Legislative Council. A Royal Commission Report in 1887 supported this notion, but it was promptly rejected by the Colonial Office. By 1895, after similar debates in the Legislative Council, Chamberlain rejected the arguments for reform.

It was at about this time that more broadly-based opposition to the Crown Colony system emerged with the formation of the Trinidad Workingmen's Association (TWA). The TWA, the first "genuine working-class movement", was founded in 1897 and played a "pioneering role in radicalizing the urban masses" in the colony.[7] Its founder Walter Mills, a pharmacist, gave evidence before the 1897 Royal Commission, explaining that his organization supported reduced taxes on food imports, the development of roads, the promoting of light industries and, importantly, the introduction of elected members to the Legislative Council.[8] While very active in its early years, the TWA was negatively affected by the waterfront strike of 1902 and the Water Riots of 1903 in which 16 people were killed. By 1906 its membership had fallen from the 1,000 claimed in 1900, to 223. It was not until the end of World War I, after Captain Arthur Cipriani assumed the leadership, that the TWA began again to play a significant role in the reform movement in the colony.

In the intervening period, another broad-based group, the Rate Payers Association (RPA), attempted to meet the needs of the frustrated middle class in Port of Spain, especially after the abolition of the city council. The RPA was founded in 1901 by leading businessmen in Port of Spain. Its membership included merchants and professionals who were white, coloured and black.[9] For its 185 rate-paying members, water had become a major issue. The government, in an effort to control wastage, prepared legislation which would introduce water meters into homes. At that time water in the home was primarily a luxury of the middle class. Yet by defining the issue as one of citizens' rights, the RPA was able to mobilize the working class as well.

For the next two years the central government struggled with the citizenry of Port of Spain over the regulation of water supplies. On March 23, 1903, the government attempted to introduce the Water Bill into the Legislative Council. Crowds massed around the Red House, the site of the Council meeting. A riot ensued. The police fired into the crowd, killing 16 and wounding 43. The Red House was burned to the ground. Ironically, the victims of the police action were primarily RPA supporters from the lower class, since the leaders had already left the scene.

While the immediate issue in the riot was water, it was clear that non-representation of the citizenry was at least of equal importance.

The Commission of Enquiry that examined the riot recognized this, recommending to Chamberlain the restoration of the Borough Council (which did not occur until 1913). In 1904, C. P. David, a prominent black supporter of the RPA, was appointed an unofficial member of the Legislative Council. Another coloured professional, Stephen Laurence, was seated in 1911. These piecemeal palliatives were meant to assuage the demands of the reformers, while leaving the political system under the control of the colonizer. This was of course necessary to maintain economic control and to preserve the existing social order.

During the first century of British rule over Trinidad, plantation sugar was king. The planter-dominated political system therefore promoted legislation that enhanced the position of sugar to the detriment of other agricultural products. The epitome of this legislation was the decision to introduce indentured labourers from India, in a scheme that lasted from 1845 to 1917. Ironically, funding for this experiment was provided by the local taxpayers during the almost 75 years of its existence. And even though the Royal Commission of 1897 acknowledged this, and the output of cocoa had surpassed that of sugar by the beginning of World War I, the political system strongly supported sugar interests and demonstrated "hostility to the small farmer."[10] Fifteen years earlier, the Commission in its most famous recommendation stated:

> It seems to us that no reform affords so good a prospect for the permanent welfare in the future of the West Indies as the settlement of the labouring population on the land as small peasant proprietors . . . the chief outside influence with which the Governments of certain colonies have to reckon are the representatives of the sugar estates, that the establishment of any other industry is often detrimental to their interests . . . under such conditions it is the special duty of Your Majesty's Government to see that the welfare of the general public is not sacrificed to the interests . . . of a small but influential minority.[11]

But the political directorate was determined that sugar must maintain its premier position in the economy of the colony. And even though peasant farming was developing in the new century, the political system made it difficult for farmers to obtain Crown lands. While different Commissions recommended that larger plots of land be made available to the small farmer, official leadership in the colony took precisely the opposite position. The price of Crown lands was increased from £1.10.0 an acre in 1900 to £2.10.0 in 1911.[12] Thus did the dualistic character of the Trinidad economy emerge. On the one side was state-supported sugar and, later, petroleum. On the other side was the steadily expanding cocoa industry, largely dominated by the French Creole sector, and coconuts and food crops, which were in the hands of the small farmers.

By the early 20th century, the British navy still depended upon coal to fuel its ships. Winston Churchill, the First Lord of the Admiralty, feared that the dwindling supplies of coal were unable to meet the navy's demands. In 1910, he ordered the conversion of the fleet to oil. At that time, Burma was Britain's only source of oil. Trinidad's first oil well had been dug in the 1860s — indeed, Charles Kingsley had reported seeing the remains of it on his trip to Trinidad in 1870.[13] Britain now began to look to Trinidad to meet its demand for oil, as it had done with sugar. It would use the local government to achieve this purpose.

The Trinidad government offered attractive inducements to British oil investors. Overly generous leases of 50 years, with the option of renewal for another 30 years, were granted — a time span that was longer than the life of an average oil well. Royalties were to be paid to the local government on a sliding scale: as production increased, fees were reduced. These rates, already low, were about half those of Burma. Not surprisingly, the oil industry in Trinidad took off rapidly. The year 1911 saw the first commercial shipment of Trinidad oil. Production that year amounted to 125,000 barrels. Nine years later, output had increased by over 1,500 percent to about 2,000,000 barrels; and a mere seven years later, in 1927, production was 250 percent over 1920 at about 5.4 million barrels. King sugar had given way to "black gold". But with neither industry did benefits trickle down to the wider society.

While employment in the sugar industry is seasonal, in the oil industry it has historically been low, as a consequence of the high level of technology required. Benefits for the state, especially in the case of oil, arise mainly in the form of taxes from this wasting asset, for redistribution to the wider population. But, as already noted, the oil industry was introduced into the colony on very generous terms, which were maintained for much of the century. Eventually, as the natural resource was depleted, and the industry shifted its focus to refining, benefits to the state were further reduced.

The colonial structure of the evolving Trinidad economy, characterized by its enclavistic and dualistic features, would have significant implications for social relations and the structure of the emerging society.

Two Trinidadian writers, C. L. R. James in *Beyond a Boundary* and P. E. T. O'Connor in *Some Trinidad Yesterdays*, have provided poignant portraits of Trinidad's society, from two very different perspectives, in the early 20th century. James was from a black lower-middle-class Tunapuna family which employed education, discipline and determination in its drive for upward social mobility. O'Connor, of French Creole heritage, was born into the colony's traditional elite, but under 19th-century British domination, the family's fortunes and status had fluctuated. The French in Trinidad focused on the production of cocoa, while the British favoured the sugar industry. Naturally, the British also favoured people of their heritage.

At the turn of the century, the decline of the sugar industry was accompanied by the rise of cocoa, and with it the fortunes and status of the French Creole community in the colony. La Chance was the O'Connor family compound near Arima. O'Connor fondly recalled his visits there.

> La Chance typified the old order of the French Creole with its accent on close family life and gracious living which had been the hallmark of colonial New Orleans from whence the de Gannes had sailed to the Caribbean. The fortunes of the French families in Trinidad had fluctuated over the years but with the re-birth of the cocoa industry in the 1890s they were again in the ascendancy and La Chance was a symbol of the renaissance.[14]

O'Connor, two years older than James, completed his high school education in Ireland, while James earned a place at Queen's Royal College (QRC) in Trinidad through one of the four "college exhibitions". In the early 1920s, O'Connor completed his university degree and obtained employment as an engineer with Kern Trinidad Oilfields at Guapo. He lived in the bachelors' quarters and his social life revolved around the oilfield club with a group of young English and Scottish engineers. He observed:

> While we in the camps enjoyed our social round and worked in relatively comfortable surroundings, the conditions in the neighbouring villages were poor and squalid . . . There were no social amenities in these villages, no recreational

facilities other than the rum shops and no public transport. Few workmen could afford a bicycle and a worker, after his twelve hour shift, might have to walk four or six miles to get home.[15]

In 1918, James was in his last year of high school. It was also the last year of World War I, and James decided that one way to see the world was to sign up for the war effort. He attempted to sign with the Merchants' Contingent in which young men from the middle class were sent directly to join the English regiments. He thought himself physically fit and well-known, having represented his school at cricket and football. He remembered very well the recruitment scene: "When my turn came I walked up to this (recruitment officer's) desk. He took one look at me, saw my dark skin, and shaking his head vigorously motioned me violently away."[16] At age 17, James had run head first into the colour bar, something that he was aware of but had not personally experienced before. Yet he claimed to be "not unduly disturbed"[17]; issues of colour mattered much less at QRC.

James would face the same problem again when he sought to pursue his dream — to play first-class cricket in Trinidad. As he examined the different cricket clubs in Port of Spain, he quickly realized that "the various first-class clubs represented the different social strata in the island within clearly defined bounds."[18] Colour, again, was the primary defining variable. Obviously excluded from the white Queen's Park and Shamrock clubs, James also excluded himself from Stingo. He said "they were plebeians."[19] His choice was narrowed down to Maple, "the club of the brown-skinned middle class", and Shannon, "the club of the black lower-middle class."[20] He sought the advice of friends and eventually joined Maple. He was not very happy with his own decision, however, admitting later:

> My decision cost me a great deal . . . Faced with the fundamental divisions in the islands, I had gone to the right, and by cutting myself off from the popular side, delayed my political development for years. But no one could see that then, least of all, me.[21]

It is interesting, even amusing, that James would scold himself for going "to the right". This might be the only time he would face such an accusation — later he would emerge as one of the leading spokesmen of the left in the entire region. Yet he had earlier admitted: "Two people

lived in me: one, the rebel against all family and school discipline and order; the other, a Puritan who would have cut off a finger sooner than do anything contrary to the ethics of the game."[22] These apparently schizoid tendencies were probably not very dissimilar to the experiences and behaviour of James's contemporaries at that period in Trinidad's history. For while the colonials were socialized into the ways of the British, the colour of the black majority determined its low and unequal status in the society. Consequently, this group confronted serious identity problems. By contrast, P. E. T. O'Connor faced relatively little difficulty: his identity was anchored in the French Creole elite. His skin tone and university education further assured him of his superior status.

This was the world in which Thomas Henry Williams, black and poorly educated, was born in 1878; he married a mulatto, Eliza Boissière, ten years younger than himself, in 1910. Eliza was determined, by her behaviour and her demeanour, to let the world know that she was of French Creole ancestry. Thomas Henry, on the other hand, believed that his colour determined his status. In a very particular sense, their marriage unwittingly attempted to reconcile the worlds of the James and O'Connor families.

The first child of this marriage was Eric Eustace, born on September 24, 1911. In him would reside the hopes of a father who believed that "what he had never been given an opportunity to achieve with his brains, he might with his loins",[23] and the aloofness and coldness of a mother who viewed herself as superior to those around her.

The Williams family: Eric is in the back row, left

LIFE IN THE WILLIAMS HOME

The ethnic heritage of Eric Williams has always been an intriguing issue for many in Trinidad and Tobago, largely because of the important role of race and ethnicity in national politics, at least since the 1950s. Soon after the formation of the People's National Movement (PNM), when it was generally perceived as representing the interests of the black sector of the society, the few East Indian foundation members of the party, believing that Williams was not totally black, pleaded with him to declare on the public platform that "he had Indian blood" in him. This was a way of broadening the base, and thus the party's appeal to the two dominant ethnic groups. Williams steadfastly refused — though in actuality he did have "Indian blood" in him. But not the Indian blood to which those party members were referring. There were elements of Carib Indian ancestry, and European ancestry, in the genealogy of Eric Williams.

Eric's grandfather, on his father's side, was Thomas James Williams, who was born in Nevis in 1855. Thomas's mother, Sarah Jane, was of Carib descent, with long straight hair; his father, of African descent, was nicknamed "Old King", and worked as a turnkey at the prison in Nevis. Thomas moved to Trinidad with Gaston Johnson, a famed criminal lawyer who later became mayor of Port of Spain, and operated a real estate agency. His wife, Onemia Wilhemenia Hunt, Eric's grandmother, "looked like a white person" and was disowned by her relatives after her marriage to dark-skinned Thomas. She had "long, straight, light hair and a straight long nose."[1] She spoke French and French Patois fluently, but had more difficulty with English. She was born in Trinidad in 1853, but moved to St Vincent, presumably after the death of her husband, with her daughter Phillipa, and died there in 1931. Her son Henry, Eric's father, remained in Trinidad.

Eric's mother, Eliza, considered herself a French Creole. Her forebears were from France, with more immediate relatives from the French colony of Guadeloupe. Her father, Jules Arnold Boissière, was the son of John Nicholas Boissière and a black woman in Trinidad. John Nicholas's grandmother, Claire Beaulieu, was born in Guadeloupe and lived there from 1760 to 1830. Eliza was born on the Palmiste estate, a few miles south of San Fernando, in 1888. Her father served there as an overseer. He had apparently received the position because the estate's owner, Sir Norman Lamont, was a close friend of the Boissières of Champs Elysées.

Jules Arnold Boissière and his wife Evalina (née Redford) eventually moved to Port of Spain. But Evalina died while only in her 40s, leaving Jules Arnold to look after a family of ten children. Eventually, these duties fell to the second oldest child, Eliza, who while still a teenager assumed the responsibility for all her brothers and sisters. She may have married Eric's father Henry, who was ten years her senior, partly to evade the responsibility of taking care of nine children. Ironically, she and Henry had twelve children themselves, six boys and six girls.

Henry, Eric's father, was born in Port of Spain on April 1, 1878. He attended Eastern Boys Government Primary School, after which his formal education ended. He began an apprenticeship with the Post Office at the age of 17, serving without pay. Two years later, he was placed on the daily-paid staff until he assumed permanent employment, at the age of 21, in 1899.

By the turn of the century, much political activity was taking place in Trinidad, of which Henry Williams could hardly have been unaware. From the working-class perspective, what was probably most significant was the formation of the Trinidad Workingmen's Association in 1897.

Henry Williams would have known of this group, and of the Rate Payers Association, organized two years later. The infamous Water Riots of 1903 would have had some impact. By this time, too, the first international cricket match had been played, the "first car arrived in Port of Spain, and the first oil well was drilled."[2]

In 1910, when he was 32, Henry Williams and Eliza Boissière were married in Port of Spain. Henry's salary at this time was about $56.00 per month. On his retirement, 25 years later, he was earning a salary of $180.00. In his autobiography *Inward Hunger*, Eric Williams repeatedly emphasizes the difficulties his parents experienced in trying to maintain a growing family on what he considered to be an extremely low salary: "the daily problem of making ends meet dogged the family as a whole and determined the fate and fortune of individual members."[3] According to Eric, the struggle for survival was the major challenge faced by the family each day.

But was this struggle any different from that faced by most of the population around World War I? Was the Williams family significantly better off, or worse off than the average Trinidad family at that time?

At the time of World War I, Trinidad was almost entirely an agricultural society. Oil exports had only just begun. Employment in that industry was miniscule. Sugar still dominated the economy, with contributions from cocoa, coffee and coconuts. In all these sectors, employment was seasonal, though the sugar industry maintained a small percentage of its labour force to look after the growing crop and the processing mill between seasons. Most of the agricultural workers were daily-paid. P. E. T. O'Connor recalled that when he worked as a shift overseer at the Woodford Lodge sugar cane factory in 1919, he received a monthly salary of $40.00.[4] Henry Williams was a permanent employee of the Post Office, receiving, as we have seen, a salary of $56.00 per month in 1910. It would appear, then, that the living standards of the Williams family may have been somewhat above those of the majority of the population who were employed in agriculture. Two additional points bear this out.

In order to supplement the family's income, Eric wrote, "my father took to auditing books of Friendly Societies." Bright student that he was, Eric assisted his father with this assignment, compiling figures. The gratuities which his father "handed over on receipt of his fees were my first earnings." His mother, too, supplemented the family's income, for she "made bread and cakes not only for home consumption but for sale on a small scale to regular customers." Eric assisted her in two ways: "in the first place I was my mother's assistant in baking. In the second place I was the seller of the produce. With a servant boy or girl carrying the basket, I walked around to the various houses filling orders or getting new ones."[5]

If the family faced a daily struggle to survive, how could a servant boy or girl be employed? Other family members do not recall having the assistance of a servant. They remembered that they all assisted with the weekend baking activities, and were also assigned another task, "cleaning the cutlery every Saturday morning."[6] Yet another sign that the family's financial situation was not as dire as stated in the autobiography.

Of course, the family's size would have caused a huge burden. Between 1911 and 1931, Eliza Williams gave birth to 12 children, of whom 11 survived. By any standard, the family's size was large. The parents did not practise birth control. Eric continues: "Not only were they [his parents] Catholic, but my father was one of the leading figures in the erection of a new church in Woodbrook, St Theresa's, after whom he named one of his daughters."[7]

The late Archbishop Anthony Pantin attested to Henry Williams's devotion to the Roman Catholic Church. He recalled that as a very young priest he celebrated Mass at St Patrick's church in Newtown each morning. He saw the quiet, balding Williams there every day, and knew that this man was the father of Dr Eric Williams.[8]

The Williams family was faced with a familiar dilemma: should they be faithful children of the church, even though they would be unable to provide for the large number of children they would have as a consequence? They made their choice. In this context, it is revealing that one of Eric Williams's first challenges as a politician in 1956, about 25 years after the birth of his youngest sister Lucille, was from the Catholic church in Trinidad over the issue of birth control. As a consequence, some gave Williams's party, the PNM, the derisive title "Pre-Natal Murderers".

Eric was the first child in the Williams family. This has given rise to provocative speculation about the implications of birth order for his personality and career choices. Research into the age-old idea that a relationship exists between birth order and personality has concluded that "tightly circumscribed statistical tests of birth order effects have begun to show some substantiation of the theory."[9]

While heredity must account for some of the differences among siblings in a family unit, it is recognized that environment also plays a part. Birth order theorists tend to believe that "a key part of anyone's environment is the ordinal position in the family that they occupy by reason of their birth."[10] This influences their functioning in school, among friends, at work, and especially within the dynamics of the family. Indeed, if the theory holds, birth order must have an influence on leadership qualities. In that context, the theorists suggest that "political power . . . is merely a variant of that power with which the individual became familiar with as a child in a family context." They continue:

> Within the family, partly in response to birth order position, children will learn lessons about dominance, conformity, rebellion, punishment, persuasion, strategy, frustration and control. Children who grow up to be world leaders will carry these lessons with them into office.[11]

Four general principles have emerged from the research of birth order theorists. With regard to the probability of attaining a leadership position, first-borns and middle-born children are more likely to be found in office than only children or last-borns. Concerning power style, first-born children tend to rely on their strength and intellectual advantages. Concerning beliefs, first-born and only children will be more attached to the heritage imparted to them by their parents; in political leaders, this allegiance is transferred to the trappings of nationalism. Regarding behavioural style, first-borns, consonant with their style of power, will be much more direct and confrontational in achieving their policy goals. Researchers believe that first-borns are most likely to resort to threats and punishment.[12]

This theory comes amazingly close to explaining the behaviour of the first-born Eric Williams. The first principle shows the close relationship between the first-born and the prospect of leadership; the second relates power to intellectual strength; the third links beliefs to parental heritage and its manifestation in nationalistic appeal; the fourth links birth order to a direct and confrontational style. Leadership, intellectual strength, appeals to nationalism and confrontation, threats and punishment, all characterized the adult behaviour of Eric Williams, the first of twelve children.

It is clear that Eric was held in special esteem by his parents, and also by his siblings. This provided him with special use of the family's scarce resources. For instance, books, clothes and shoes were handed down from one child to the next. But, as one sister emphasized, "Eric never had used clothes etc., he was first, so he had the first use of everything."[13] So did the oldest surviving daughter, Angela.

The Williams family's second child was Mervyn, considered to be as "bright as Eric." He also attended Queen's Royal College (QRC), having won a College Exhibition. The third child, and first girl, died at nine months. Angela was the fourth, the one upon whom much of the family's burden fell, especially during the periods when Eliza was pregnant or recovering from birth. Flora was the fifth child, the petite one in the family, and was both her father's and Eric's favourite. John, the sixth, was considered a "black sheep" of the family; like Mervyn, he lived much of his adult life in England.

The seventh child was Eileen, the family rebel. She was thrown out of the family home while still a teenager, when she became pregnant. Ralph, number eight, was the mother's favourite. She considered him her "attorney"; he looked after her affairs, not without controversy during her later years. Victor, the ninth child, lived at Eric's home for some time while the latter was Prime Minister, and served as an assistant. He repeatedly attempted to use his proximity to his brother to seek to accumulate power. Theresa, named after the Catholic church in Woodbrook, was the family's tenth child. She too was thrown out of the family home at age 14, and went to live with her brother Mervyn; she eventually moved to Ciudad Bolivar, in Venezuela, but frequently returned home to participate in Carnival celebrations until she suffered a stroke. Tony, the last boy, number eleven, became a sports announcer in Trinidad. The youngest of them all, born in 1931, was Lucille. She was actually brought up by Angela, and in some ways viewed Angela as her mother rather than her sister.

The Williams family was clearly a complex unit, not only because of its size, but because of the conflicting personalities of its individual members. It appears that the personality that impacted most dramatically on the behaviour and dynamics of the entire family was that of the mother, Eliza.

Eliza Williams was tough, aloof, imperious, and a firm disciplinarian. She was very demanding of her children, and was firmly in command of her family. Henry Williams was also firm, but possessed a warmer personality. Eliza viewed herself as a French Creole, and believed that she was superior to those around her. As one daughter recalled,

> she had the French embedded in her. She had the French style. She had the many French ways. She thought that she was an aristocrat. She believed she was better than others. We called her "Madam" (behind her back). She was very proud.[14]

Thus, although each parent had at least one child who was favoured, there was apparently little warmth, and even less overt love, within the family. Of course, the primary preoccupation was "to make ends meet", as Eric himself wrote; and the family's size probably made organization and discipline more necessary than in many other families. Beyond that, however, it is clear that Eliza was cold and brusque. The threat of punishment was always present. One daughter recalled with sadness the militaristic nature of the household:

> You had to know what you were doing! You could not "skylark". You had to have your head on your shoulder . . . You had to follow her [Eliza's] instructions immediately. If not, too bad for you, "left hand box".[15]

No one was permitted to argue with the mother: "whatever she said, our father went along with. She was the boss, she gave the orders."[16]

In order for the family to function efficiently, each member was assigned particular responsibilities, before and after school, and on weekends. The two oldest boys for instance, Eric and Mervyn, were required to bottle-feed the youngest children before they left for school each morning. It was not unusual for their school clothes to be dirtied by the babies after a feeding.

The girls in the family were assigned the cleaning, cooking and washing. One recalled having to wash large amounts of diapers on a daily basis. She was still too small to reach the clothes line, and needed to stand on a wooden box to hang the diapers out in the sun. Because

Eliza was so often pregnant or recovering from giving birth, on many occasions the blue-flame kerosene stove was placed in her bedroom, so she could oversee the daily cooking from her bed.

On Saturdays, everyone was required to help in giving the house a general cleaning. Floors were swept and mopped. Furniture was dusted and cutlery and other silver cleaned. Because Eliza was generally unsociable and unfriendly, she discouraged her daughters from inviting their friends to the home: "You do not need others, you could talk to each other." After one Saturday cleaning, she announced: "I do not want anyone to come here and hot up my chairs." The daughters decided to stop dusting and cleaning. Their mother asked later, "Aren't you cleaning the house today?" One daughter, at a safe distance, replied, "No, no one is coming to hot up the chairs."[17]

Saturday was also the day when the family undertook large-scale baking. This included two types of breads and an assortment of cakes, both for home use and for sale in the neighbourhood. This appeared to be very much a family project. One daughter recalled: "All my brothers could cook, bake and clean." Neighbourhood sales were Eliza's way of supplementing the family's income. Four times a year, also on Saturdays, the family changed its house curtains, another family project that involved hand-washing and ironing. This was certainly a house-proud family.

It was a standing joke among the daughters and their friends, especially of the opposite sex, that no one dared to visit the Williams home. One Saturday evening, one young man, apparently very attracted to one of the now teenaged daughters, decided to accept the challenge. He arrived at about 8.00 p.m. and was entertained by the sisters. But about 9.00 p.m., father Henry entered the room and began fussing with the chairs and closing the windows. His signal to the young man was clear: it was time to leave. A heavy shower was falling at the time, but the young man, seeing the father's demeanour, promptly left, walking into the rain.

Eric's father supported the tough discipline meted out by Eliza. He too was a firm individual, deeply religious, with very traditional values. Yet while Eliza's behaviour was generally characterized by condescension and aloofness, he was perceived as a more caring person. "He was a peaceful man," one daughter recalled. Yet no one doubted that the primary focus of his attention was always Eric.

Eric suggested that his father lacked the necessary "social qualifications" for advancement in the civil service. These were

> colour, money and education in that order of importance. My father lacked all three. In colour he was dark brown. His three great expectations for money failed him. Unfortunate in his colour, disappointed in his hopes of a legacy, he had no more than primary school education.[18]

As a consequence, Henry Williams languished at a relatively low civil service level during his 35 years of employment at the Post Office, with little recognition and a small salary. He was determined that his first son would achieve all that he did not have the opportunity to do. As Eric stated succinctly: "Greatness, Trinidad style, was thrust upon me from the cradle."[19] One daughter put it another way: "Our father lived his life through Eric."[20]

From a very tender age, Eric was groomed by his father for greatness. From an intellectual perspective, he responded magnificently. Henry Williams was well aware that education was the way to transcend colour and encourage social mobility. He plotted Eric's educational path as a general would plan a war. His goal was the island scholarship. Speaking of his father, Eric admitted: "The island scholarship for his son became the dream of his life."[21] Neither his son nor his church would deter him from his dream. This is illustrated by two incidents.

In 1922, Eric won one of the only eight college "exhibitions" which granted tuition-free high school. Among the two prestigious male high schools in Port of Spain were the Catholic St Mary's College, and the "state" school Queen's Royal College (QRC, which was actually of Anglican foundation). As a devout Catholic, Henry Williams was expected to select St Mary's as the high school that his son would attend. He apparently consulted with his parish priest on this decision; the church may have hinted that the family could face censure if St Mary's was not selected. But on this rare occasion, Henry overrode the advice of the church. He believed that QRC was the more prestigious school. So Eric was sent to QRC at the tender age of 11. He was not involved in the decision.

In high school, Eric was as successful at soccer as he was in the classroom. By his senior year, he was the captain of the school's soccer team. He had also been injured while playing; indeed, when his father arrived on the field that day, he was still laid out on the ground. This may have been the occasion when Eric suffered the damage to his ear that later resulted in his partial deafness. Henry would not let anything stand in the way of his son competing for the island scholarship. Well aware of Eric's earlier mishap, Henry ordered his son not to participate in the 1931 Inter-Collegiate soccer match between QRC and St Mary's, the premier high school soccer event each year.

Eric did attend the game, accompanied by his close friend Halsey McShine. Seeing his team go out on the field short-handed, Eric made an instant and bold decision: he would defy his father. He ordered Halsey to rush him to his family home close by, sitting on the handlebars of Halsey's bicycle. He quickly changed into his soccer outfit and hurried back to the soccer field. Not only did he participate in the game, but he also scored the winning goal "with a left foot bullet," and at the end of the game was "carried shoulder high across the Savannah to the college."[22]

There is no record of Henry Williams's reaction to his son's disobedience. But this much is known: Eric scored the winning goal in one of the most important soccer games that year. His father must surely have been proud. And Eric had not been injured during the game.

Soccer did add an interesting dynamic to the life of the Williams family. After Eric assumed the captaincy of QRC's soccer team, the family home on Woodford Street became the meeting place where team members reviewed previous games, planned strategy, prepared balls for the games, etc. This continued for a year. By this time, several of Eric's sisters were teenagers; there should have been a natural attraction between them and the soccer players. But in the Williams home this was not permitted. The sisters were required to remain in the back bedrooms and out of sight. As one recalled, "If we came out it would be licks like peas!"[23] This was typical of everyday life in the Williams household, especially for its female members.

After morning chores were completed, the children went off to school, returning home at lunchtime. The girls were not permitted to walk home with other children. The reason was that Eliza "did not want to hear complaints from others about us." The children believed that since their mother was an unsociable individual she expected her daughters to be the same.

Eliza was a stern disciplinarian. One of her favourite statements was "When I speak let no dogs bark!" The children constantly tried to stay on her right side. If they didn't, one said, "Crapaud smoke your pipe!"[24] Even after chores and homework were completed, Eliza required the girls to remain within the yard. No one was permitted to go out. Occasionally this resulted in rebellious behaviour, and the offenders were promptly thrown out of the house.

The strict upbringing imposed by both parents did not soften as the children moved through their teenage and later years. As one said, "Our teenage years did not make much of a difference to us." Even after some of the girls obtained their first jobs, they were still required to be in by 7.00 p.m. This put serious stress on their ability to go out on dates. The accepted ruse was to tell their parents, "We are going to visit Mervyn at his home" and then go and meet their various boyfriends. Without telephones, the parents remained unaware of their daughters' activities.

If dating was difficult, planning for marriage was even more so. Male friends were not permitted to visit the home. When a young couple decided on marriage, a formal letter was written to the father. This was followed by a formal visit by the intended. In most cases, Eliza disapproved of the selected mate, and refused to attend the formal marriage ceremony.

In one case Eliza was particularly upset since the proposed mate was not a Catholic. She referred to non-Catholics as "saved souls". Neither parent attended that particular wedding. The couple, a priest and two witnesses were the only participants. This daughter had become so annoyed with her parents, particularly her mother, that she left the family home four months before her marriage, and did not return until her father's death seven years later. Eliza was especially upset by this marriage, since it was this daughter who had carried the biggest burden of household duties.

The sons of the family, in accordance with the local culture, had fewer restrictions placed upon them, particularly with regard to their social life. Eric, for instance, was permitted to have his entire soccer team spend the afternoon at his home. By this time he had carved out for himself a special place of honour with both parents. Not only was he the first child, which automatically conferred special privileges, but he performed so brilliantly, both in primary and at high school, that the family's status was elevated even before he won an island scholarship. His achievements in soccer and cricket further enhanced his status at home. The other sons simply left the family home as they grew older, however, discouraged by the strict regimentation demanded by both parents. Two eventually migrated to England.

Yet a certain degree of regimentation was inevitable because of the family's large size and limited financial resources. For instance, clothing and shoes were purchased at the Johnson store sale each August. Family members had to be ready and willing to accept handed-down clothing. School books had to be maintained carefully, so that as many members of the family as possible could use them. Eventually, the children developed their own secret system of sharing food resources. Naturally, each had a favourite food; food items moved around the table according to likes and dislikes without the parents being aware of what was happening.

The Sunday meal was a special event. It began with both parents enjoying a cocktail, a combination of rum, eggs and syrup. The children were sometimes served Gilbey's wine. Meat was always served, along with vegetables. Sometimes this meal was followed by home-made ice-cream or snowballs and milk. More or less the same fare was prepared for birthdays, especially cake and ice-cream. Gifts were apparently not exchanged. Again, this is not surprising, considering the family's income level and size.

Housing remained a perpetual problem. Eric stated it very bluntly:

> We disputed our way all over Port of Spain, seeking living space at low rentals. In my first 21 years in Trinidad we changed houses eight times, and it is possible to identify members of the family not only by name or by sex but also by the house in which each was born . . . in one bad case the bailiff appeared.[25]

The family was unable to purchase its own home until Henry retired in 1932 and received a gratuity of $4,000.00, which was used for that purpose. By that time a few children had already left.

In 1946, Henry Williams developed cancer of the prostate. It remained undiagnosed for some time, largely because he refused to go to the hospital. Mervyn unwillingly returned to his parents' home, at the instigation of other family members, and persuaded his father to be hospitalized. Eric's friend Halsey McShine and Dr Shepherd performed the surgery. McShine was well aware that Henry was seriously ill and contacted Eric in Washington, encouraging him to return home. Eric had left Trinidad in 1932 and had returned only once since then. That was in 1944, while he was travelling through the Caribbean. His father's greeting to him then was "So you are a doctor after all!"[26] Eric's reply to McShine in 1946 was that he would be very busy for the next three weeks, but would visit after that. Henry died the day before Eric returned.

Henry's death placed the family under new psychological stress. Even though many of the children had left the family home by this time, some remained in contact. Henry had been the tenuous link that held the family together. Eliza was left at home alone with Ralph and Lucille. She had never had many friends; now she had even fewer. Eventually, she turned to drink; with her French Creole tastes, she enjoyed brandy, but as funds dwindled, she substituted rum. Already a diabetic, she became an alcoholic; after a stay at the public hospital, then Park's Nursing Home, she died in 1972.

The environment in which Eric Williams was born, nurtured and functioned, from his birth in 1911 until he travelled to England in September 1932 at the age of 21, had a huge impact on his personality. After all, personality is largely the "engraved and habitual ways of psychological functioning that emerge from the individual's entire developmental history."[27]

There are certain broad and recurring patterns in Williams's developmental history. His childhood was characterized by a perception of deprivation, and he believed that colour was its major cause. He was the first in a family of twelve children. His father was determined that his son would succeed in a manner that he himself was unable to; his cold, imperious mother believed that she was superior to those around her. There was extremely rigid family discipline, and a church that sought to shape and dominate the family's life.

The Williams family could probably have been classified as lower middle class. But even though the father maintained permanent employment, this unusually large family was unable to enjoy much more than the basic necessities of life. Adequate housing remained a permanent problem, and health care was focused almost entirely on the child-bearing mother. Eric's father insisted that a lack of social qualifications — colour, wealth and education — was the direct cause of the family's circumstances. Eric later applied this argument to his own struggles at Oxford University and the Caribbean Commission.

Henry Williams was convinced that the only escape for his eldest son, and for the family, was through education. As Eric wrote: "The island scholarship for his son became the dream of his life."[28] Henry was not deterred even by the risk of excommunication from his beloved church or the alienation of his favoured son by prohibiting him from playing soccer. Later, he would attempt to select his son's career choice. This single-minded determination and his total focusing upon goal attainment characterized Eric's own behaviour in adulthood.

The influence of Eliza was no less significant. In his public behaviour, as leader of the nation, Eric Williams was generally perceived as cold, aloof, even arrogant. Eliza was similarly described by her children. Yet in his private behaviour, especially with young people — including, for instance, friends of his daughter Erica — Eric was variously described as very warm, easy to talk to, and down to earth.[29]

Those who worked with Eric described him as stern, highly disciplined and methodically organized. These traits were also Eliza's. One daughter said: "There was a method to do everything." In a sense, Eric Williams ran his cabinet as his mother ran the home. Like his mother, he did not tolerate inefficiency. No one dared to question his directives. He remembered Eliza's favourite expression, "When I speak let no dogs bark!" His concern was with results.

To a large extent, the Williams family was obedient to the Catholic church and upheld very traditional values. The parents did not practise birth control. But one of Eric Williams's first confrontations, as leader of the PNM, was with the Catholic church over birth control; he was opposed to state support for denominational schools, and fought the church on this issue also. Much of his opposition to the church, as party leader, was probably rooted in his childhood perception of its undue influence over his family.

Eric Williams was a product of his heredity and environment; birth order, family dynamics, the colonial condition, class and colour, all contributed. The personality that developed from these influences had a huge impact on the society and the state as Trinidad and Tobago moved from colonialism into independence.

*Established in 1870, Queen's Royal College was Eric Williams's
stepping stone to an island scholarship and Oxford University*

SCHOOLING IN TRINIDAD

I t was Eric Williams's belief that he was destined for greatness, and that the initial choices made by his father shortly after his birth pointed him in that direction. He wrote:

> Some are born great, some achieve greatness, some have greatness thrust upon them. Greatness Trinidad-style was thrust upon me from the cradle. My father knew that what he had never been given an opportunity to achieve with his brains, he would with his loins. The island scholarship for his son became the dream of his life.[1]

Henry Williams had long concluded that education was the only means to break the constraints of the colonial career treadmill. But since family resources were severely limited, the scholarship was the only means — for those less fortunate, and dark-skinned, like the Williams family — to achieve the education that Eric and his father desired. While primary education was state-funded, the cost of secondary education was simply beyond the family's means. The challenge for Eric, then, from childhood, was to earn the necessary scholarships.

At the primary level, Eric was enrolled at Tranquillity Government School. Later he expressed great admiration for his education there. He recalled: "The intellectual discipline to which I was exposed at

Tranquillity emphasized grammar, spelling, dictation, arithmetic and geography . . . I received a firm foundation in grammar, vocabulary and spelling."[2] He singled out one teacher in particular: J. J. Mitchell. Mitchell had begun working at the school in what was then known as the pupil-teacher system. With little more than an elementary school education, an apprentice teacher could be promoted through a system of monitoring, special courses and examinations. Partly because of this, Williams admired Mitchell enormously.

> He was one of the old brigade of primary school teachers whose dominant personalities could not be circumscribed by the humble social position they filled, and who, unhonoured and unsung, helped to mould thousands of young Trinidad boys, many of whom achieved distinction in one form or another . . . He was a stern taskmaster if there ever was one. He firmly believed in the old adage "spare the rod and spoil the child".[3]

Mitchell was important in Williams's life for another reason. He coached his student in "private lessons", a system Williams termed "one of the principal articles of the educational faith of the Trinidad parent, then and now."[4] While these private lessons were relatively expensive, a dollar per month, it was so much a part of the education culture of the society that parents willingly sacrificed for it; Henry Williams paid "cheerfully".

One other individual impacted on Williams's life at Tranquillity, and later upon the lives of many other schoolchildren in Trinidad. He was J. O. Cutteridge, appointed principal of Tranquillity during Williams's last year at the school. In Williams's view his impact was negative, even though Henry Williams believed Cutteridge was a patron for his son. Eric's reaction was based on the belief that since Cutteridge was non-degreed, his only qualification for the position was that he was an Englishman — yet another attempt by the British to dominate life in the colony. For the next decade, Cutteridge did dominate educational life in Trinidad. He became Director of Education for colonial Trinidad and published West Indian readers and geographies which were ultimately read by all students.

At Tranquillity, Eric developed two friendships which remained with him throughout his life. One was with Ray Dolly, who was senior to Eric, though both were in the same exhibition class. Dolly was making his last attempt at the examination, and Williams his first. The age limit for this scholarship was twelve. The two friends were among those competing for eight exhibitions. Ten years earlier, C. L. R. James had won one of only four such scholarships, which provided tuition-free education at the secondary level. Eric won on his first try, before he was eleven. Dolly did not. They attended different high schools, but would meet in London many years later. Dolly recalled having "a good friendship with Eric" at primary school, partly because "we had a common interest in sports".[5] As Prime Minister, Eric Williams made frequent visits to the Dolly family home at Pointe-à-Pierre, where Dolly was employed as Medical Officer at Texaco.

Eric also befriended a student one year his junior at primary school, Halsey McShine, who remained one of his closest friends, and later became his private doctor. They both attended Queen's Royal College (QRC), and were together in England for seven years. At Tranquillity, McShine remembered Eric as a "quiet little boy, who did not have very much to say".[6]

To be able to attract the attention of his teachers and his new principal, Eric Williams must have been a brilliant student at Tranquillity. Certainly, he won a coveted scholarship at his first attempt. His father, of course, expected nothing less; he had always paid very close attention to his son's progress.

> My father took the steps necessary for the realization of the pious hope he shared . . . the first was an unrelenting domestic pressure. It began in the cradle. He had read . . . about teaching a young child the alphabet and nursery rhymes. He promptly bought an alphabet card and began to put me through my paces. When I could recite the alphabet I received a treat.[7]

Eric crossed the first hurdle towards his father's dream when he won a college exhibition in June 1922. But, as already noted, the family immediately faced a minor crisis, a choice between the Catholic St Mary's College and the secular Queen's Royal College. "My father drew a distinction between religion and education," Eric wrote, and Henry chose QRC, a decision in which "he was warmly supported by my mother."[8] Even so, Eric soon faced another challenge: the special kind of environment he was about to experience at QRC.

Upset by Cutteridge's effort to make Tranquillity "more English" in its outlook, Eric now entered a school which, in his words, was "qualitatively British."[9] Not only was QRC British in quality, it was almost entirely white in colour. There were just two black teachers, Trinidadian W. D. Inniss and Barbadian G. E. Pilgrim. While Eric was there, a few other black staff were appointed, including C. L. R. James and Arthur Farrell in 1927.

In 1926, four years after Eric began attending QRC, Victor Stollmeyer, aged ten, joined the preparatory form. "Perhaps the most noteworthy thing about prep was that all the pupils were white or apparently more or less so," he recalled.[10] The next year, as he moved into the First Form, "there were a few boys of darker hue — even black." In 1928, in the Second Form, Stollmeyer found himself

> with the "exhibitioners", the bright boys emerging from the primary schools. I found myself for the first time part of a white minority, and what is more with a black Form Master . . . being none other than C. L. R. (Nello) James.[11]

To say that QRC was qualitatively British and predominantly led by whites is to say that it was un-West Indian. This was reflected in the curriculum's content. As Williams developed his interest in British colonial history, he soon realized that the subject taught was much more British than colonial. He noted that "there were some references to the West Indies, but they were in terms of European diplomacy and European war. What I knew of slavery and the plantation economy came from Roman history."[12] He continued: "The British education of the young colonial was not distracted by the West Indian environment."[13]

But Williams's early primary academic interest was in languages, especially Latin. He recalled that on his first day at QRC — his eleventh birthday — his exhibition class was assigned to memorize the conjugation of a few Latin verbs. He wrote:

> Within a short period at home that night I had learnt not only all the tenses of 'amo' [his assignment] but of 'moneo', 'rego' and 'audio' . . . I walked up and down the house, reciting all these tenses . . . my father beaming indulgently the while.[14]

It was partly this interest in History and Latin which led him to develop a very close relationship with W. D. "Billy" Inniss. "In his quiet unobtrusive way," Williams wrote, "he was the soul of Queen's Royal College, the secretary general, the chief administrative officer, of the institution."[15] Williams later conceded that "more than any other teacher in Queen's Royal College, he [Inniss] shaped my destiny." He claimed that "in one way or another, directly or indirectly, every student at the college was touched by WD."[16]

Stollmeyer also remembered Inniss with much fondness. He was "small and 'soft' with a quiet piping voice . . . a wonderful teacher, and [he] could impart . . . not only the facts but the love of the subjects he taught." Stollmeyer summarized Inniss's contribution this way: "He did more for QRC than just teach. He did all kinds of work behind the scenes. He was a very worthy man."[17] But Inniss possessed yet another quality that probably drew Eric and others toward him: he was excellent in preparing students for examinations. Williams was determined, as was his father, that he would win an island scholarship. Inniss was extremely knowledgeable in guiding students in their subject selection, and the areas within the subject material upon which they should focus. Later, expressing his gratitude to Inniss, Williams wrote that this teacher "took particular pride in my annexation of the island scholarship — and well he might, for he had contributed to it much more than any other individual except myself."[18]

The fact that Inniss served both as guide and mentor was psychologically very important to Williams, coming out of an authoritarian and otherwise deprived home situation. Inniss provided structure, care and even love for his student. Williams, like any human, needed all of these. Inniss was the first of many who would serve as his academic mentors.

It is interesting that a soft and mild-mannered individual, as Inniss apparently was — Williams referred to him as "dainty" — had such an enormous influence. Both his imperious mother and his elementary school teacher J. J. Mitchell had been powerful personalities, and his father's ambition had been a driving force. While Eric obviously had no choice regarding his parents, he probably chose Inniss as his mentor because, among other factors, Inniss was genuinely caring and more willing to listen to him. His parents simply demanded. Under Inniss's tutelage, Williams performed brilliantly at QRC.

"This man [Eric Williams] was far and away the most popular, charismatic and brilliant boy during my years at QRC," Victor Stollmeyer recalled. "Most stood in awe of his achievements, a few were envious, but hardly dared to show it."[19] The lengthy list of awards and prizes earned by Williams during his days at QRC included the Jerningham Gold Medal, for placing first in the island scholarship examination, and special prizes for subject performance in French, Classics, English, History and Spanish. Williams won the Gerald Doorly prize in 1930, awarded to the boy "who in the opinion of the Masters and the students has been the best example to the College for the year."[20] Stollmeyer concluded: "I will wager that this performance has never been bettered or even equalled. It may never be!"[21]

Williams evaluated his own performance quite candidly. It took him two years to earn the house scholarship and three for the island scholarship. He wrote:

> For the next five years my examinations provided the island with one of the most extraordinary patterns they have ever taken in their long history; whilst I topped the students with respect to the number of distinctions, I always placed third in the order of merit until I won the 1931 (island) scholarship.[22]

Excellent as Eric was in his academic work, his performance in sports was equally impressive. His passion for sports had begun in his primary school days, and was one of the early bases for his friendship with Ray Dolly. In his early years at QRC he attracted the attention of opponents in intramural soccer matches. Within a few years he earned a place on the first eleven soccer team, and in 1929 was made captain of the school soccer team. At this time he was not as proficient at cricket, playing on the second eleven cricket team in 1929.

But in now typical manner, he was unwilling to settle for the second eleven. Some of Williams's schoolboy friends, including George Edwards and Cecil Pouchet, were in the first eleven team, then captained by Joey Ribeiro (whose sister Elsie would become Williams's first wife in London some ten years later). Edwards recalled that Williams "always expressed his admiration for the ability of Ralph [McGregor], Cecil and me, and was determined to get into the first eleven."[23] To achieve this, Williams "used to come down to my home at Fitt Street armed with a bat." Williams spent long periods in the Edwards family's backyard as he sought to improve his cricketing skills. Sometimes this coaching took place in the backyard of Cecil Pouchet, whose family lived on the same street. This was typical of Eric, always striving to do better, a lesson he had learnt from his father: ever to be the best. In late

1929, Williams did earn a place on QRC's first eleven in cricket. Edwards noted that he was "an excellent cover-point fieldsman."

QRC's excellence in sports led to an invitation by Harrison College in Barbados to compete in a soccer, cricket, shooting and athletics tournament. Williams's small circle of athletic friends were all selected to represent their high school. The group included schoolboy supporters like Halsey McShine, and stayed at the Savoy Hotel, sharing one room. Edwards recalled: "We all excelled in our various fields, Bill [Eric] being responsible for our victories in the two football matches played, scoring in both games."[24]

This youthful group of sporting enthusiasts, about eight to ten teenage boys, eventually named themselves "the Ranchers". They generally congregated at Cecil Pouchet's home on Fitt Street on Friday and Saturday evenings. There were refreshments — two cents for a glass of mauby, one cent for a rock (cake), and two cents for a glass of snowball. An additional cent was added for some condensed milk on the snowball. Edwards recalled that when discussions and arguments became heated, Williams, who was the acknowledged scholar of the group, was called upon to mediate: "If Bill says so, it is so, man!"[25] Over 15 years later, when Williams returned to Trinidad, working with the Caribbean Commission, one of his early activities was to host a lavish dinner party for his youthful friends of the Ranchers.

While Williams had some close friends in high school, he also served as a tutor to some classmates during his last year, and in 1932, before he left for England. Halsey McShine, also hoping to earn an island scholarship, felt that he was not sufficiently proficient in Spanish; he asked for some private lessons, but startled his father by insisting "I only want to take lessons with Eric." His father was understandably surprised, since QRC had on its staff some excellent teachers of Spanish. He nevertheless agreed, and Halsey began going to Williams's home on Woodford Street for private tutoring. Other students included Frankie Pierre, two Gaskin boys and three Mendes brothers. Thus Williams accumulated some funds for his study in England.

Williams was very pleased with McShine's improvement in Spanish, and prophesied that he would eventually win the island scholarship. This McShine did, one year after Eric; he was so pleased that he immediately went to the Williams home to share the news with the family. But Eric had left the previous week for England, so their rejoicing did not take place until they met in London a few weeks later.

As was customary in Trinidad, Williams made repeated attempts to win an island scholarship. His father's anxiety increased with each try. After Eric's third attempt, in 1931,

> his concern over my performance in each paper, the rest of the family listening the while, was such an intolerable strain that I refused point blank to answer any question and remained silent; at the end of the examination he asked me, not unkindly, whether I wished to discuss the prospects, and I told him that I did not.[26]

The results were announced in October. Williams had completed the examinations some months before, and was serving as a temporary master at QRC. On October 19, he learnt he had finally won an island scholarship. His father's joy was even greater. Eric recalled that there was

> jubilation, for my father, who arrived home for lunch bewildered by the congratulations from people on the way. His twenty-year-old dream had come true ... he looked upon my victory as a decisive proof of his manhood. His bearing was more erect thereafter, his confidence in himself restored, and he often told me that whatever his rivals had, they had not an island scholar as their son.[27]

Henry Williams had been preparing for this day for many years. He had directed his son's academic life from primary through high school, and by this time had also selected a career for his son. His choice was that Eric would pursue a medical degree. Indeed, he had previously consulted with his friend Dr Hayes on this issue. They had agreed that Eric would work with Hayes on completion of his degree. Advised by Hayes, Henry had surveyed possible medical schools for his son.

Henry Williams, of course, had engaged in no discussions with his son on career choices. Two factors influenced this. It was the nature of the society at that time that the elder, be it the Governor of the colony or the father of the home, would make decisions which must be accepted without discussion or question. Secondly, many parents in the colonial Caribbean were determined that their children should pursue careers in medicine or law. The perception was that these professions provided financial security, brought a measure of individual independence even within the colonial framework, and, most importantly, enhanced the social status of the family. Thus the only issue that concerned Henry

Williams, once his son had won the scholarship, was what medical school Eric would attend.

By this time, though, the determined, single-minded, stubborn, independent child had grown into a 20-year-old man of similar qualities. There was also the very practical consideration that Eric could not stand the sight of blood.[28] The showdown between Henry Williams and his son continued for several weeks. Neither side was willing to budge. What drove Henry Williams was his need to shape a son after his own unfulfilled aspirations. What drove Eric was that he had developed a love for teaching. He had tutored while at high school, and taught at QRC briefly. During the months before he left for England in 1932 he was assigned to teach English and History at the Government Training College. He put it simply: "I was determined to be a teacher."[29] And, as he observed during an interview with the BBC many years later, "It was I who had won the scholarship, not he!"[30]

In seeking to finalize the decision on his career, Eric Williams held discussions with many people. He went to his favoured teacher W. D. Inniss, who was doubly pleased — his student had selected both his alma mater and his profession. Eric also "consulted two coloured nominated members of both the Legislative and Executive Councils . . . one a physician, the other a lawyer."[31] They agreed with his decision to pursue a career in teaching and research.

Having obtained the island scholarship, Williams sought entry into Oxford University. Letters of recommendation were provided by former teachers at QRC. Among these was C. S. Doorly, who wrote that Williams's "final mark of 1732 (out of 1800) was one of the best ever seen at QRC". In his recommendation, R. Cambridge emphasized that Williams had achieved an "exceptionally brilliant school record".[32] Yet Williams was quite aware that his application to Oxford did not meet with the approval of his father.

Eric Williams approached the confrontation with his father, the most serious they had ever had, as he had done everything previously, and as he would do in his later life. That is, he was thoroughly prepared. He was ready "for the showdown with my father. Aptitudes, interest, my personal experience, the advice of others, the signs of the times, all cried out for my support."[33] But what he faced was his father's dreams and hopes, which had been nurtured for 20 years. Henry Williams "protested, remonstrated, argued and sneered, cajoled and persuaded." Eric refused to back down; eventually, his father did, and in a show of solidarity decided to accompany his son on the boat trip to England.

Eric served as a teacher during the year before he began his scholarship. George Edwards, still a student at QRC, and by 1932 captain of the school's cricket team, remained a close friend during that year. He recalled that when Eric received his first salary, he lavishly treated Edwards and two young ladies at a cake and ice-cream shop on Frederick Street named the Patisserie. Eric later spent a weekend at the Edwards home in Longdenville, where both young men made their first appearance at a public dance, accompanied by two sisters named Beckles.[34] They were able to renew their friendship in 1944, 12 years later, when Eric made his first return visit to Trinidad.

Eric had good company on his first trip away from Trinidad. His father had not travelled previously, and his imminent retirement from the Post Office allowed him to travel with his son. Eric's childhood friend, Ray Dolly, studying medicine in London, was home on vacation, and Eric changed his boat tickets so that they could travel together. They left on the *Simon Bolivar* together with some other students who had been vacationing in Trinidad. It was a difficult trip for father and son, for both suffered from seasickness during the voyage.

As Eric Williams left Trinidad, to begin a new period in his life as a university student in England, he did so with the firm assurance that he had conquered all the challenges that had so far been placed before him. These included a childhood characterized by scarce resources and a strictly regimented home life; parents who sought almost absolute control; a school environment alien to local conditions; and competing for the island scholarship. Even so, having won, he had been forced to debate with his father furiously to be able to pursue his academic interests.

Additionally, the racial issue persisted. As already noted, Eric had come to believe that the family's financial deprivation was a direct consequence of a discriminatory colonial system. Because of colour and limited education, Henry Williams believed that he was destined to a low-status and low-paying position at the Post Office. The perpetual challenge for the family was "how to make ends meet." Eric believed that he had faced a similar situation when an Englishman was appointed principal of his primary school simply because he possessed the necessary "social qualifications"; the situation at QRC was fundamentally the same.

Williams had demonstrated a very high degree of resilience in the face of all these adversities. He had found his sense of purpose, guided by his father, in a brilliant primary and secondary school record. In an important sense, education would indeed provide him with the means of control. He began to view himself as a leader, an example to others, especially among the black youth. His performance in sports and education had helped to groom him for this role. This self-confidence and sense of purpose would serve him well as he confronted the new challenges in England. He had little doubt that he would conquer these as he had successfully conquered all others before.

In 1935, Eric Williams was awarded a First Class degree at Oxford University

ACADEMIC PREPARATION IN ENGLAND

T he stormy weather which Eric and Henry Williams experienced on their boat trip to England was something of an omen of the life that Eric would encounter during his years of university study. Both father and son were seasick on the voyage, and absent from the dining room for many meals; but they arrived safely in England, and were looked after initially by Ray Dolly, who was about to begin his third year of medical school. Eric roomed with Dolly until he left for Oxford, while his father was accommodated nearby.

Henry Williams, on his first trip away from home, remained in England for a few months. After Eric left for Oxford, Ray Dolly arranged some interviews for Henry, and showed him around London. Henry was curious about the British postal system. He thoroughly enjoyed this brief sojourn in England, and returned home very excited and "very British."[1] By this time Eric had rented a room in a family home in Oxford, and had begun to settle into the routine of university life.

High school education in Trinidad had provided Eric with an excellent foundation for Oxford. Not only because of the huge doses of history and literature at Queen's Royal College, but because personal discipline had been paramount in preparing for the island scholarship examination. This reliance on personal study and discipline proved vital as Williams adapted to the method of study at his Oxford college, St Catherine's. "The core of the Oxford system," he wrote, "was the weekly tutorial."[2] He acknowledged that the "tutorial system . . . admirably suited my temperament."[3] Under this system, the tutor provided the general guidelines, while responsibility was placed on the student to do the research. This was an ideal system for Williams, who was both a brilliant student, extremely conscientious with regard to his studies, well organized and goal-oriented. He was aware that Oxford would provide him with the means, and the education, to achieve his goals: he simply needed to be guided in the right direction. He wanted to pursue knowledge on his own, and paid little attention to formal lectures. He admitted that he covered the "entire history course, except the special subject, in tutorials."[4]

He selected four areas of study during his first term: Latin, French, European History and Political Economy. But he attended lectures occasionally in only two of them, at the insistence of his tutor, R. Trevor Davies, a Welshman who Williams described as "my guide, philosopher and friend, during my three undergraduate years."[5] According to Williams, "My weekly tutorial hour at noon on Fridays — which grew longer and longer until it ran into nearly two hours — represented my sole connection as an undergraduate with the Oxford dons."[6]

Just as W. D. Inniss had served as Williams's mentor in high school, R. Trevor Davies became his first mentor at Oxford. He needed a guide and a friend. Yet he was not a follower. He was willing to accept advice from those he respected, but was very focused on the path he had selected. He had led his high school in sports, he had studied assiduously and privately to earn the island scholarship: he did the same at university. He possessed enormous self-confidence and had established clearly-defined goals for himself. His immediate objective was to obtain a First Class undergraduate degree.

While goal-oriented, Oxford provided Williams with a more integrated perspective on education. The study of history at QRC had been "a record of battles and politicians, dates and events."[7] But as Williams gained a new appreciation for literature and art "as sources for the understanding and appraisal of historical development", he now began to view history as a "record of the development of humanity, of life and of society, in all their various manifestations."[8] He found it easier to appreciate the divine right of kings from a study of Shakespeare's *Richard II*. Visits to the National Gallery and the Tate and Wallace Collections contributed to his understanding of history. Three years after his arrival at Oxford, Williams was well prepared to undertake his final examinations.

While Williams approached his studies very seriously, he was not merely a bookworm. He was determined to live a balanced life, as he had done during his years of high school, when active involvement in sports complemented his rigorous studies. However, he was uncomfortable with his immediate social surroundings.

In the England of the 1930s, a black student at Oxford was still something of a novelty. Unfortunately for Williams, he was always sensitive to issues of race and colour. This, of course, was the consequence of listening to a lifetime of complaints from his father concerning the negative implications of race for advancement in the colonial civil service. Williams's relationships with his fellow students were therefore sometimes difficult. London remained a refuge for him, because there he could interact with his friends from the Caribbean. But he recalled that during his first Christmas vacation there, children would "touch me as they passed me in the street and say 'First luck!'"[9]

Williams was very fortunate to have Trinidadian friends in England. Ray Dolly and Halsey McShine were studying in London. Later Joey Ribeiro, who had been his high school cricket captain, and within a few years would become his brother-in-law, began to room with Dolly and McShine. Another close friend, John Pillai, had been a member of the football team which Williams captained at QRC. Thus, during his college years, Williams's closest friends were men he had known at least since high school. He interacted somewhat less with his fellow English students.

This small group of Trinidad students remained in close contact during their university years in England. Williams travelled to London regularly to spend the weekend with them; and since Dolly owned a car, the London group, with their various girlfriends, made occasional one-day trips to Oxford. Because the group was relatively large, they did not stay over. Williams would show them around the university and the town, and they shared a meal together. McShine remembers that occasionally Williams would discuss with them the discrimination he felt at the university.[10]

In London, Williams, Dolly and McShine spent much time travelling around and socializing. Williams's appreciation for art matured at this time through his frequent visits to the art galleries. McShine recalls one amusing incident. They had gone into a public bathroom, but into separate areas. Suddenly he heard Williams shout, "If you do not stop this I will put my boot into you!" Apparently a homosexual in the bathroom had attempted to interfere with Williams, but made a hasty exit when the young student began to shout at him.[11]

These friends, especially Dolly and Williams, also made time for sporting activities. They joined a group that called themselves the "Catamarans" or wanderers, which comprised West Indian, African and Indian university students and played cricket against various colleges and other friendly teams around London.[12] The group also made time for intellectual pursuits with a more radical perspective than that of formal university lectures, though this seemed to have less impact on Williams than on the other colonial students. Oxaal noted:

> The intellectual and political Zeitgeist which greeted James and Williams in the England of the Thirties was perhaps more strongly to the left than it had even been before . . . The Western democracies were entering a period of intense political ferment and crisis . . . In this highly-charged political period the education of colonial students tended to acquire great ideological intensity and significance.[13]

One forum for this kind of education was WASU (the West Indian, African Students Union in London). Here Williams and his friends attended informal lectures by radicals including George Padmore and C. L. R. James, and by future leaders including Jomo Kenyatta and Kwame Nkrumah. The extent of Williams's involvement in this group is, however, questionable. For instance, James, after his falling out with Williams, later wrote,

> Williams also knew George Padmore; Jomo Kenyatta; that monster, C. L. R. James, and others of the kind. He came to our meetings, read our books, magazines and pamphlets, took part in some of our discussions. He studied and wrote history. But he never joined anything.[14]

Williams later confirmed this view. In his famous "Let Down My

Bucket" speech in Woodford Square, Port of Spain, in June 1955, when he formally entered the national political scene, he was aware that it was necessary to present himself as ideologically pure. He told the assembled crowd, "I had never had any connection whatsoever with any political organization at all, except that at Oxford. I had attended regularly, meetings of the Indian nationalist students in their club, the Majliss."[15]

If Williams was less involved, and consequently less influenced by the radical movement of the 1930s, the question remains: was this because he had determined that obtaining a university degree, First Class, was his only priority, or was it simply that the politics of the left held little appeal for him? His academic concerns were probably paramount, though that does not mean the ideological issue was irrelevant. Williams had an enormous capacity for very diligent study, as he had already demonstrated. This same diligence was applied to his study at Oxford. He later wrote,

> I worked steadily throughout the entire period . . . and in the excessively long vacations . . . I made it my practice to spend three weeks at Christmas, three at Easter, six in the summer in Oxford, which was at those times like a dead city, reading steadily in my rooms and in the college and university libraries.[16]

Williams was thus thoroughly prepared when he took his final undergraduate examinations, and was duly awarded a First Class degree in 1935. He placed among the top three students in that class. Part of the examination was a *viva voce*, and Williams was asked where he had come from and what was his favourite subject. When he volunteered that he most enjoyed colonial history, his examiner pressed for a reason. To which he responded, "Well, I am a colonial."[17] The examiner then asked "whether I meant that there was a connection between one's study and one's environment. I replied I could not see the value of study unless there was a connection to the environment."[18]

This issue of the relationship of study to the environment gained salience when Williams embarked upon the research for his doctoral degree. The expected path, after his first degree, was to proceed to a diploma in education in preparation for a secondary school career in Trinidad. But both his college principal and his tutor agreed that Williams's academic promise would be stultified by this career path.

The principal therefore prepared a letter for Williams to present to the Trinidad government, explaining that Williams had just

> crowned a successful career . . . by getting a brilliant First Class in Modern History . . . he was one of the best three men . . . Mr Williams . . . has not been a mere bookworm, but has distinguished himself both in cricket and in football . . . He is capable of advanced academic work, such as teaching teachers, not boys . . . he should be encouraged to fit himself for that sort of work, either by taking another Honour School in Oxford or by taking a research degree there . . . Williams is an exceptional man who deserves, if possible, exceptional treatment.[19]

Oxford was obviously very impressed by Williams's performance. But initially the Department of Education in Trinidad was not. Williams himself wrote to J. O. Cutteridge requesting an extension of his scholarship in order to pursue post-graduate study.[20] Cutteridge's response was negative.[21] Later however, probably because he received a testimonial from Dr J. K. Brook in September 1935, Cutteridge sent a cable to Williams extending the scholarship so that he could proceed to work toward a second Honours degree.[22]

In the fall of 1935, Williams enrolled in the Honours programme of the School of Philosophy, Politics and Economics. He also decided to attempt the All Souls Fellowship examination that October. He later wrote that these decisions turned out to be hopeless mistakes.[23] Up to this point in his life, Williams had triumphed over every challenge he had faced; but both academically and socially, All Souls presented a challenge to which he would eventually succumb. He said succinctly, "I simply did not belong." For "no 'native', however detribalized, could fit socially into All Souls." He felt ill at ease in the classroom, but even more so in the dining room, admitting that "I have always lacked the social graces."[24]

For Williams, the fundamental issue was again racial discrimination, a problem, he believed, that had persisted for much of his life. Upon seeking entry into All Souls he had been told that his race would prevent him from obtaining a "social" fellowship (one "involving principally tutoring"). However, he remained eligible based on merit. Because of his race, he believed he was not accepted socially at All Souls. After completion of his Fellowship examination, he was taken aside by the College Warden and politely told that the "greatest service I could render to my people . . . was to return to Trinidad."[25] Williams summarized his situation at All Souls this way: "The entire episode, capped by the Warden's advice, convinced me that I would never get an All Souls Fellowship, and that the racial factor would dispose of me in 1936 as the examination factor had in 1935. I was very angry."[26]

Williams was quite aware that he had performed below his own expectations in the Fellowship examination. One reason, he believed, was that this was his second very rigorous examination in four months (the previous one had been his undergraduate finals). He also found that the strain of an oral language examination, surrounded by 40 Fellows, presumably all English, was too much. Compounding his problem was the loud laughter of these Fellows when he made a crucial mistake in his oral translation. Toward the end of this ordeal, he simply refused to continue. For him, the predominant issue, again, was race.

He had done quite poorly in his Fellowship examination, and the academic year which he spent reading for his second Honours degree followed the same course. He did not enjoy his study of Philosophy and Economics, though he did fare better in his classes in Politics, partly because he developed a close relationship with his professor and tutor, D. W. Brogan. Eight years later, Brogan would write the introduction to Williams's classic *Capitalism and Slavery*.

The year 1936, then, was a very difficult one for Williams. He was convinced that racial discrimination had prevented him from obtaining a fellowship at All Souls College. He did not enjoy his courses. And he was handicapped by limited finances. In January of that year, as was his style, he "blazed out in a letter to his principal". Shortly afterwards, he was awarded a Senior University Studentship, which eased the financial strain. But in order to balance his finances he was forced to take a job teaching English to Burmese students at Oxford. At the end of the 1935–6 academic year, Williams decided to abandon his study toward a second Honours degree and switch to doctoral research. He considered this "the most important decision I had made in my life",[27] along with his previous decision to study at Oxford.

During 1936, Williams began to develop his connections with Howard University in Washington, which would lead to a two-year position in the fall of 1939[28], later converted into a tenure-track Assistant Professorship in the Social Sciences. Between 1936 and 1939 Williams maintained a steady stream of correspondence with Abram Harris, Alain

Locke and Ralph Bunche, all "outstanding internationally respected African-American scholars,"[29] and ideally placed to introduce Williams into their professional circle and to provide advice on his research efforts.

The subject that Williams chose for his doctoral research was the abolition of the West Indian slave system. The prevailing view was that slavery was abolished in the British Empire after a group of English humanitarians had publicized the issue of man's inhumanity to man, thereby appealing to the conscience of the British. It was Williams's position that this view "could claim no support from the historical records."[30] He therefore advanced the thesis that the demise of slavery was due primarily to economic, not ethical, factors. More specifically, he would argue, the rise of industrialization had introduced a new labouring class whose interests were different from those of the older capitalist sugar barons. It was they who encouraged the anti-slavery movement.

How did Williams develop this thesis? He provided at least a partial answer in the bibliography to *Capitalism and Slavery*, the revised version of his thesis. In commenting on the sources for his work, he mentioned two studies: the first was a Master's thesis and the "second and more important is C. L. R. James, *The Black Jacobins* . . . On pages 38–41, the thesis advanced in this book is stated clearly and concisely and, as far as I know, for the first time in English."[31]

It is clear that James and another Trinidadian-born revolutionary, George Padmore, interacted with Williams as he wrote his thesis. Williams and James had known each other before they both left for England. They met again at meetings of the WASU group, and it is believed that in 1937–38, when Williams was conducting his research in London, he met with James on numerous occasions. It appears that James was Williams's mentor during this period.[32] Williams also consulted with that other Trinidadian revolutionary, George Padmore, formerly Malcolm Nurse. In his letters to Alain Locke in 1938, he writes about "long conversations with George Padmore."[33] Interactions with these two radicals must have contributed to the radical slant of Williams's thesis.

During the 1937–1938 period, Williams lived in London, close to his old friend Halsey McShine, and spent much of that time in the

Public Record Office, probing the various official papers, and in the British Museum, researching in the unpublished manuscripts of Liverpool, Clarkson, Windham and Melville. At the conclusion of this research he noted that his thesis, *The Economic Aspect of the Abolition of the West Indian Slave Trade and Slavery*, was in his opinion "an important contribution to research on the subject."[34]

Yet while Williams worked diligently, he also found time for other pursuits. In London he saw his friends McShine and Dolly frequently. McShine recalled that he and his future wife Eileen, together with Williams and his girlfriend Elsie Ribeiro, "were a friendly foursome who spent many Saturday evenings dining and dancing in London."[35] Elsie's brother Joey roomed with McShine and Dolly: McShine's recollection was that the relationship between Williams and Ribeiro never appeared to be serious to the point of marriage. Williams dated a Jewish lady named Julie before developing his relationship with Ribeiro.

Nevertheless, Williams and Ribeiro were quietly married while he was completing his doctoral research.[36] Dolly claimed that he was quite astounded to learn of Williams's marriage. He considered himself "like brother and sister" with Elsie, yet had no idea that the couple had decided on marriage.[37] Williams simply announced it to him shortly after the wedding.

While in London, and maybe as a form of diversion and relaxation from his research, Williams requested McShine to teach him the game of chess. He was a quick learner, and they progressed rapidly to competitive games. McShine recalled that Williams was always disappointed when he was unable to win. But, as he said, "How could Bill expect to beat me, he had just learnt the game while I had been playing it all my life!"[38] What McShine did not realize was that Williams expected to win every challenge he faced. He had already compiled an impressive record, and was unaccustomed to not winning. In fact, he was a bitter loser on those few occasions in his life when he was defeated.

His doctoral thesis having been completed and successfully defended, Williams was awarded the Doctor of Philosophy degree in December 1938. The obvious issue for him then was, where could he find employment? Since 1936, he had been developing his contacts with Howard University. The British had already made it clear to him that he would not be employed at Oxford. While working on his thesis, he had approached the Japanese Ambassador in London, seeking a position of lecturer at a university in Japan.[39] He wrote similarly to the Siamese legation in London.[40] In his letter to President Radakrishnan of India, Williams emphasized that he was "familiar with Indians long before I came to England."[41] This, Williams believed, would have enhanced his qualifications for a lectureship in India.

Clearly, Williams was much too qualified to return to a teaching position at his old high school in Trinidad. He had written to the President of Dilliard University in the US seeking a position.[42] But eventually his three-year correspondence with Howard University paid off. Ralph Bunche, head of the small Political Science department, offered him a position to teach Social Sciences. Williams readily accepted. He spent the next eight months, until August 1939, conducting private research in the field of his thesis, before leaving for Washington.

Published in 1944, "Capitalism and Slavery" was Eric Williams's
seminal work on the abolition of slavery

AMERICAN SOJOURN: HOWARD AND THE CARIBBEAN COMMISSION

The ship that brought Eric Williams to the United States arrived in New York on August 7, 1939. After a very brief visit with relatives in Harlem — his first experience of the difficult life of black Americans — Williams went directly to Washington to begin preparation for teaching at Howard University. His arrival at Howard was the culmination of a three-year effort by some influential faculty there to secure a position for him. Yet his first choice for employment had been an academic appointment in England.

Clearly Williams had hoped to obtain a position at his old university, but he quickly concluded that "there were too many senior people at Oxford." Moreover, it was his belief that the English were anxious for him to return home. The Dean of his college had remarked, "Are you still here? You had better go back home. You West Indians are too keen on trying to get posts here which take jobs away from Englishmen."[1] It was his view that discrimination had prevented him from obtaining the necessary scholarships at Oxford, and would also preclude his prospects for employment. Many years later, he complained to Norman Manley: "I was denied a fellowship at Oxford . . . it was on racial grounds . . . every conceivable pressure was brought to bear on me to leave and return to Trinidad."[2]

So Williams had built a relationship with senior faculty at Howard. By 1938, with his doctoral degree soon to be completed, the need to find a job was becoming more urgent. He had cast a wide net, including an interview with the Japanese Ambassador in London, who was interested in increasing trade relationships; the Burmese government; and even a personal letter to President Radakrishnan of India. He had also been interviewed by the Colonial Office for a position at his old high school in Trinidad, but was deemed to be overqualified.[3]

Eventually, as Williams himself observed, "as the war clouds began to gather more ominously, I turned to the U.S.A. [and] . . . landed a job . . . at Howard University."[4]

It is possible that the impending war in Europe encouraged Williams to move to the other side of the Atlantic. One sister expressed the opinion that "he left England because of the war. He did not want to be involved in the war."[5] Nevertheless, Williams's search for a position at Howard had begun "sometime in 1936."[6]

It was not surprising that Williams sought employment at Howard. Most university-trained black West Indians, and those aspiring to attend an American university at that time, accepted the view that Howard was the leading black institution of higher learning. Williams would also have known that many black intellectuals in the United States found a haven at Howard, away from the discriminatory practices of the wider American society. For Williams, Howard University would become the "negro Oxford"; there he would be converted from an assiduous but somewhat timid researcher into a "brilliant internationally respected scholar, a formulator and leader of the West Indian decolonization struggle . . . and a dominant figure in post-colonial West Indian politics."[7]

The radicalizing of Williams was due in part to the relationship he developed with three influential scholars at Howard: Ralph Bunche, Abram Harris and Alain Locke.

Ralph Bunche had begun teaching at Howard in 1928. When Williams initiated his correspondence, Bunche was head of the Department of Political Science. He enthusiastically supported Williams's application since his department "had a pressing need for a scholar in the foreign field", and he noted that "Williams was well-prepared to fill this role."[8] The relationship was short-circuited when Bunche left Howard in 1944 to begin a diplomatic career, which resulted in a Nobel Peace Prize in 1950. By the time of his departure, his relationship with Williams was tense, but he had already "helped Williams break into Washington's international circles."[9]

Abram Harris was chair of the Economics Department. He was the most radical of the three, and contributed much to liberalizing Williams's perspectives on economic issues. But it was Alain Locke, Professor of Philosophy, with whom Williams would develop the closest relationship. He served as Williams's mentor much as W. D. Inniss had done during those high school years in Trinidad.

Alain Locke taught philosophy at Howard for some 40 years. Williams befriended him while he was already a senior professor serving his last years at Howard. Williams maintained a ten-year correspondence with him, including the years they were together at Howard. These letters display the warmth, affection and abiding respect in which Williams held Locke. In a letter dated November 1938, almost a year before Williams arrived at Howard, he wrote:

> In a recent letter from Dr Harris I learnt that you are still making persistent representations on my behalf. I would like to say how deeply I appreciate your attitude, and hope, for my sake at least, that your efforts will at last be successful.[10]

Writing to Locke a few months earlier, Williams had referred to him as one of his "godfathers", probably due to the determination of this senior professor to assist a struggling graduate student.[11] He constantly wrote about his difficult financial situation, and the necessity to find permanent employment after receiving his degree. Williams apparently served as a go-between for Locke and George Padmore over the publication of a pamphlet on the West Indies. He repeatedly referred to his lengthy conversations with Padmore, and assured Locke, in typical Williams manner, that before the final manuscript was sent "George and I will go through it microscopically."[12] Eventually, it was Williams who completed most of the work on this pamphlet, for which he was paid by Howard. He needed the funds to pay Oxford before his degree was conferred.

In March 1939, Williams happily informed Locke that "Dr Bunche wrote me recently saying that he was recommending me for an assistant professorship." He went on to express the hope that "this means that the united efforts of close on three years will at last bear fruit."[13] In fact, they did, for by June Williams was able to express his delight at obtaining the appointment. This for him was "the realization of a long-cherished dream, and I shall do my best not to let you and my other sponsors down." He continued: "It would be churlish and contrary to my natural feelings not to add how deeply I appreciate the efforts which you, along with Ralph and Abe, have persistently made to get me into the charmed circle."[14]

This letter to Locke is also important for two additional reasons. Firstly, Williams wrote openly about his personal outlook on life. With war increasingly imminent, Williams told Locke: "I am by nature inclined to be pessimistic." He expressed the view that he was "getting worse everyday" as the "international situation deteriorates." He admitted to having a "more gloomy view of human nature."[15] These admissions may seem surprising: Williams had recently secured a job, and he had come to know Locke only through an exchange of letters. Yet at each stage of his educational experience — in primary school, secondary school, and at Oxford — he had sought out and developed a close relationship with a particular teacher who would serve as his mentor. And even though in June 1939 he had not yet had a face-to-face meeting, he had certainly selected Locke to play a similar role. Perhaps these mentors provided Williams with the emotional connection that he did not have with his father.

Secondly, in this letter, Williams wrote that his wife had left for a short trip to Trinidad to visit her mother, whom she had not seen for many years, and hoped to rejoin him in Washington shortly after his arrival. It is not known whether Locke was aware that Williams was married, since earlier letters make no mention of his wife. What is known is that Williams made a deliberate effort to suppress awareness of his marriage, fearing it would compromise his scholarship.[16] It therefore testifies to Williams's respect and regard for Locke that he shared information with him about his marriage and his state of mind.

As a position at Howard appeared more likely, Williams recognized the necessity of making his research more relevant, especially to the black population of the United States. This was probably a pragmatic decision, since increased relevance could only enhance his prospects.

In connection with his thesis, Williams had conducted research "on the humanitarian side", hoping to do a "biography of Wilberforce" later; but he now decided to concentrate on an "authoritative economic history" of the British West Indies, since he believed that this "will be of great interest to American negroes."[17] In this continuing quest for relevance, he explained to Locke, a few months later,

> I want to draw conclusions as to the capacity [of] the West Indian negro for advancement and estimate to what extent his white master has fulfilled his . . . mission of civilization and trusteeship. Perhaps if I get to Howard some Negro organization may find it a subject of importance to Negroes generally.[18]

He repeated this position a year after his arrival at Howard, when he began to conduct the research that was later published as *The Negro in the Caribbean*. He wrote Locke that he used that title "in line with my constant argument that events in the Caribbean are of vital importance to Negroes in the U.S."[19]

Williams was given a joint appointment at Howard University, with three-quarters of his time in the Division of Social Sciences and the remainder in Political Science under Ralph Bunche. Initially, the appointment was for two years, with an annual salary of US$2,300.[20] In the Social Sciences, he was given the monumental task of designing a new course on the evolution of civilization, a requirement for all freshman students. He had only about two months' notice to prepare for this class.

The task was extremely challenging, not only because of the limited time for preparation but also because there was no model to follow and no suitable textbook was available. Williams's biggest challenge, though, was himself: the extremely high standards that he maintained, and the thoroughness and completeness with which he undertook any task. He interpreted his assigned courses as "the evolution of humanity through recognized historical periods."[21] He compiled his own body of readings, drawing on original writings from Plato to Hitler, which he eventually produced as a three-volume anthology. He considered this "a major accomplishment . . . the product of nine years' labouring in the field."[22]

Volume II, for instance, provided a formidable challenge to his students.[23] It surveyed the period 1689 to 1880, with a brief introduction by Williams. It began with the economic basis for civilization, then proceeded to other manifestations. It covered the growth of industrial capitalism; the rise of political democracy; the domination of Great Britain in world affairs; the supremacy of science. Altogether, 852 items were included in a volume of 567 pages. The completeness and thoroughness of the volume, while an immense challenge to new students, was vintage Williams. It reflected the way in which he approached each assignment: to be well prepared and to give of his best.

If preparation of this new course in a compressed time frame was difficult, delivery of the lectures, to a relatively large student body, was no less a challenge. Williams himself did most of the formal lecturing, and was joined by other professors in leading the discussion groups. The student body for the course grew immensely in the immediate post-World War II years, as large numbers of ex-soldiers returned to college at government expense.

During the 1946–47 school year, Williams reported that 1,003 students attended two sections of Social Sciences I, and 1,494 attended three sections of Social Sciences II. His largest class consisted of 733 freshman in a day class, to which he lectured "with little audio help."[24] It is clear that this exercise in mass education was excellent preparation for Williams; some ten years later, he undertook the task of educating the masses at his "University of Woodford Square" in Port of Spain.

Two students recalled attending Williams's Social Science classes at Howard with fond memories. Both noted that the classes were large and conducted in a large auditorium. One remembered that Williams "was great, a born teacher, always thoroughly prepared."[25] The other found the lectures to be "very stimulating," and even though the course content covered very abstract ideas, "the information came to us, we did not have to get it from him as he was speaking . . . his ideas came over very clearly."[26]

Effective as a teacher, Williams also displayed a personal concern for West Indian students at Howard and indirectly served as a mentor for many of them. His home, near the campus, became something of a home-away-from-home. Students were invited for informal social gatherings and to play bridge. One recalled Williams getting together with students in the dormitory for general discussions.[27] He encouraged these students to form a Caribbean Student Association, for which he served as faculty adviser. He served as a soccer coach, presumably to these same students.[28]

Williams's relations with faculty, especially his peers, were more formal. He described them as "cordial, even though few friendships were developed." He attributed this to the "inevitable jealousy of the outsider, particularly one from Oxford."[29] The view of others was that "Williams's aloofness was the result of his feeling that few equalled him in intellect."[30] But Williams had made a very conscious decision to take no part in campus feuds between junior and senior faculty, in union activity, or in faculty attacks upon the university administration. He explained his strategy towards campus politics this way: "I maintained correct and even friendly relations with many [faculty], but I concentrated on my work, and I soon came to be regarded as a worker doing his work and minding his own business."[31] While this strategy tended to insulate Williams from the difficulties of campus life, it was not always successful. In a letter to Locke in 1946, he explained that while "I largely steered clear" of campus problems, on one occasion "someone came right up to me and deliberately punched me." If this is what occurred literally, it says something of the intensity of the conflict among faculty at Howard during those years.[32]

Nevertheless, Williams maintained a close relationship with Ralph Bunche and Alain Locke. Bunche, chair of Political Science, had lobbied the university president, Mordecai Johnson, for a position for Williams, who was required to contribute a quarter of his time to that department. Recognizing his enormous potential, Bunche encouraged him to diversify the department's programme by offering a course on Latin America. He also helped Williams make contacts in official Washington, and involved him in the conference and other public speaking activities of the university. This was the primary means by which Williams was able to develop a relationship with the US State Department.

Yet over the years, the relationship between Bunche and Williams deteriorated, apparently over Williams's efforts to balance his teaching at Howard with his employment at the Caribbean Commission, the organization that was set up to strengthen cooperation between the US and Britain in the wartime Caribbean.

Williams undertook a one-year part-time position with the

Caribbean Commission, commencing in March 1943. He was then appointed Secretary to the Agricultural Committee at the Caribbean Research Council, a branch of the Commission. This new position seriously compromised his full-time position of assistant professor. He requested part-time leave. This was granted, and Williams received a one-third salary decrease.[33] He also asked to deliver his lectures at night. Bunche was displeased, since the majority of students attended day classes. Yet Williams prevailed.[34]

When new classes began in March 1944, Williams was absent. He was in the Caribbean on behalf of the Commission, and spending time in Trinidad on his first return visit. He had informed Bunche he would be away for three weeks, and arranged for a substitute teacher to conduct his classes. In fact he stayed away for over six weeks. Bunche was irate and reported to the Dean that "the sole source of difficulty . . . is to be found . . . [in] the intemperature and unconscionably bigoted attitude of Mr Williams in this matter."[35] Bunche had recommended that Williams's paycheck be withheld, Williams had responded angrily,[36] and this was Bunche's riposte. Williams had suggested that half of his paycheck be given to the substitute teacher, to which Bunche responded, "I fail to see how he can, with any sense of propriety or decency, claim the right to profit from salary which someone else had earned for him."[37] He termed Williams's arrangement to employ a substitute teacher as "academic peonage or share-cropping."[38]

Because of the growing conflict, Williams requested and received leave of absence from the university for the 1944-1945 year. When he sought to return in mid-1946, he was careful to ask the Dean about the status of Bunche, who by this time had left Howard.[39]

Williams's relationship with Professor Alain Locke, by contrast, deepened. Over the ten years of their professional relationship, he developed a deep admiration and respect for the elder man. This is apparent from the voluminous correspondence he carried on with Locke, even while they were colleagues. Both professors maintained very heavy travel schedules as a consequence of their research and public speaking demands, and letters served to keep them connected. The correspondence had been initiated by Williams's search for a faculty position, and continued partly as a consequence of mutual research interests. It blossomed as Williams gradually turned to Locke for advice on a wide range of issues. Eventually, Locke became something of a father figure to Williams.

In May 1943, Williams wrote to Locke, who was lecturing in the northern Caribbean, to inform him of the birth of his son Alistair. He also expressed his distress because he had not received a Rosenwald Fellowship that year, and mentioned that someone had recently termed him "your boy!"[40] Within two weeks Locke replied:

> Sorry about all those complications re: grants etc. There is too much politics and too much personalities in all of it . . . I think you should just calmly stick things through and win out, as merit always does . . . with the family situation on your hands you should take it easy, and . . . just enroll for teaching at summer school. As a regular session it ought to be fairly well compensated. I can see the Rosenwald point of view even though I don't agree with it.[41]

Locke's advice to Williams here clearly transcended that of one academic to another, on purely intellectual issues. Indeed, he appeared to be gently suggesting that, with the birth of Alistair, Williams might need to re-order his priorities. By this time Locke was well aware that Williams was almost constantly concerned about having adequate funds to meet his needs. Williams had referred to this problem in previous letters. Hence the suggestion about summer school. By informing Williams that he understood why there was no grant that summer, Locke was countering another of Williams's perpetual fears — that there was a conspiracy against him.

Williams shared his research and writing with Locke, seeking critiques, comments and eventually approval. Many of the letters focused on the issue of publication, something to which Williams devoted much effort. It has been stated that, while at Howard, Williams published or co-edited at least one major article every year in leading US journals.[42] As late as January 1948, a few months before he left Howard for a position in Trinidad, he continued to seek advice from Locke as he modified the reading requirements for his introductory Social Science course.[43]

It is obvious that research and writing were as important to Williams during his American sojourn as his teaching was. He developed five additional spheres of activity during his ten years in Washington: research into West Indian history; a lecture programme on West Indian affairs; work at an international organization dealing with the

Caribbean; proposals for a West Indian university; and research in colonial questions generally.[44]

At Oxford, Williams had worked with George Padmore on a contribution to Locke's Bronze Booklet Series on "The Negro in America". Within six months of his arrival at Howard, he was awarded a $2,000 Rosenwald Fellowship, which allowed him to travel and research in the northern Caribbean during the summer of 1940. The result was his popular but controversial The Negro in the Caribbean, again part of Locke's series. Williams was very pleased with this effort. He believed that "the book established my reputation"; appearing as it did "a little over two years after my first appointment, there was nothing like it in any language."[45]

The stage was now set for Williams's magnum opus — Capitalism and Slavery, "the elaboration and expansion of my thesis on the British abolition movement."[46] In April 1942, he received another Rosenwald grant, which furthered his research. Much of this was conducted in the United States since, as he said, "American scholarship in this field was quite remarkable." He mentioned in particular Elizabeth Donnan's "monumental anthology of documents" illustrative of the slave trade in America, and Leo Stock's edited anthology of debates in the British Parliament regarding North America up to the 1800s.[47] What Williams did not mention was that the "research that occupied the first half of Capitalism and Slavery was richly stimulated by the intellectual environment" at Howard University.[48] He did state that "ultimately the first half of Capitalism and Slavery was entirely new research on the period antecedent to that selected for my doctoral dissertation."[49] But he did not give credit to Howard for this new thrust in his research.

By the time Williams arrived at Howard "social science enquiry . . . was dominated by the presence of Abram Harris Jr., the first academic economist of note among black Americans."[50] Harris, it may be recalled, was one of the three senior faculty who encouraged and supported Williams's application for a position at Howard. Harris wrote at the beginning of his The Negro as Capitalist that it was one part of a projected three-phase study that would include "Africa and the Rise of Capitalism", "The Accumulation of Wealth Among Negroes prior to 1860", and "The Economic Basis of the Negro Middle Class". William Darrity, an economist and researcher on the Atlantic slave trade, observed that "the first phase of the three-part study was the part that intersected directly with the first half of Eric Williams's *Capitalism and Slavery*".[51] While Harris did not write a comprehensive study of the importance of African slave labour for the evolution of capitalism, one of his graduate students, Wilson Williams, completed a master's thesis in 1938 on the subject "Africa and the Rise of Capitalism". In his bibliography to *Capitalism and Slavery*, as we have seen, Eric Williams wrote:

> Special mention must be made of two studies which present in a general way the relationship between capitalism and slavery. The first is a Master's essay by W. E. Williams: Africa and the Rise of Capitalism . . . The second is C. L. R. James, The Black Jacobins: Toussaint L'Ouverture and the San Domingo Revolution.[52]

Darrity, with reference to Wilson Williams, stated: "There are often passages of the two works that bear a strong resemblance in tone, phrasing and sentiment",[53] and he concluded: "Eric Williams apparently seized upon Wilson Williams's thesis and ran with it to develop a far richer and more detailed analysis of the contributions of the West Indian slave plantation system to British development."[54]

Eric Williams also gave credit to C. L. R. James's *The Black Jacobins*, stating that "the thesis advanced in this book [*Capitalism and Slavery*] is stated clearly and concisely [in James's book], and I far as I know, for the first time in English."[55] The thesis to which Williams refers is what James termed "the truth about abolition" which, according to Darrity, "is, in all essentials, the same 'truth' that is replicated faithfully in Chapter VIII of *Capitalism and Slavery* . . . titled "The New Industrial Order.""[56]

The relationship between James and Williams was an intriguing one.[57] The bond between the two writers strengthened while Williams was writing his thesis at Oxford, and intensified when both arrived in the United States. James came a year before Williams to give some lectures, but stayed on after he became ill. James remained an unabashed Trotskyite, while Williams, who generally favoured an economic determinist perspective, studiously avoided being labelled. The entire intellectual environment at Howard, and particularly his friendship with radical economist Abram Harris, probably encouraged Williams's movement to the left, and therefore closer to James. More pragmatically, since Williams was assisted by James in the preparation of his doctoral thesis, it is understandable that James's assistance would be sought again as he rewrote his dissertation as *Capitalism and Slavery*.

Yet Williams did not write effusively about his relationship with James. Other than complimentary comments made to his mentors, especially W. D. Inniss at high school and Alain Locke at Howard, Williams was not an individual who freely dispensed credit to those who contributed to his development, personally or intellectually. However, on one occasion in 1944 he sent a note to James, in which he referred to himself as "Your godchild!"[58] This was a rare admission from a very private individual. It may be recalled that Williams had earlier termed Alain Locke "one of his godfathers."[59] One must conclude that Williams reserved that expression for the few who played special roles in his life.

In addition to teaching and research activities, Williams, like other young scholars, recognized the importance of participation in conferences to promote his professional career. While publications "opened wide the doors to lectures and writings", he participated in his first conference on "Negro Studies" within eight months of his arrival at Howard; his contribution focused on research priorities for the Caribbean. He became involved in the annual Social Science conference at Howard: at the first after his arrival, in May 1940, he was asked to present the opening address, with a lecture on "The Negro in the Caribbean". It was obvious that the authorities recognized Williams's broad intellect, even though he was only in his first year at Howard, and offered him the special honour of opening the conference.

Williams served as programme chairman of the 1943 Social Science conference, which had as its theme "The Economic Future of the Caribbean". At this gathering he made a presentation on economic development in the region. In an interesting footnote, the published report shows a minor contribution by Dom Basil Matthews: this may have been the first meeting of these two powerful figures, who would meet again, eleven years later, in a historic debate in Trinidad.[60]

With the publication of *The Negro in the Caribbean* in 1942 and *Capitalism and Slavery* two years later, the demand on Williams for lectures and conference participation increased. He wrote: "I broadened my contacts and saw more of the country than I would otherwise have seen."[61] He travelled to Boston, meeting with the Jamaican nationalist movement, and through them met Norman Manley. The Jamaican leader would be of much assistance later, as Williams faced difficulties with the Caribbean Commission. Later still, as Prime Minister of Trinidad and Tobago, Williams would value Manley's advice. On a research trip to Puerto Rico, Williams also met with its dynamic leader Muñoz Marin, who would become a firm friend in later years.

Williams's increased popularity resulted in invitations to speak at two major black universities: Fisk in Nashville, Tennessee and Atlanta University in Georgia. As the relationship with Fisk developed, Williams was offered a position there. By this time, however, his interest in the establishment of a West Indian university had deepened to the point where he decided that, if he were to resign from Howard, he would do so only to accept a position at a new West Indian university.

The idea for a West Indian university emerged in 1944, when the British government established a commission to consider higher education for its colonies in Africa and in the Caribbean. The five-member West Indies Committee included three English representatives, among whom was Sir James Irvine of St Andrews University and two well-known West Indian educators, Hugh Springer and Philip Sherlock. The Committee visited Howard University after a tour of the British West Indian islands, and Williams asked to present evidence to the group. His two primary points were that the university's curriculum must be relevant to the Caribbean environment, and that the university should be self-governing. That is, it should be unaffiliated to any British or Canadian university.[62] Irvine strongly disagreed with Williams on the second point. Nevertheless, Williams requested permission to submit a formal memorandum to the Committee, outlining his conception of a West Indian university.

He had once told Locke in a letter that "I put all that I have in anything that I do", and that was precisely his approach to his memorandum to the university Committee.[63] He studied the historical development of university education in former colonial areas, and, with an understanding of pre-university education in the West Indies, proposed a university "to suit the needs and aspirations of their people."[64] He continued his strong opposition to the idea of affiliation to any foreign university.

In order to add further weight and credibility to the memorandum, Williams consulted with the famed American philosopher and educator John Dewey, who was by this time in his mid-80s. Williams gained much from their meetings. A few years later, when the memorandum was published as *Education in the British West Indies*, Dewey wrote the foreword, in effect signalling his strong support for the project.

Williams submitted an 80-page memorandum to the Committee, the Colonial Office and the Caribbean Commission in March 1945. The only response he received from the Committee was that it was "in agreement with my views". The response that Williams had apparently wanted was the offer of a position at the new university, but according to him "I heard nothing more of the question of an appointment."[65]

In mid-1945, the Caribbean Commission contemplated moving to the Caribbean. Williams admitted that he seriously considered resigning from Howard University and moving to the West Indies with the Commission, pending the establishment of the West Indies University.[66] At that juncture, however, Howard offered him a full professorship, and he quickly decided "that it might be more strategic to transfer to the West Indian university from a United States professorship than from a research job with the Commission."[67] But even though the university actually began classes in 1948, Williams was not offered a position. Instead, in that year he accepted a full time position with the Caribbean Commission in Trinidad.

Kent House in Maraval, Port of Spain, where Eric Williams was based

with the Caribbean Commission from 1948 to 1956

INTERNATIONAL CIVIL SERVANT

T he Caribbean Commission, formerly the Anglo-American
Caribbean Commission, was the organization in which Eric
Williams served in various capacities for over twelve years. It
had its genesis in a Lend-Lease agreement between the United States
and Great Britain in March 1941. Under this agreement Britain received
50 mothballed US destroyers, while the US was granted land in Antigua,
St Lucia, British Guiana, Trinidad and Jamaica on which to build sea
and air bases under 99-year leases. While the British government was
of the view that the United States had received "far in excess of what
was required for military defence,"[1] the US expressed some scepticism
about the arrangement. The US President wrote:

> I am not yet clear in mind, however, as to whether the United States should consider
> American sovereignty over these islands . . . as something worthwhile or as a distinct
> liability. If we can get our naval bases why, for example, should we buy with them
> two million headaches, consisting of that number of human beings who would be
> a definite drag on this country, and who would stir up questions of racial stocks by
> virtue of their new status as American citizens.[2]

A similar arrogance had been displayed a few months earlier when
President Roosevelt sent his friend Charles Taussig on a fact-finding

mission to the region.[3] Taussig reported that since there were problems of concern to both the American and the British governments, a joint commission should be created.

In a joint communiqué, the two governments established the Caribbean Commission on March 9, 1942, and announced that its purpose was:

> Encouraging and strengthening social and economic cooperation between the United States and its possession and bases . . . in the Caribbean, and the United Kingdom and the British colonies in the same area . . . Members of the Commission will concern themselves primarily with matters pertaining to labour, agriculture, housing, health, education . . . and related subjects.[4]

A somewhat more sceptical view of the organization was provided by Jenny Pearce, who stated in her 1982 study, *Under the Eagle*, that the Commission's "purpose was to maintain 'stability' in the region during the war but also to consolidate the growing United States influence in the area."[5]

Nine months after the establishment of the Commission, Eric Williams, then Assistant Professor of Social and Political Science at Howard University in Washington, as he put it, "offered my services to the British representative in Washington."[6] From Williams's correspondence during that period, it appears that he was very anxious to leave Howard. But working at the Commission was not his first choice.

Between September and October 1942, Williams wrote letters to his old contacts in England, including Vincent Harlow, D. W. Brogan and V. J. Brook. He told Harlow: "I want to take a more active role in the War. I feel that I have a contribution to make."[7] He asked Brogan to try to obtain a position for him at the BBC, to which Brogan replied, "I don't see anything I can do at the moment."[8] Both Harlow and Brook suggested that Williams make an application to the Caribbean Commission. Williams accepted this advice and wrote to J. Huggins at the British Colonial Supply Mission in Washington.[9] He was interviewed in November 1942, and took the opportunity to present a copy of his recently published *The Negro in the Caribbean* to the British representative. The ideas presented in this text would cause Williams serious aggravation in the years while he worked at the Commission.

Williams believed that the British were reluctant to employ him at the Commission, partly because of the critical conclusions he had expressed in his doctoral thesis. It was also his view that a colonial would be confronted with much difficulty in reaching high office in a metropolitan-dominated organization. Williams held to this belief from the time of his interview in November 1942 until his dismissal in June 1955.

To support his job application, Williams turned to D. W. Brogan, his professor and tutor at Oxford, and to Professor R. H. Tawney for recommendations. But it was Charles Taussig, "the live wire at the Commission" and a man familiar with Williams's academic achievements, who was instrumental in obtaining a part-time position for him. Williams worked part-time at the Commission for a year, starting in March 1943. Initially, this involved one afternoon each fortnight, while he maintained his permanent professorship at Howard. His first assignment at the Commission was to bring West Indian laws up to date and to keep a check on price movements on the basis of price lists sent in by the British colonies in the Caribbean.

Towards the end of that first year, Williams stated, "my duties were steadily increased, both in quantity and in quality, until the month before my permanent appointment, I was working a 30-hour week."[10] The expansion of his responsibilities at the Commission led to discussions about full-time employment there. As he saw it, the British were so opposed to this that they offered him a post as an Agricultural Economist in Jamaica. "I declined the offer, on the grounds that I am not an agricultural economist."[11] The British then raised the issue of his selective service classification. The Americans responded by giving him a deferred classification. Next, there arose the issue of his salary, which was to be paid jointly by the British and the Americans. Williams had apparently decided to continue teaching in Howard University's evening programme, even though he would be employed full time at the Commission. The British appeared to be concerned that his total income should not exceed a specific amount.[12]

Eventually, in March 1944, Williams was appointed Secretary to the Agriculture Committee of the Caribbean Research Council, a branch of the Commission. He insisted that an important condition of his employment was his continued freedom to pursue his intellectual activities with regard to writing and public lectures. He agreed to submit advance copies of lectures to be delivered in the Caribbean to the American and British heads of the Caribbean Commission. In late 1944, the British edition of *The Negro in the Caribbean* was published, on the instigation of Williams's friend George Padmore. Williams's superiors had been informed of this. Yet the text ignited much contention when it arrived in the Caribbean in mid-1945, and Williams was caught in the middle.

He had already been involved in controversy over his public lectures a few months earlier, while still working part-time. The British section of the Commission was upset with his lectures on independence for Jamaica. One lecture had been delivered at a conference in Boston, and a second in Jamaica, where he was in open conflict with the British governor. The American section of the Commission was generally amused by the British attempts to censor Williams's public comments, but they no longer took that position when Williams published "Race Relations in Puerto Rico and the Virgin Islands" in the prestigious American journal *Foreign Affairs* in January 1945.

By the middle of 1945, therefore, Williams was at a crossroads concerning future employment with the Commission. Two other issues complicated the situation. Howard University declined to renew Williams's leave of absence for the school year 1945–1946; instead, seeking to encourage his return, they offered him one of ten new professorships. Williams realized it would be difficult to turn this offer down; he being offered a very senior position at a relatively young age, and would be able to skip the intermediate position of associate professor.

Secondly, the Caribbean Commission was thinking of transferring its headquarters to the Caribbean, something that Williams strongly advocated; at the same time, the British had begun to investigate the establishment of a university in the West Indies. Both proposals excited Williams immensely. He believed he could combine employment at the proposed new university with working at the Caribbean headquarters of the Commission. It was a dream come true.

But the new storm over *The Negro in the Caribbean* threatened Williams's future with the Commission. Both the *Antigua Star* and the *West India Committee Circular*, publications supported by British sugar planters in the Caribbean, attacked Williams's text as propagandist. The British section of the Commission was embarrassed, since Williams was one of its employees. After a heated discussion with Williams, his superior officer concluded: "I would want to ask you to resign, but I could not do anything because of your 18 months' contract."[13]

Williams discussed his options with the President of Howard University. He decided that if he resigned, he would be succumbing to pressure from the Commission. The President agreed to grant him another year of leave. Thus fortified, Williams wrote a ten-page letter to Sir John Macpherson, the senior British officer at the Commission, in which he concluded:

> In view of these facts I see no alternative but to inform you that under no circumstances will I entertain any request for my resignation. I consider myself . . . to be under an 18 months' contract beginning March 1, 1945, with the understanding that from September 1, 1946, we shall revert to annual contracts. I may also add that I expect to be appointed Secretary of the General Research Council in accordance with various discussions that we have had . . . If through the pressure of vested interests, I am to be removed from the Commission, it will be done not only without any assistance from me but against every effort which I can make.[14]

This was vintage Williams. He would not back away from a fight, especially if he perceived racial discrimination to be the cause. His method of confrontation involved well-documented, lengthy, acerbic letters. He fought this case of perceived discrimination exactly as he had done while a student at Oxford. He took the fight to the British, in the way that his father had not been able to do 25 years earlier when confined to a low-paying position at the Post Office in Trinidad.

In spite of the tensions, Williams enjoyed some aspects of his work at the Commission. He admitted that the "travel and field work associated with the Commission was the most attractive and valuable aspect of my connection with it."[15] Some of his travelling was in connection with the West Indies Conference, an auxiliary body of the Commission, which had been conceived as a way of bringing island representatives together to discuss common problems and make recommendations to their metropolitan governments through the Commission.[16] Williams participated in the first such conference, held in Barbados in March 1944, shortly after beginning his full time position with the Commission.

He used the opportunity of this trip to Barbados to make his first return visit to Trinidad since leaving almost twelve years earlier. He gave two public lectures while he was there. The first was to the Literary Society of his old high school, QRC, and was chaired by his former teacher and mentor W. D. Inniss. The subject was "The University of the British West Indies", a subject on which Williams held strong views. Williams then made his first visit to British Guiana, seeking to develop linkages to the Commission. On his return to Trinidad, he took as the theme for his second lecture, delivered on April 19, "The British West Indies in World History". It represented a preview of his yet unpublished *Capitalism and Slavery*.

This occasion turned out to be highly emotional for Williams. It was the first public gathering he had ever addressed in Trinidad. Twelve years after leaving as a student, he had returned as a teacher. He admitted:

> These people were my own flesh and blood. I had been to school with them, played cricket and football with them, shared their sufferings, enjoyed carnival with them. I had gone away, they had stayed home. I had come back with a University education, they had none. Now I, their former classmate, was their teacher.[17]

For Williams, "the atmosphere was electric" and the crowd "lapped up the lecture". He felt that their "pent-up nationalist pride and dignity were caught up in my phrase 'Two hundred years ago we were sugar plantations. Today we are naval bases.'"[18]

This lecture, and the response of the overflowing crowd at the Public Library, must have been exceedingly gratifying for Williams, cementing in his mind the belief that his future would be with his people. Eventually, largely influenced by his travel throughout the Caribbean, he came to the belief that all Caribbean people were "his people".

However, it was this extended visit to the Caribbean, much longer than initially planned, that precipitated the dispute between Williams and his department head, Ralph Bunche, at Howard.

Williams clearly appreciated the opportunities for travel which both the Caribbean Commission and Howard University provided. He would later claim, "I was in 1940 a West Indian who had more direct and closer contact, historically and actually, with the Caribbean area as a whole than any other."[19] His vision for the region, which had begun with Trinidad in 1932, extended to all the British West Indian colonies during his Oxford years, and by the 1940s included all the island territories in the region.

Within a few months of his arrival at Howard, Williams had secured a fellowship which allowed him to spend eight weeks in Havana, between June and July 1940. By August he had travelled to Haiti, followed, a few weeks later, by the Dominican Republic. Finally, he went on to Puerto Rico before returning to Washington to begin a new school year. He occupied much of his time in each of these territories studying the available documents on their economic history. He also developed useful contacts in the academic and public sectors. His ability to work in Spanish and French facilitated his research enormously. His work with the Caribbean Research Council took him to the Virgin Islands and further south, to the Leewards. Later, he had the opportunity to visit the Dutch territories of Curaçao and Aruba, and the French islands of Martinique and Guadeloupe.

What emerged out of all these travel and research opportunities was the recognition that while Caribbean peoples might be formally separated by language and culture, their essential commonality lay in their shared experience of colonial economic organization and exploitation. The consequences of the plantation system for the lives of ordinary people made them essentially similar to each other.

With the end of World War II, it became evident to the US and Britain that there was need for a wider regional organization to deal with the problems of the Caribbean area. France and the Netherlands were invited to join the Anglo-American Caribbean Commission, which now became simply the Caribbean Commission. The agreement was signed on October 30, 1946, and the Commission's headquarters were transferred to Trinidad. But Williams soon became disenchanted with the "cumbersome administrative machinery designed to illustrate the four-power structure." The British were responsible for the Research Branch; according to Williams, when they were "getting even with me, [and] passed me over for a retired man" to head this division, he decided it was time "to sever my connection with this collective colonialism."[20]

Having lost his opportunity, a year earlier, to become a full professor of Social Sciences, Williams was now ready to return to Howard. However, his Dean, with whom he had had some serious problems before he went on his two-year leave, was not very cooperative. In July 1946, Williams applied for the headship of the Political Science department if Bunche did not return to that position.[21] The Dean responded by returning Williams to his assistant position at an annual salary of $2,650.[22] Williams was upset, and wrote to friends suggesting that "I do not consider my future career as a teacher in the US . . . exclusively associated with Howard."[23] In early August, before the beginning of the school year, Williams wrote to the President of the University requesting a full professorship, and again enquired about the position of department head. He also complained about the non-cooperative attitude of his Dean.[24] By October, he was an Associate Professor with an annual salary of $3,970.[25]

Williams returned to Howard in August 1946, but also accepted a part-time position as a Research Consultant with the Caribbean Commission in an office in Washington which he was authorized to establish. Norman Manley of Jamaica, whom Williams had met the previous year, was a member of the British section, and helped him to secure this position. Williams maintained this part-time position until May 1948. His enormous capacity for work was invaluable: "My Washington branch office was given increasing responsibility until I was working full time for the Commission over and above my duties at Howard University. I was able to do this by working nights and weekends."[26]

In May 1948, the Secretary General of the Commission proposed that Williams head the Research Branch at the headquarters in Trinidad. The Dutch opposed this offer, but a compromise was reached: Williams would serve as acting Deputy Chairman of the Caribbean Research Council for six months, after which a final decision would be made. Again Williams took leave of absence from Howard University. In his request for a sabbatical, he informed his Dean that "I am very tired, my physician has recommended a reduction of schedule, eliminating all possible sources of tension and friction, and if possible a change of climate and environment."[27] He promised to continue his work on Caribbean economies, but made no mention of the research position in Trinidad.

One of the first controversies to meet Williams in Trinidad was confirmation of his position as Deputy Chairman of the Research

Council. He believed that the British and Dutch were determined to block the appointment, and were prepared to introduce the spurious issue of communism.

In a very general sense, Williams had flirted with the left during his university years. One mentor for his thesis, C. L. R. James, was an avowed Marxist. So was George Padmore, who was instrumental in having *The Negro in the Caribbean* published in Britain. Williams had frequented the meetings of WASU in London, though he insisted that "I had never had any connection whatsoever with any political organization at all."[28] And his doctoral thesis, of course, was virulently anti-imperialist in tone. But that did not make him a communist. While he was at Howard, during the war years, his Division of Social Sciences had been summoned to the Department of Justice for questioning, though Williams himself had not been called. Interestingly, in 1944–45, while serving full time at the Commission, he was technically on the payroll of the State Department, which was partially responsible for funding the Commission.

In a document he had prepared for the third session of the West Indian Conference, scheduled for Guadeloupe in December 1948, Williams had made "some reference to the abolition of private property". He blamed it on an oversight, from being overworked.[29] But his critics seized upon this reference and demanded an investigation. The British tried to persuade another West Indian to accept Williams's position, but without success. Williams had the strong support of regional leaders. Norman Manley led the fight to appoint him and to confront the charge of communism. He was ably assisted by the Puerto Ricans, who offered a research position at the University of Puerto Rico, should Williams be released from the Commission. Eventually, in June 1949, Williams was confirmed, with a five-year contract at an annual salary of US$7,000.[30]

For him, however, all this was yet more evidence of persecution, and demonstrated a refusal to appoint local people to senior positions at the metropolitan-dominated Commission. And new problems lay ahead in Trinidad, this time concerning the relationship between the Commission's Secretariat and its Research Branch.

The issue was the relative worth of the research and administrative units. The Secretary General was the head administrator; Williams served under him, with responsibility for the research programme. According to Williams, "it was common knowledge that the Commission stressed that the research section of the Secretariat was more important than the administrative."[31] This set the stage for tension between the two units and their respective leaders, which eventually grew into open conflict.

In a letter to Robert Robbins of the State Department in Washington, Williams outlined the "profound differences" between the Secretary General and himself over a broad range of issues. These included the status of the Deputy Chairman (himself) and the position of the Research Branch in relation to the administration; personnel issues; the work of the Research Branch; and staffing needs. Williams expressed the view that "political factors" influenced the differences.[32]

Later, in a handwritten note to the Secretary General himself, Williams stated:

As I have indicated to you on several occasions, I find myself completely in disagreement with you on a number of matters . . . with respect to my position in the Secretariat . . . I have come to the conclusion that . . . it is desirable that the Commission should adjudicate these issues.[33]

Following the pattern that he had developed at Howard University — that is, a proposal to settle outstanding issues through mediation — Williams prepared a detailed report on the "Status and Responsibilities of the Deputy Chair", which in effect was a presentation of his case.[34] The method represented his belief in the power of the written word. Indirectly, he may have been setting himself up himself for martyrdom by the Commission, and therefore as a hero to Caribbean peoples.

Within a few months, Williams believed that agreement had been reached on some of the outstanding issues with the Secretary General, and that there was agreement in principle on other issues. He therefore withdrew his lengthy memorandum.[35] The output from his unit increased.

But even Williams's productivity caused problems. He had an enormous capacity for work, and had a trained staff supporting him; with increasing demands from the Commission for special studies, and the need to service various conferences, the output from his division was voluminous. Others felt threatened. One young statistician who worked with him during his first year in office recalled that Williams required that "the work had to be done as quickly as it could be done, but it had to be completed correctly."[36] Another recalled that Williams "never suffered fools gladly. He knew what he wanted and how to get it! You were required to be prompt and efficient. Excellence was his forte."[37]

Yet, even now, Williams still found time for other interests. Victor Woodstock, who arrived in Trinidad from Jamaica in May 1951 to serve as a statistician in the Research Branch of the Commission, was somewhat surprised by what he termed the average Trinidadian's "laissez-faire attitude towards life". He found Williams atypical, in that he was a hard, serious worker who demanded results from his staff. Yet Williams was "very congenial when it came to sports", and his continued love for cricket was very apparent. A Test match series was being played at the time, and Woodstock found that Williams, like others in the office, paid close attention to the progress of the individual games.[38]

Woodstock also noticed that Williams was different from other Trinidadians in the parties that he hosted at his home. "Williams did not party like the average Trinidadian. Yet he was a pleasant and very gracious host at his home." Out of office, Woodstock recalled, Williams was warm and friendly, while his parties were quiet and sociable.[39] "Williams did things his own way. Nothing disturbed his work, while nothing disturbed his recreation!"[40]

Ironically, this determination to do things his own way would lead eventually to his dismissal from the Commission. Tension between Williams and the Secretary General, which had been present since Williams assumed his formal position in 1949, had built up gradually in the early 1950s, and exploded in 1953 over the issue of the status of the Research Branch. After a tentative resolution, the relationship simmered for another year. But in April 1954 Williams forwarded a memorandum to the Secretary General concerning the overtime work of his staff. He complained about increased workload accompanied by a reduced budget.[41]

The response of the Secretary General was laced with criticism of Williams's administrative capabilities. He warned that "a recurrence of this [problem] must be positively prevented", and chided Williams on his "supervision of the staff" and for "heaping new responsibilities upon them". Implying that Williams was engaged in too many activities outside the Commission, the Secretary General stated: "Your personal preoccupation with research chores has not always enabled you to keep . . . in touch with some of your staff members." He concluded that "your staff is entitled to you fulltime."[42] This was the period when Williams was engaged on an ambitious adult education programme, which must have detracted somewhat from his ability to focus his total energy on research activities at the Commission.

Williams was irate. The Secretary General had written a two-page letter: Williams's response was fifteen pages, single-spaced. He charged: "[You] impugn my supervision of research staff" and "exculpate yourself from, and accuse me of, responsibility for taking on 'additional chores'." He expressed the view that

> the core of the whole problem [is] the divergence of views between yourself and myself as to the status of the Head of the Research Branch and the Branch itself, vis-à-vis the administrative staff.[43]

Williams concluded that "this is a vote of no-confidence in my administration. I reject your charges *in toto*."[44] He called upon the Commission, once again, to investigate the charges made by its Secretary General. He later informed the Commission that he would be unable to attend the meeting to discuss the charges, because he was exhausted from overwork and also had responsibility for his three-year old daughter Erica (see chapter 9).[45]

The four co-chairmen of the Commission did not respond to Williams's memorandum, because in their view the Secretary General was the person responsible for interpreting Commission decisions concerning operations within the organization. But since the Commission's Agreement was being revised, and all roles reappraised, and in view of the Secretary General's report on Williams, they advised that "your service contract with the Commission, expiring in June 1954, shall be renewed for a period of one year."[46] Implicitly, Williams would be on probation, with the prospect of dismissal at the end of a year.

Williams perceived the situation as a "declaration of war", but he did not provide a formal response for six months. Instead, he began to seek advice concerning possible job alternatives and the form his response should take. As he had done before, he turned to an older and wiser friend. He wrote a very tormented letter to Norman Manley, in which he presented what he perceived as his three possible responses to the Commission's order: bow down and worship; leave things as they are, and let the Commission make its final decision in a year; or fight. He continued:

> I was denied a fellowship at Oxford — I have always been convinced it was on racial grounds — every conceivable pressure was brought to bear on me to leave . . . The U.S. has not sent me my re-entry visa . . . Taylor did not want me at Mona . . . Macpherson tried to get me out of the Commission in '45 . . . Now de Vriendt does not want me . . . What am I to do, cut cane? They threatened to fail my doctor's thesis because they did not like my views; the British never ceased attacking me . . . local representatives are always opposing my views . . . I am determined once and for all to put a stop to this impertinent persecution. They suspended the B.G. [British Guiana] constitution, and now they wish to suspend me. I am sick to death of it all.[47]

Williams undoubtedly felt persecuted, even wounded, for much of his adult life. Like his father before him, he believed that the British were the primary source. But unlike his father, who suffered in silence, the son clearly believed he had the necessary equipment to take the fight back to the British.

One of the strategies that Williams decided to employ in this battle was to engage the enemy in the public political arena. His letter to Manley continued:

> I may be out of a job in a year's time. There are elections here next year, and I have already been asked to come out and join the Independent Labour Party, and the suggestion has even been made that I should be Chairman. I do not rule it out . . . If they do not want to deal with me at the level of an innocuous research worker, perhaps they prefer to deal with me as a legislator. If they insist on my being a hewer of wood and a drawer of water for a metropolitan boss, perhaps they prefer a colonial-metropolitan relationship at the level of my joining the demand for a complete responsible government.[48]

In November 1954, Williams responded to the one-year extension of his contract by sending a 29-page single-spaced memorandum, with an equal volume of appendices, to the four co-chairmen of the Commission. In it he expressed the view that the Commission's earlier notice to him was equivalent to a letter of dismissal; he regretted not being permitted to defend himself, though he had previously informed his superiors that he was too exhausted from overwork to be able to attend the meeting; he detailed his performance record, and emphasized that the Commission's decision was an implied attack on his reputation, against which he needed to defend himself.

Williams made three general concluding points. He criticised the lack of West Indian involvement in the work of the Commission; he expressed the view that the Caribbean was sceptical about the Commission's activities, and he suggested that it was his role in adult education and the promotion of Caribbean cooperation that influenced the implicit dismissal. To dismiss "Mr Caribbean" would affect the prestige of the organization in the region.[49]

The Commission replied briefly, stating that:

> the smooth working of the Caribbean Commission depends upon . . . friendly and full cooperation between senior officers . . . [the Commission] meets in six months on your contract renewal. The experience during that period would justify conclusion of a further contract with you.[50]

Implicitly, this letter was a plea for cooperation between Williams and the Secretary General, and an expression of hope that if this were to materialize, then Williams's contract would be renewed. From Williams's perspective, however, it represented a demand for him to submit to his metropolitan superiors. He had no intention of doing that. In January 1955, he sent a personal letter to Manley, which was hand-carried by one of his early supporters and advisers, David Nelson.[51] In it, Williams said he saw "no room for a modus vivendi with the Commission." Reviewing his possible political debut in Trinidad, he continued:

> The Catholics look upon me as their No.1 enemy . . . The Indians also were hostile, for I, apart from Nelson, did more than anyone else here to kill their opposition to federation, or rather to cut the ground from under their feet. The most recent consequence is an open détente from the Indian [High] Commissioner . . . there is no doubt that throwing my hat in the ring will be a sensation . . . Nelson will speak to you about assessing whether I should enter politics . . . Elections are to be postponed until September '56; this will give me more time . . . I am immersed in a vast adult education programme . . . this will help keep my name before the public.[52]

This letter, like the earlier one to Manley, reveals much about Williams's state of mind during that period. Significantly, he explained his position on Trinidad's East Indian population with particular regard to his perception of their attitude toward the impending federation of ten West Indian territories. He had taken a similar position earlier, stating that "Indian political domination of British Guiana and Trinidad might have serious repercussions on current proposals for federating all the B.W.I. territories."[53]

Williams's belief that there was "no room for a modus vivendi" with the Commission meant that his primary alternative was to enter the political arena. In that context, he may have believed that to be dismissed by the Commission would enhance his political status, and provide him with a launching pad to political office. Thus he wrote Manley: "I am biding my time here, pushing off as best as I can all the work that de Vriendt tries to push on me."[54] Meanwhile, his leadership of the adult education programme helped to keep his "name before the public."

In one sense, therefore, the Commission played into Williams's hands when it wrote to him on May 26, 1955, stating that "your service contract with the Commission, due to expire on June 21, 1955, will not be renewed."[55]

Williams with members of his first Cabinet,1956, including Learie Constantine

(centre) and Dr Patrick Solomon (left)

EMERGENCE AS
NATIONAL LEADER

W as Eric Williams's entry into the political arena motivated primarily by his conflicts with the Caribbean Commission? Among those who were close to him at that time, views still differ. According to one student in Williams's first class at Howard in September 1939, Ibbit Mosaheb, Williams had been planning his entry "for a very long time."[1] Mosaheb remained one of Williams's closest friends for the next 25 years, and suggests that one reason why Williams cultivated friendships throughout the region, during his academic travels and while serving with the Caribbean Commission, was that they could be useful to him when he entered politics.

The view that Williams had a long-standing interest in politics is shared by Winston Mahabir, another early close ally who began a correspondence with Williams while he was a student at McGill University.[2] The two met formally in 1945 when Williams lectured at McGill, and the friendship continued after both returned to Trinidad. Mahabir and Mosaheb were Williams's closest friends in the early 50s, along with Halsey McShine, who was by then a surgeon based at the San Fernando Hospital. Since all three lived in San Fernando, Williams made frequent trips and spent weekends there. According to Mahabir, "Williams, Mosaheb and I initiated a weekly study group which we named the Bachacs."[3] On the basis of this close relationship to Williams, Mahabir concludes: "I am certain that the political ambitions of Williams were latent for as long as I knew him."[4] In Mahabir's view, dismissal from the Caribbean Commission only served to sharpen Williams's ambition.

For Elton Richardson, who with Mahabir and Mosaheb joined Williams as founders of the People's National Movement (PNM), Mahabir's assumptions are not convincing. Richardson, a medical doctor like Mahabir, had returned to Trinidad in 1948, and soon began attending Williams's early public lectures. A friendship developed, and Richardson was asked to join the Bachacs. According to Richardson, "Eric did not appear to me to be interested in politics" — though he later conceded that "I knew little about Bill", who played his cards "close to his chest."[5] Interestingly, these three co-founders of the PNM — Mosaheb, Mahabir and Richardson — disappeared from the political scene less than ten years after the formation of the party.

After being placed on a one-year probation by the Caribbean Commission, Williams had written to Norman Manley about possible involvement in domestic politics: "I have been asked to come out and join the Independent Labour Party, and the suggestion has even been made that I should be chairman. I do not rule it out . . ."[6] The suggestion that Williams should chair the ILP probably came from Richardson, who had helped to form the party a year earlier. Winston and Dennis Mahabir were also members. Williams had prepared a proposal on agriculture which was presented by Richardson to the ILP, and had discussed the party with Winston Mahabir — he had apparently "poured scorn on our efforts," wrote Richardson.[7]

If Williams did indeed pour scorn on efforts to organize the ILP, the reason is not clear, since at about the same time he was suggesting to Manley that he might soon become its chairman. Yet it is not surprising, for it would have been Williams's position that, without him, the ILP would amount to very little. Of course, Williams never did lead the ILP: after surveying the array of political parties, he and his small group created their own.

But there is another view of Williams's motives for entering national politics. He was an academic and a researcher at heart, and had found fulfilment in his work at the Caribbean Commission. He had the research staff, the autonomy and the salary. But what he did not have, and what he thought that he thoroughly deserved, was the status and recognition that would come from being Secretary General. Not only was he not granted this position, he was placed on probation and eventually fired. Selwyn Ryan writes:

> Dr Williams hesitated a long time before finally deciding to enter upon a career of political activism. His indecision angered some of his colleagues, who felt that for all his expressed concern for the people of Trinidad and Tobago, he preferred the cushions of his lucrative post at the Caribbean Commission. His dismissal from the Commission, however, brought to a dramatic end his reluctance to plunge into the uncertainties of politics. He had been handed a ready-made issue with which to build a political career.[8]

One of Williams's daughters, Erica, has provided the most intriguing explanation for her father's entry into politics: that it was the tragic death of her mother Soy, just three years into their marriage, that propelled her father onto the political scene. Soy Moyou was Williams's second wife (see chapter 9); he clearly loved her very deeply, and repeatedly told Erica that, had her mother lived, he would not have entered politics — his marriage and his job provided him with total fulfilment. According to Erica, her mother would have preferred Williams to remain politically uninvolved, and he would have respected her wishes. But when Soy died suddenly, Eric Williams the man gave way to Eric Williams the politician.[9] This was precisely the time when Williams's most serious problems with the Commission began; for by early 1953 he had become both a popular and a controversial figure in colonial Trinidad.

Williams himself explained that the "official boredom and metropolitan hostility" he experienced at the Commission in Trinidad drove him to seek refuge in intellectual pursuits and the adult education of ordinary Trinidadians.[10] Shortly after arriving in Trinidad in 1948, he accepted the presidency of the Historical Society of Trinidad and Tobago, and within a year he began publishing a Caribbean Historical Review, followed by two sets of documents on Trinidadian and Caribbean history. Simultaneously, he agreed to write a series of articles for the daily *Trinidad Guardian*. After some 40 articles had been published in 1950, the newspaper ended the agreement; the pieces stirred up controversy with the economic adviser to the government, Arthur Shenfield. In 1950, Williams agreed to serve as a consultant to the Teachers Economic and Cultural Association (TECA), which promptly served as the publisher of his *Education in the British West Indies*. These activities obviously increased Williams's visibility in the society, and were pursued in addition to his full-time position at the Commission. But this visibility was truly enhanced when he began a series of lectures and seminars across Trinidad.

Between 1950 and the launching of the PNM on January 24, 1956, Williams delivered over 100 lectures on a wide variety of themes and an equally wide variety of platforms. He lectured under the auspices of the Extra-Mural Department of what was then the University College of the West Indies; the Teachers Education and Cultural Association, through its political arm, the People's Education Movement (PEM); and the Political Education Group (PEG), the successor to his study group, the Bachacs. To a large degree, the PNM was a synthesis of the PEM and the PEG.

During those five years, Williams related to the Trinidad population at two levels. On the private face-to-face level he interacted with, and sometimes led, study groups like the Bachacs, and worked with the small PEM and eventually the PEG. This served to build personal relationships, especially with members of the emerging black professional group, which would be particularly useful later as he sought lieutenants for the building of his party.

At the public level, Williams lectured to groups ranging in size from a few hundred at the Public Library, encouraged by his friend (and later mortal enemy) Albert Gomes, to thousands in open public meetings. The culmination of these public lectures was his famous "Let Down My Bucket" lecture to an assembled gathering of some 20,000 at Woodford Square, Port of Spain, on the evening of his firing from the Commission.

Why did Williams undertake such an enormously rigorous and demanding schedule, even while he was employed at the Commission?

He was totally committed to the belief that education was the primary means for career advancement in a colonial society. He knew how limited education had stultified his father's career and had overshadowed the fortunes of his family. His father had been determined that his eldest son would not experience the same limitations. Having gained the best education possible, the younger Williams felt a need to assist others. Engaging in a massive programme of adult education was an attempt to compensate for what his father lacked, and became a source of deep psychological satisfaction.

Williams gained as much in adulation as he gave to the crowds attending his lectures. Writing about them, he noted:

> The people have come in crowds to listen to the clarification of various topics, whether current, complex or abstruse . . . I have become the centre of a lively and encouraging movement for an enlightened democracy, and the central figure in an active programme of community education.[11]

He warned the Commission in a memorandum that it would "not be possible for people to reconcile my role in the adult education movement with my dismissal from an organization designed to promote regional cooperation."[12]

But the original question remains: did Williams have a political agenda? Was the education of the masses a part of this agenda?

He provided a partial answer with his statement, "If war is a continuation of politics by other means, politics was for me a continuation of education by other means."[13] He had already told Manley about his "vast adult education programme" which would "help keep my name before the public."[14] And he was thrust further into national prominence through his famous debate with Dom Basil Matthews.

Williams had delivered a lecture at the Public Library on September 28, 1954, entitled "Some World Famous Educational Theories and Developments Relevant to West Indian Conditions". In it, he quoted from Aristotle's *Politics* in defence of his now familiar thesis: that state control over education was desirable. Sitting in the audience was the popular Catholic educator and monk, the Reverend Dom Basil Matthews. This tall, distinguished black churchman, himself in possession of a Ph.D., rose to challenge Williams's use of Aristotle's ideas to support his argument.

Williams was incensed by the challenge from Matthews, and saw it as criticism from the Catholic Church. His hostility to the Catholic

Church was long-standing. He had discussed the issue with his friend Elton Richardson, who recalled:

> He [Williams] was determined to attack the church. I argued against such an attack. He was adamant. He would not budge . . . Then, in desperation, I said, if you must attack, attack the man. He loved this, and this is how the famous attack on the then good old Dom was launched.[15]

On November 9, Matthews was given the platform at the library, and presented a rebuttal of Williams's argument in a lecture on "Aristotle, Education and State Control". The issue was joined. Much of the country watched this duel between two intellectual giants.

The date for Williams's response to Matthews was November 17. Ellis Clarke, then Solicitor General and acknowledged as one of the bright rising stars in the colony, was asked by Matthews to chair the session: he had known both Matthews and Williams briefly. The meeting room was overflowing hours before the presentation. Williams, speaking on "Some Misconceptions of Aristotle's Philosophy of Education", turned the tables on Matthews by pointing out that Aristotle's ideal state supported slavery, the subordination of women, and so forth. One commentator, much later, noted that "the debate was a piece of intellectual stick-fighting that was totally irrelevant to the concrete issues of Trinidad and Tobago", yet necessary to build a new party.[16] The popular view, including that of Clarke, was that Williams triumphed over Matthews, by attacking Aristotle and implicitly aligning the Catholic Church with some of Aristotle's reactionary ideas. It was a deceptive approach, but one that played extremely well with the crowd. Clarke halted the session somewhat abruptly. Some believed he was attempting to protect Matthews from further humiliation. In fact, he claimed, the meeting room had become a fire hazard because of the crowd, and he was asked to end it.[17]

Patrick Solomon, later a deputy leader of the PNM, attended the debates. It was his view that the entire lecture series provoked much public discussion and had far-reaching political consequences.[18] For Williams, the road ahead was very clear. He was now a national figure. If the Commission did not renew his contract in May 1955, it was inevitable that he would enter politics. A few months earlier he had admitted as much in a private letter to Manley.

The final lecture in the series focusing on education was delivered the following week. Williams presented "An Analysis of Recommendations of Education Commissions and Experts in Trinidad, 1869-1954: State versus Denominational Control". This was a favourite theme, and he used it to build on his victory in the historic debate the previous week. Again, the crowd was massive. Over 700 people filled the Library, while the overflow heard the lecture through loudspeakers in next-door Woodford Square.

After this very successful presentation, Williams proposed that all voluntary groups, teachers' organizations, youth councils, women's organizations and trade unions should come together to establish a non-partisan Committee on Education for Citizenship. The purpose of this organization, he claimed, was "to rationalize the adult education movement and spread it throughout the islands of Trinidad and Tobago."[19] But as a prominent PNM party member later stated, "Anyone with eyes to see could deduce what was going on: they were preparing to form a political party."[20] Williams knew that his contract with the Commission was due to expire on June 21, 1955. That was his D-day. Instead of simply waiting for the day to arrive, he intensified his adult education campaign in early 1955. Implicitly, he was intensifying his political campaign. In the first five months of the year, he ran four separate lecture series, focusing upon "Famous Personalities in Caribbean History", "The British West Indies Federation", "Democracy and its Relevance for the British West Indies" and his popular theme, "Recommendations of Education Commissions and Experts in Trinidad". Additionally, he gave occasional lectures to various groups, and wrote articles for the *Trinidad Guardian*.

The lecture series had specific primary objectives, including the building of nationalism, which Williams defined largely in terms of anti-colonialism, and "the imperative necessity of federation." "Nationalism" was defined in regional, not in insular, terms: in effect, Williams was arguing for the emergence of a Caribbean man reflecting a regional personality. Williams was not simply promoting the idea of a political federation: for him, the economic dimension was just as important. The lectures also focused on West Indian educational problems, with particular reference to the dichotomy between secular and religious-controlled educational systems.[21]

Williams was brought back to harsh reality on May 26, 1955, about a month before the expiration of his contract, when he received his letter of dismissal from the Secretary General of the Commission. Sitting at his home on Lady Chancellor Hill, he made telephone calls to Richardson, Mosaheb and Mahabir, the original members of the Bachacs, asking them to come to his home later that evening. Mosaheb and Mahabir drove up together from San Fernando. When they arrived, Richardson was already there, together with one of Williams's brothers, probably Victor. It is interesting that Williams turned to these old friends, and not to the TECA group, especially de Wilton Rogers and John Donaldson (though they would be included within a few months). His other two oldest friends in Trinidad — Halsey McShine and Ray Dolly — were steadfastly non-political.

According to Mahabir, this first meeting went on for about ten hours, or until dawn the next day, during which time "we were administering conjoint psychotherapy to Eric during his spontaneous marathon abreaction."[22] Mosaheb recalled that the obvious question was: where does Williams go from here? To answer that question, it was quickly agreed, or simply ratified, that Williams would formally enter the political arena. The only question that remained was: what should be the vehicle for doing so? The group of five reviewed the existing political parties, finally coming to the conclusion that since none met their criteria, they would build their own independent movement.[23]

Richardson recognized that to build a mass movement demanded a restructuring of the leader's lifestyle, at least outwardly. For instance, Williams lived in the posh confines of upper-class Lady Chancellor Hill: the spatial and class separation from his anticipated followers was painfully obvious. He also drove a huge American automatic Buick, so attractive that it had been used to transport Princess Margaret on her trip to Trinidad two years earlier. Richardson said to Williams, somewhat pungently, "What you have to realize is that all you are now is just another poor Negro boy!"[24] Williams responded with much laughter, and accepted the recommendation that he should move to the middle-class district of Woodbrook. But with his passion for large vehicles, which served as status symbols, he baulked at the idea of turning in his Buick. He eventually bought a more modest Vauxhall, which caused him some practical problems because he was unaccustomed to a vehicle equipped with standard transmission.

Williams suggested a few names which might be added to this nascent group. They included Donald Granado, a trade unionist whom Williams had befriended during his lectures and meetings with the local trade union movement, and David Nelson, political writer of the *Trinidad Guardian*, whom Williams respected. Nelson, however, was dropped within a few months.[25] Williams agreed to mark his dismissal from the Commission with a large public gathering at Woodford Square. He also agreed to present his speech privately to the group before the public presentation. This appears to be somewhat out of character, but it was to be a regular practice at least until the elections of 1956.

Richardson claimed that Williams did present his "My Relations with the Caribbean Commission" lecture to the group in advance. "It was a beautifully done speech, but I felt it lacked the quality of identification. I said that he ought to couch it so that all poor struggling folks could see their own struggles reflected in his experiences. Eric hesitated long before he accepted, but finally he did."[26] While this information is uncorroborated, it is extremely significant if it is accurate. For until that time, Williams's public lectures had suggested a learned professor teaching an untutored crowd: there remained a distance between the professor and his students. But now, apparently on the advice of Richardson, Williams destroyed the barrier. He was able to present his personal conflict with the Commission as a symbol of the struggle of all colonial peoples with their metropolitan overlords. He persuaded the crowd that his struggle was part of a larger struggle in which they were all involved. That evening, the learned professor was converted, in the eyes of the assembled thousands, into the charismatic leader of the oppressed masses.

Williams had relied on the organizational skills of TECA, and on the commitment of its leaders, de Wilton Rogers and John Donaldson, for staging many of his public lectures over the previous four years. But it was given minimal credit by Williams for the success of the public meeting which effectively launched his political career. He states in his autobiography that he simply "got in touch two days later with two teacher friends" who agreed to organize the public meeting under the auspices of TECA.[27]

For Williams the meeting was a resounding success. He took the crowd through a lecture of 51 printed pages, explaining "the whole sordid story of my relations with the Commission", and at the end was able to claim: "I had crossed the Rubicon."[28] One commentator later described Williams's presentation this way:

> Eric Williams boldly presented himself to his audience in Woodford Square that evening as a martyr in the anti-imperialist struggle. Though neither threatened with imprisonment nor compromised in his eligibility for other employment, his dramatic narrative of his vicissitudes within a quasi-colonial establishment nonetheless served to project the image of one who had suffered in the anti-colonial cause.[29]

This was the beginning of the political genius of Eric Williams. For the next 20 years or more he would mesmerize friends and foes alike by manipulating power with rare skill. "Mr Caribbean" had also become "Mr Trinidad".

Williams moved rapidly to consolidate his position. At the private level, he oversaw the gradual building of the party, while at the public level he developed a seven-lecture series, which ran from June 21 in Woodford Square to January 1956 and the formal launching of the PNM.

A second private meeting was held at Williams's home following the successful Woodford Square "celebration", to plan strategy for the party's development. The two new participants were Granado and Nelson. Winston Mahabir was absent, and would remain so for many future meetings. He had discussed his many reservations about Williams with Richardson,[30] but allowed himself to be drafted into the election campaign as a candidate because he believed the party "was especially lacking any Indian of stature to lend a semblance of genuine multi-racial solidarity, one of the most loudly proclaimed precepts of the PNM."[31]

This second meeting agreed to establish the Political Education Group (PEG), the forum that Williams would employ to take political education to the population. Until that time, Williams's public lectures were largely sponsored by TECA and its political arm, the People's Education Movement. It is possible that Williams decided to lecture through the PEG and not the PEM because the latter was under the effective control of Rogers and Donaldson. But it was precisely these two individuals, together with the Alexander brothers, Wilfred and Felix, who were next invited to bring the membership of the PEG to nine. With the formation of the PEG, the Bachacs went out of existence.[32]

Granado vividly recalls attending his first meeting at Lady Chancellor Hill, when the PEG was organized.[33] He admitted to being naïve about Williams's political agenda, but "I knew I liked the man. I liked what he was saying, how he was saying it." What he particularly remembered about Williams was that "he would share what he knew with everybody who wanted to listen. He was willing to share and take as long as necessary to do so." While this picture of Williams does not approximate to the public persona, it is repeatedly corroborated by his students at Howard University and many who attended informal sessions at his home. He was at heart a dedicated teacher.

By the time a third meeting was held, on July 3, the membership of the group had increased to 13. Mosaheb was appointed Chairman. Gerard Montano (who had been a member of the Bachacs), Kamaluddin Mohammed, Isabel Teshea, and Andrew Carr, Williams's neighbour in Woodbrook, had been recruited. This meeting outlined criteria for membership of the new party. Members must be men and women of integrity in broad agreement with [the group's] views; they must in general have no affiliation or political past; they must be opposed to racial discrimination or bias; they must be willing to accept the discipline of the party; they must be willing to work, make sacrifices, study and organize. Priority would, at that stage, be given to persons with a following and influence in the community. Selection would be made with a view to achieving a balanced racial representation, so long as it did not compromise the basic aims, principles and objectives of the party.[34]

Two observations are in order concerning this list of qualifications. The first is that, being broad, general, and all-inclusive, the criteria were not distinctive. The emphasis on "integrity," "opposed to racial discrimination" and "willingness to work" is applicable to most groups. Secondly, and more importantly, the PEG did not take any particular ideological position. To what, then, did "broad agreement with [the group's] views" refer? One writer has suggested that an earlier draft stated "in agreement with broadly socialist views".[35] If so, the omission of the term "socialist" from the final text would probably have been due to Williams. Throughout his career as a student, university teacher and international civil servant, he had studiously avoided labels. He had always insisted that he had joined no group. While Williams wrote and spoke the language of socialism, he did not consider himself a socialist. In fact, some months later a meeting of the PEG was called for the precise purpose of developing a consensus on major issues, in case it became necessary to defend the group on these points. With regard to the possible question "Is the party socialist?", group members were requested to reply: "No! It is nationalist!"[36]

The list of qualifications was interesting, too, for what it did not state. The unwritten rule was that loyalty to Williams was a primary qualification. After all, the initial purpose of the PEG was to advance his candidacy in the general elections expected in 1955. Granado recalled:

> We were very conscious of the fact that if the elections were called in 1955, we would not have been able to contest many seats, and so we set our sights on contesting only one seat and the candidate was to be Eric Williams. As time went by, it was agreed that we should contest three seats, just to form a token Opposition in Parliament, and to learn how things were done in that august institution.[37]

In a remarkable turn of events, the government, entirely unaware of the growing strength and organization of the incipient PNM, postponed the elections for a year. The developing party was thus given the time it needed to organize and field candidates in every constituency the following year, the only party to do so. Had the elections been held as scheduled, it is unlikely that Williams and the PNM could have maintained the momentum for another five years, and their fate might have been entirely different.

Another meeting of the PEG was held at Williams's home on Lady Chancellor Hill on July 28. Twenty-three members were in attendance. Mosaheb, now Chairman, reported that Mahabir "preferred to remain outside the group". The membership was organized into six committees. It was agreed that each member would pay a fee of $5.00 per month. On the question of Williams's public lectures, the group agreed that he was "free to accept or reject all comments on said lectures as they were his personal responsibility."[38]

Williams also influenced other aspects of decision-making. His control over membership was exercised through a rule that any prospective member had to be invited to join the PEG. This defined the composition and texture of the group; because much of the initial group was drawn from the black middle class, so too were the invitees. Williams appeared to have the final word.

In the early stages of recruitment, Williams proposed the membership of the youthful Ulric Lee. Granado noted that he "dared to oppose" this nomination, both the first and second time Lee's name was proposed: Lee was not admitted. But before the third meeting, Granado was called to the home of one of Williams's closest allies, Wilfred Alexander; there he was politely told that he should not oppose Lee's nomination when the proposal was reintroduced because "you have made your point." Granado acceded and Lee was accepted as a member.[39]

Williams did make some effort to widen the race and class bases of the party, even seeking to incorporate the white business sector. Cyril Merry, a respected white cricketer and businessman, arranged a dinner party at his home where Williams presented the party's objectives and its desire to incorporate all groups into the movement. Some, including Victor Stollmeyer, were enthusiastic, and agreed to be involved, but the majority remained sceptical, seeing Williams as a threat: his agenda challenged the interests of the entrenched elite, and his nationalistic objectives were viewed as anti-business.

Stollmeyer recalled that Williams was literally "begging the white people to come along, he wanted everybody."[40] But Stollmeyer was not particularly representative of his group. He had known Williams, and his reputation, since high school days at Queen's Royal College (Williams was four forms ahead), and had been taught by Williams during his brief teaching stint at QRC. He had followed Williams's career, and as a Trinidadian "whose paternal ancestors settled in this island more than a century ago"[41] believed that he had a responsibility to contribute. Though he did not become a member of the party, his support for Williams, especially through his letters in the newspapers, caused some sensation. After all, Stollmeyer was a member of one of Trinidad's older, most distinguished white families. Moreover, he was captain of the Trinidad cricket team, which would have further enhanced his status.

Stollmeyer's support for Williams was not appreciated by some. He wrote that "an old friend of my school and cricketing days has asked me, laughingly, [if] it is true, whether I wished to be ostracised."[42] But it was not a laughing matter when a member of his law firm wrote to him while on a trip to England:

> I was horrified to learn that you have associated yourself with that "drip" Eric Williams, more especially as our three star clients . . . have definite views of his activities. Unless you hasten to pull out of that mess . . . [we] are likely to suffer a serious setback.[43]

The letter-writer urged Stollmeyer to give the matter "serious consideration" and to "take prompt steps to let it be known that you are no longer interested in master Williams's activities."[44] It is difficult to gauge whether such views were widely shared among the elites in the society.

They were however, shared by the Catholic Church. In a pamphlet released shortly before the September 24, 1956, general elections, the church urged its members not to vote for candidates of the PNM. The two long-standing issues between Williams and the Catholic Church were artificial methods of birth control and denominational control over education. In his public statements, Williams had long championed the need for birth control, largely arising from the huge size of his parents' family, and had strongly supported state control over education, again partly as a result of his childhood experiences. The position of the church was that

> These rights are conferred by God, no Government or Legislature can abrogate them. Any candidate or "Party" that will not make a clear and unequivocal statement in regard to the recognition and defence of these rights is by the very fact, according to the law of the Catholic Church "suspect" and therefore, unworthy of support by Catholic voters.[45]

Williams's adamant position was not reflected in the party's election manifesto. Under the section "The Citizen and the Child", it stated: "The giving of religious education shall be compulsory in all schools maintained or assisted by Government." It endorsed "the maintenance of the right of the citizen to send his child to a school of his own choice."[46] The manifesto did not equivocate on the issue of birth control.

Under the section on "PNM Code of Public Morality" it stated: "PNM considers the question of birth control a private and religious matter and it is absolutely false to say that the Movement has ever advocated birth control."[47] But the Catholic Church refused to accept the PNM's statements on education and birth control; it branded them "evasive and misleading", and termed the party "suspect", recommending that "no Catholic should vote" for the PNM.[48] The basic problem was that the Church was deeply suspicious of Williams's own hard-line position. Simply stated, it refused to accept the manifesto as the true position of the party.

With these two important interest groups — the entrenched elites and the Catholic Church — opposed to the PNM, and with the party's refusal to align itself with the other major interest group, the trade union movement, it is somewhat surprising that the PNM performed as well as it did in the general elections of 1956. Credit for this was entirely due to the leadership skills of Eric Williams.

Meeting the people

CHAPTER EIGHT
PERSONALITY AND
POLITICAL BEHAVIOUR

HOW 2 OUT MSNG + B HEALTHY

PAUL FLEX
OR DETER

It is generally agreed that political behaviour is influenced by the many factors that comprise "personality". Personality itself may be defined as "the acquired and relatively enduring dynamic configuration of one's predisposition to behaviour."[1] Yet the degree to which personality shapes political behaviour, and the ability to measure its impact, have remained imprecise.

Since politics is largely the struggle for power, the study of political behaviour must examine the way power is shared among political participants. Power, here, is taken to mean "a capacity or ability to control others, and, in this context, to control the decision-making process."[2] Indeed, it has been suggested that the possession of power is part of an individual's personality.[3] In that context, personality, political behaviour and power are all interacting variables in the make-up of political man. This discussion inevitably leads to a consideration of the authoritarian personality, for the primary characteristic of this type of personality is its attitude toward power.

Authoritarianism has been defined as "an attitudinal system which consists of inter-related anti-democratic sentiments including ethnic prejudice, political conservatism, and a moralistic rejection of the unconventional."[4] But because it is a continuous variable, authoritarianism is an ideal type found at one end of the spectrum. Its antithesis is the "democratic personality" at the opposite end.[5]

It follows, therefore, that an individual cannot be simply classified as either authoritarian or not, since personality exists as a continuum. It has been noted that "certain circumstances may serve to raise or lower the mean level of authoritarianism."[6] Thus, for instance, one school of thought holds that the severity of discipline meted out by parents can affect the extent of authoritarianism displayed by a child in adult life.

These issues contribute to an understanding of the leadership style and so-called "political personality" of Eric Williams.

A very popular view in Trinidad held that Williams possessed an authoritarian personality. But closer examination of his total relationships reveals an individual who was, to a large extent, "selectively authoritarian". For instance, while he tolerated no opposition from within his party, the media and popular culture, calypso was allowed surprisingly broad latitude despite its ability to comment and criticize.

Ken Gordon, one distinguished media personality in Trinidad, is not as charitable in his analysis of Williams's relationship with and respect for the media. While

> Dr Williams was always very careful to uphold what he saw was the letter of the law, [he] frequently violated what I think is the spirit of the law. I suppose that is the difference between how a journalist would handle something and how a politician would handle it. He was a very strong man who wanted his way and was satisfied that his way was the right way for the country. In many cases it was, but that was his weakness.[7]

A devoted disciple of Williams, Ferdie Ferreira, who worked assiduously for the party until he was unceremoniously expelled some 20 years after its formation, summarized Williams's domination of the PNM this way:

> The key is that he [Williams] worked very hard. He generated the ideas and plans and wrote the proposal. The party was dependent upon him: physically, intellectually and financially. He had to threaten council members to pay their dues. At one point he declared: "How long am I going to play party bailiff?" He put in more than others. He therefore demanded authority and loyalty. He was "Papa".[8]

It is revealing that Ferreira continued to rationalize Williams's domination of the party, even though he himself had been crudely dropped from the unofficial inner circle of Williams's advisers, without explanation. Such was the awe in which Williams was held by those close to him.

While it is true that most of Williams's supporters held him in awe, one member of the group that cleared the way for the party, Donald Granado, argued that his own relationship with Williams was based on mutual respect, not submission.[9] He recalled Williams presenting a speech to the Political Education Group before delivering it on the public platform. He commented to Williams: "It is all right to speak about the university, but the people who are not in the university are simple and would not understand." He recognized that "Williams was definite about what he had written"; yet "without saying a word . . . that preparation was completely changed by Williams."[10]

Granado developed an interesting theory of people's relationship to Williams. With particular regard to party members, he observed:

> Some people sort of worshipped the man so much that they said "yes" to whatever he said. It wasn't that they had to say "yes", it wasn't that he wanted them to say "yes", but this is what happened. The only people who questioned him was myself and a few other people.[11]

In fact, Granado emphasized,

> whether you are a fifth standard boy or a seventh standard boy or just a junior Cambridge, he believed that you must have a point of view and he wanted to get that point of view. He would not have necessarily agreed with it, but he wanted to know your thinking and feeling on a particular point. That was the Williams I knew.[12]

While Granado did seem to have had an unusual relationship with Williams, he fully recognized that "there were very few who would do that . . . In fact, you could probably count them on one hand."[13] In that context, Ferreira stated: "Williams tolerated opposition in the country but not in the party."[14]

The question remains: why was Williams to some degree an authoritarian individual? Why did he enjoy being in control?

Harold Lasswell has provided an explanation for this form of behaviour. Different schools of dynamic psychology, attempting to formulate a general hypothesis concerning the "power seeker", have seen this personality type as one who "pursues power as a means of compensation against deprivation. Power is expected to overcome low estimates of the self, by changing either the traits of the self or the environment in which it functions."[15] Drawing on these findings and theories, Lasswell emphasized the significance of low self-esteem, thereby presenting the argument for "ego motives" in the striving for power. This does not rule out the possibility of exploring deeper levels of motivation and psychodynamic processes. Indeed, an understanding of ego needs could provide a useful beginning for probing deeper motives. Obviously, the factors which encourage low self-esteem are themselves important in understanding the personality and behaviour of an individual.

One case often studied is that of former US president Woodrow Wilson. Some of the critical childhood experiences which led to damaged self-esteem lay in the character of Wilson's relationship with his very distinguished and successful father. Joseph Wilson, a preacher, was a strict disciplinarian. He placed on his first son the burden of living up to his very high expectations of moral and intellectual accomplishment.[16] A former professor, he did not permit his son the use of incorrect words and phrases, forcing the multiple rewriting of essays until he was satisfied. He met his son's imperfections with caustic wit. While young Woodrow never openly rebelled, his self-esteem was deeply affected by this relationship.

There are some interesting parallels between the childhood experiences of Woodrow Wilson and Eric Williams, especially with regard to the role of the father.[17] While Henry Williams was not distinguished in a intellectual sense, he was apparently a man of much dignity. Partly because of his strict adherence to Catholicism, he was, like Joseph Wilson, a strict disciplinarian. In this, he was fully supported by his wife Eliza, who was as cold and aloof as she was strict. Like Joseph Wilson, Henry Williams set exceedingly high intellectual goals for his first son, leading one daughter to assert that "our father lived his life through Eric."[18] As Eric wrote many years later: "The island scholarship for his son became the dream of his life."[19]

From the cradle until Eric wrote his island scholarship

examinations, Henry Williams maintained a steady pressure on his son to be successful. On one occasion, when Eric earned third place at a prize-giving day during his elementary school years and was awarded a book prize — ironically, *Great Expectations* — his father sneered at him. Henry demanded nothing but first place from his son. He desperately hoped that his son would become a medical doctor. Even when Eric was awarded his doctorate, his father — greeting him with "So you are a doctor after all!"[20] — was apparently still unsatisfied: Eric had earned a Ph.D. degree, the significance of which his father probably did not fully comprehend, but he was not the prestigious medical doctor of whom Henry had dreamed. Eric's inability to satisfy his father during and after a brilliant academic performance must have damaged his self-esteem and otherwise hurt his relationship with his father.

Woodrow Wilson apparently adored his father, but Williams's relationship with his father was more complex. On the one hand, there would have been the obvious respect for Henry Williams, mixed with a certain degree of fear. On the other, Henry, though he demanded much of Eric, did not himself achieve, at least economically. He succumbed to the many pressures, particularly those imposed by colour and class, which Eric, to a very large degree, overcame. These conflicting images of his father may have impacted on Eric's ability to relate to others. In that context, if Williams saw someone as demanding or as a threat, he would react against them out of a narcissistic need for power. But if they were not perceived as a challenge, he could listen to their advice with equanimity.

Eric had begun to establish some distance from his parents, if not his siblings, as he grew older. His father argued with him for over three weeks, unsuccessfully, about his intended course of study in England — and then accompanied him on the boat trip. Eric stayed away from Trinidad from 1932 to 1944, even though he conducted research trips elsewhere in the Caribbean. When he was told of his father's grave illness in 1946, while he was in Washington, he professed to be "too busy" to visit Trinidad.[21] Perhaps this reaction was due as much to his obsession with his job as to indifference to his father's health. He did arrive the day after his father's death.

It was also from his father's beliefs that Eric's claim to social and economic deprivation arose. From the evidence available, it is unlikely that the Williams family was more economically deprived than most Trinidad families at that time.[22] But the father, and later the son, believed that it was. As Eric saw it, the necessary "social qualifications" for advancement were "colour, money and education, in that order of importance. My father lacked all three."[23]

It is understandable that Eric Williams believed colour was the most important qualification for advancement, because in fact it was, especially during that period. Sensitized by his father to the problem, and even though he eventually reached the pinnacle of educational performance, he insisted that colour was the source of his problems at university. During his many years of service with the Caribbean Commission, he believed that the same issue affected his opportunities for promotion.

Thus Williams, to some degree, believed he was a deprived individual. He perceived himself as the victim of racial and social oppression at university, and suffered the constant fear of having insufficient funds to complete his studies. Though academically superior to most of his colleagues at the Caribbean Commission, he believed that it was his colour which impeded his advancement. According to Lasswell, to the degree that Williams felt deprived, he would seek power to compensate for these feelings. In this context, power is not necessarily an end in itself, but can be a means to achieve other needs, such as affection, approval, respect and accomplishment.

The issue is how this compensatory process can be measured empirically. The psychoanalytical work of Freud and Fenichel on the political manifestation of the need for power resulted in a list of six indicators of a striving for power gratification on the part of a compensation-seeking personality:

- unwillingness to permit others to share in the actual or assumed field of power
- unwillingness to take advice
- unwillingness to delegate tasks that are believed to belong to his field of power
- unwillingness to consult with others who have a claim to share power

- unwillingness to inform others
- desire to devise and impose orderly systems upon others in the political arena.[24]

With regard to the first indicator — unwillingness to permit others to share power — Winston Mahabir, one of the founders of the PNM, writing about Williams, said, "The PNM was effectively built by Williams, built around Williams, with his unmistakable stamp, bearing the imprint of his strength and weakness, his conflicts and his contradictions, his brilliant intellectual insight and his recurrently confusing behaviour."[25]

In this context, it is also appropriate to recall Ferreira's cogent summary of Williams's role in the PNM: "he was Papa."[26]

A party secretary recalls an early incident which at the time was probably amusing, but which reveals much about Williams's need to control. A meeting of party leaders, chaired by Ibbit Mosaheb, was being held at the party's Queen Street location. Williams announced that he wished to speak on a particular subject, saying: "As political leader I have something that I have to talk about." The group, recognizing that another item was being discussed, responded: "You are the political leader, but you are not chairing the meeting. You cannot speak on that subject now." To this Williams declared, "If I am not speaking then I will leave!" The group invited him to leave, knowing that he had been driven to the meeting, and thus would need to be driven back home. Williams was horrified that the group simply continued with the meeting while he stood outside the building waiting to be driven home.[27]

The popular view in Trinidad was that Williams was unwilling to take advice (the second indicator) and was unwilling to consult (the fourth indicator), thereby enhancing his status as an authoritarian leader. However, it has already been suggested that Williams was selectively authoritarian; Donald Granado noted that his relationship with Williams was based on mutual respect, not submission. George John, Public Relations Officer of the Williams government for six years, supported Granado's view that Williams's seeming authoritarianism was engendered, at least in part, by the peculiar personalities of some who surrounded him. According to John, Williams permitted individuals with particular expertise the opportunity to exercise and develop ideas and to employ their own initiative. But he added:

> My impression is that there were people who were afraid of him. If they were to say something that [they thought] he would not like, they would not say it . . . my impression is that something would come up and he would expect the Minister in charge to handle it, and the Minister would be waiting for a signal from him to start. He would give no signal, and the fellow would not do anything.[28]

While Williams's colleagues in the political sphere appeared to be largely intimidated by his domineering personality, his personal and technical advisers dispute the notion that he refused to accept advice and consult with them. Eldon Warner, formerly chairman of the Industrial Development Corporation, emphasized that Williams "was a good listener. He made you feel that your input was appreciated . . . He challenged us to exercise our minds and ideas. He inspired us to develop independent thought on the issues being considered."[29]

Warner's view is echoed by Dr Kenneth Julien, who served as a personal adviser to Williams for ten years until the latter's death. Julien insisted that their relationship was based upon "mutual respect", and consequently he had "no difficulties" working with Williams. "I was always 'Professor Julien' and he was 'Prime Minister Williams', because I was an adviser, and he kept it at that level." Julien speculated that he may have earned Williams's respect partly because "I never asked for a favour. I think that meant something to him."[30] The implication is that Williams may have had little respect for many of those around him, believing that each sought to pursue private and personal agendas.

While Julien served with Williams during the Prime Minister's last ten years in office, J. O'Neil Lewis was an adviser for about the first ten years, during the trauma and demise of the West Indies Federation and the movement toward independence. He was also a personal friend who rented Williams's home on Cornelio Street in Woodbrook. Working intimately with Williams on major economic policy issues and constitutional reform, he too was of the opinion that Williams willingly accepted the advice of his experts. He especially recalled the internal debates over the 1960 Budget speech. Williams had provided a draft of this speech to a small advisory group, which included Lewis, working out of the leader's home. The group modified every page of the draft. When Williams saw the major modifications he declared,

"Aren't you people leaving anything of the original? However, this is a democracy, and if you don't like something, I'll change it!"[31] He proceeded to make changes in the speech according to the advice of his consultative group. A general and tentative conclusion might be that while Williams displayed respect for the professional and technical staff working with him, he did not necessarily show the same respect in his political relationships. Possibly, too, the technicians were not perceived as potential challengers to power as the political figures were.

With regard to the third indicator of the power-striving personality, unwillingness to delegate, it was George John's experience that Williams allowed him much latitude in the organization and running of the Public Relations Office and in the exercise of his individual initiative.[32] But with regard to party affairs, where Williams was apparently ably assisted by part-time secretary Nicholas Simonette, he was generally unwilling to delegate tasks that he believed belonged to his field of power. He may also have questioned the level of competence of many around him.

During Williams's later years, the interest and energy he devoted to details of party affairs appeared to wane significantly. The administration of party affairs deteriorated, though he would probably have argued that it was only he who could hold the group together.

One of the primary hallmarks of Williams's penchant for control manifested itself in his desire to devise and impose orderly systems on himself, and on those around him. While he was very efficient and disciplined, his major complaint about his fellow citizens was probably that they were frivolous, careless and undisciplined. He was not alone in recognizing these characteristics. He challenged himself to introduce discipline and order to the society. Everyone who worked with him described him as efficient, orderly, prompt and organized. He demanded much of his co-workers, and no less of himself. His personal secretary of many years recalled that "there were deadlines to be met and you had to be as accurate as possible. He was demanding to an extent. If there were errors on final drafts, he was very particular about that." She recalled having to work the same long hours that he did; she was called out to work many weekends, and even on some public holidays. She admitted that this rigorous schedule affected her family life, but she accepted it as part of her employment.[33] Another secretary recalled: "He was demanding, you had to be on your toes. He maintained the highest standards."[34] Orderliness characterized his lifestyle.

His political secretary recalls the trauma of moving residence from Williams's private home on Mary Street to the Prime Minister's formal residence. This move, she said,

> was traumatic for him. He was concerned that his papers would be put back in the same position on his desk. So that as you cleared up his [old] desk and wrapped everything, there were notes that said, for instance, "left hand side, near drawer", so that everything was replaced exactly as before.[35]

This orderliness extended to his library at the new residence. When he

> moved into the Prime Minister's residence, I went there to fix his library for him. He told me what books he wanted out . . . when I had completed the work, I typed a list for him. He asked me to walk him through his new library. Everything was in an orderly manner so that he could get up in the middle of the night and put his hand [on what he wanted], including his detective stories. Everything had to be orderly for him.[36]

If there was a problem with Williams's desire for orderliness, it was the degree to which he demanded it of others as well as himself. The underlying and subconscious motive was his need to control the environment. He was largely successful in this because of the almost mesmerizing hold he maintained over much of the population. He was truly a charismatic leader.

It was Max Weber who introduced the term "charisma" into sociology; Weber was the first to analyze the inner content of the charismatic character, and the first to argue that charisma implies a relationship between the great man and his followers.[37] He emphasized that "the charismatic . . . can exist only in relationship to his adoring followers."[38] Thus for Weber,

> "charisma" shall be understood to refer to an extraordinary quality of a person, regardless of whether this quality is actual, alleged, or presumed. "Charismatic authority" . . . shall refer to a rule over men, whether predominantly external or predominantly internal, to which the governed submit because of their belief in the extraordinary quality of the specific person.[39]

In general, the charismatic leader-follower relationship arises in times of psychic, physical, economic and political distress. During these times people tend to feel that they are helpless, alienated and distorted, and that the society in which they live is meaningless.[40] In that context, Oxaal commented on mid-century Trinidadian attitudes:

> After the 1950 elections there . . . developed a general mood of pessimism among many . . . professionally employed coloured middle class. The prospects seemed poor for creating in Trinidad a responsible, educated political leadership such as Norman Manley symbolized for Jamaica. The Trinidad Creole community lacked a middle class hero like Manley who . . . had emerged in times of social crisis to declare [his] common cause with the lower class at considerable personal risk and sacrifice.[41]

In Trinidad, this void was filled by Eric Williams; it was felt not only by the black middle class, but even more by the larger black lower class. As Oxaal observed, "For many lower class negroes, particularly creole women, Dr Williams was nothing less than a messiah come to lead the black children to the Promised Land." This sentiment was captured in a placard at a pro-PNM rally: "The Master Couldn't Come So He Sent Williams!" The placard carried a drawing of Williams titled "Moses II".[42] Ferdie Ferreira, one of Williams's important links to the ordinary people, said that the crowd "always saw Williams as a modern-day Christ."[43] He recalled that, after a political rally in Mayaro in 1956, Williams, Ferreira and others sat around having drinks, with a crowd mingling outside. Ferreira suggested that he and Williams take a walk on the beach. Within minutes, the scene had turned to near chaos, causing much apprehension from the policemen assigned to protect them. As Williams began his walk, the crowd pressed forward, each, according to Ferreira, attempting to "touch the hem of Williams's garment", an allusion to the sick wanting to be healed by Christ.[44]

Williams's status as a leader grew steadily over the five years between 1950 and 1955. The themes that he introduced into public discourse all resonated with an increasingly receptive audience: the origins, nature and consequences of slavery; the exploitative nature of colonialism and imperialism; the role of education in building a democracy. His legendary debate with Dom Basil Matthews pitted the diminutive doctor against the imposing churchman.[45] After he was fired from the Caribbean Commission, he could present himself to the assembled thousands as a martyr. In his Woodford Square speech, he successfully converted his frustrations into the frustrations of the masses;

his hurts into their hurts; his need to conquer into their need to conquer. His assortment of props — hearing aid, dark glasses, monotone voice — only added to the mystique.

One characteristic of the charismatic is a detachment from the particular, including the relative unimportance of the individual and of individual events. This was very evident in Williams's personality and behaviour. The traumatic "Black Power" uprising of 1970 illustrates his attitude toward individual events.

While Williams's Cabinet remained ensconced in the relative safety of the Hilton Hotel from the first day of the crisis, Williams remained at home, surrounded by his unofficial advisers, including Carlton Gomes, Ferdie Ferreira, Ivan Williams, Bertie Ballantyne and Irwin Merritt, with Rolf Moyou and Carl Tull in infrequent attendance. Each night he lectured to this group on the historical precedents of the uprising, discussing with them, for instance, the details of the Haitian Revolution. As Gomes recalled, "every night he placed the Black Power problem in the context of world history."[46] Williams's universal perspective, and his apparent inability to relate to the domestic uprising — the cultural contradictions engendered by his government, for instance — exacerbated the basic issues involved. Yet this was the expected behaviour of a charismatic-type leader. That no single individual represented an absolute value to Williams is probably what most characterized his leadership.

Williams's path to power, and his 25-year national leadership, were strewn with the bodies of people who at one time or another had found favour, but who were later discarded. Patrick Solomon, one of the senior casualties, put it this way: "No one or nothing was left untroubled if he or it could serve Eric Williams's purpose. As the years rolled by, person after person was used and discarded . . . in Eric Williams's triumphant march to the top of the political ladder."[47] Winston Mahabir was among the group of five that met with Williams on the evening of his dismissal from the Commission; Mosaheb, Richardson and one of Williams's brothers were the other participants. Within a few years, these three co-founders of the movement had been forced out or were no longer involved. Mahabir himself commented that "the list of those whom Williams lifted to high places and then destroyed was terrifyingly long." After Williams had discarded C. L. R. James, Mahabir — who described

James as Williams's "spiritual father" — was moved to ask:

> Does Williams care at all about people apart from their value as manipulative
> political objects? To retain power, would Williams not continue to be completely
> ruthless to the point of being unresponsive to the chords of 30 years of friendship?
> These are some of the questions that caused a shudder in some who, even while
> they were objects of current favours, feared the unpredictable day of doom.[48]

Mahabir also noted Williams's narcissistic personality.[49] This is a characteristic of many charismatic leaders, who believe that they possess great power, physical appeal, and the right to assert their will. In these personalities, two different experiences of the self co-exist. One is the insecure self, characterized by low self-esteem and insecurity, while the other is a grandiose self, driven by the need for achievement and recognition, by fantasies of self-confidence and control. They continually seek public approval and have an authoritarian style that permits them to present their views with more self-confidence than available information warrants.[50]

Not all these characteristics were evident in the personality of Eric Williams, but the force which drove him seemed to be a yearning for the redress of grievances which represented a narcissistic injury to his self-image. That is, he perceived throughout his life that he was treated as inferior, when he knew he possessed superior intellectual endowments.

Williams was a driven individual with an abundance of energy, and expected the same level of energy, production and efficiency from those around him. His energy level was legendary: he repeatedly told his advisers that he could function effectively on five hours of sleep. In that, he was similar to Fidel Castro, who has found three or four hours of sleep quite sufficient. This type of personality oscillates through a cycle from mania to depression. Of such leaders, it has been noted that "when manic, they overwhelm those around them with their massive energy and a flood of instructions about all the things that must be done at once. Everything is a crisis."[51]

Nicholas Simonette, the party secretary, recalled an interesting instance of Williams's manic behavior. After the controversial "African Safari" tour, Williams reported to the nation in a public lecture, "A Small Country in a Big World". The speech was taped and later transcribed. When Simonette visited the Prime Minister's home, he gave Williams a copy of the transcribed speech and suggested that it should be published. Apparently, Williams had been presented with beautifully bound photo albums of the tour by leaders in the various countries he had visited. He became so excited by the possibility of publishing this speech that he retrieved a kitchen knife and proceeded to cut pictures from the bound albums to be included in the publication. Simonette was astonished at this behaviour and the mutilation of the albums, and suggested that the pictures could be obtained later, to which Williams responded, "No, get it at once!"[52] Shortly afterwards, Williams left for a trip to London; on his return, the publication project was no longer discussed.

Personalities of this type do not maintain close relationships and generally avoid true intimacy. As previously shown, people are replaceable. Psychologist Ramon Rios pungently stated: "They are also hell to get along with because their nature is so changeable and unpredictable."[53] Rios could have been employing Williams as his subject, so well do the characterizations fit.

It is useful to recognize, however, that Williams did have a brief intense relationship with his second wife, which ended abruptly with her sudden death, and that he enjoyed a close personal relationship with his third child Erica, at least until the last years of his life. His efforts at developing personal relationships, both as a husband and as a father, are the subject of the following chapter.

Eric Williams's three children: Pamela, Alistair, Erica

Soy Suilan Moyou, Eric Williams's second wife

HUSBAND AND FATHER

Sometime in June 1939, Henry Williams, Eric's father, answered a knock on his door, to see an attractive light-skinned young woman standing on his doorstep. He asked what she wanted, and she replied, "I'm Mrs Williams!" Taken aback, Henry asked, "Which Mrs Williams?" To which she answered, "I am Mrs Eric Williams!" In this way, Henry and Eliza Williams learned that their first son was married.[1]

Eric and Elsie Ribeiro were married, very quietly, in Hampstead, England, on January 30, 1937, while Eric was still a postgraduate student at Oxford and Elsie was pursuing studies in music. Eric had known Elsie in Trinidad, before they both left for England. Her brothers Oscar and Joey were actively involved in the sports programme at QRC; Eric was a member of QRC's cricket team, which was captained by Oscar. But Eric had not dated Elsie in Trinidad. His girlfriend before leaving home was his best friend's sister, Elsie McShine.

Elsie Ribeiro's mother, from the Iverson family of St Vincent, had arrived in Trinidad during the early years of the century. She worked as a housekeeper for J. J. Ribeiro, a Port of Spain merchant, with whom she eventually had three children: Oscar, Joey and Elsie. Although she was born in Trinidad, Elsie identified with St Vincent. It was her wish to be buried there.

Joey roomed with Halsey McShine and Ray Dolly in London; Williams visited London frequently, and lived there while doing research for his thesis. He and Elsie, with McShine and his future wife Eileen, had often dined and danced together on Saturday evenings.[2] But McShine was very surprised to learn of Williams's marriage. He did not think the couple were "friendly enough to marry."[3] Dolly, too, expressed much surprise, since he considered himself "like a brother to Elsie."[4] Even when Williams visited McShine before leaving for Washington, he did not disclose his marriage. McShine learned of the marriage from John Pillai, who had attended QRC with Williams and was a member of the school's soccer team that was captained by Williams. He too was a university student in London at this time, and served as best man for the wedding ceremony.

Williams apparently selected Pillai as his best man, rather than McShine or Dolly, because they would be returning to Trinidad after completing their studies. But Pillai's family roots were in south-east Asia. Williams was very concerned that the terms of his scholarship might have prohibited marriage; he feared that if word of his marriage reached Trinidad, the scholarship could be terminated. So almost no one in England or in Trinidad was informed of his marriage to Elsie Ribeiro.

Once Williams had obtained a position on the faculty of Howard University, he and Elsie decided that he would proceed directly to the US while she would first visit Trinidad before joining him in Washington. He could thus find proper accommodation before his wife arrived, and she could spend some time with her mother. Thus on June 2, 1939, he wrote to Professor Locke at Howard: "My wife is on her way to Trinidad on a short visit to her mother whom she has not seen for many years, and is hoping that things could be arranged so as to allow her to leave Trinidad to join me in the USA about a day or two after I get there."[5] It was on this visit that Elsie met the Williams family and told them of her marriage to Eric, more than two years after it had taken place.

Elsie spent about two months in Trinidad visiting her mother and her many friends from Bishop Anstey High School. One of Eric's sisters, who was employed at a photography store in Port of Spain, recalled purchasing many rolls of film and processing the pictures Elsie took during this trip.[6] In August 1939, Elsie boarded a ship sailing to New York. Also on board, to begin university study at Howard, was Ibbit Mosaheb; the trip provided him with an introduction to Williams, whose student and close friend he became.

Eric, always friendly with West Indian students at Howard, both male and female, invited many of them to his home. During these visits Mrs Williams seemed friendly, yet somewhat reserved. Later, when Mosaheb was pursuing his dental studies in Montreal, Canada, at Williams's request he played host to Elsie Williams for two weeks; one reason for the visit may have been that "things were not right with the [Williams] marriage."[7]

Elsie gave birth to a son, Alistair, the first of Williams's two children with her, on May 6, 1943. Williams had hoped to have a daughter. The son's birth was therefore a surprise, and he expressed this in a letter to Locke.[8] Young Alistair occasionally accompanied his father on trips to Trinidad, where he was looked after by an aunt, Williams's sister Angela Jeffers. She recalled taking Alistair with her to the convent to meet some children: on seeing a garbed nun little Alistair blurted out, "Is she an Arab?"[9]

Probably because of his extensive travel during the mid-1940s, on behalf of the Caribbean Commission, Williams's relationship with his wife did not improve. The problems were exacerbated by the birth of their second child Elsie Pamela, on July 22, 1947, and the issue of paternity. Here, Williams's characteristic weakness, his affinity for gossip, displayed itself; it would later be the source of some of his most serious problems as a political leader. He acted on the gossip: he took leave of absence from Howard,[10] and in less than a year had accepted a permanent position in Trinidad with the Caribbean Commission and separated from his wife.

When Williams left Washington for Trinidad in May 1948, he left his wife and two children, aged five and one, in faculty housing near the university. As a department head, he could have arranged with the university for his family to remain in the house for at least one more year; but he made no such arrangement, and his family was required to vacate by October.

With the approach of winter, two small children, and no means of earning an income, Elsie took in three university students as boarders. Her neighbour at the time was Warner Lawson, head of the music department at Howard. Lawson arranged a part-time position in music for Elsie — she had studied music in England. She, her children and her boarders moved to a house on Bryant Street, which would serve as the family home for the next 50 years. After renting it for a while, she was able, with the help of her brother in London, to purchase the home. At about the same time she took the US federal government's civil service examination, passed, and obtained a permanent position with the General Accounting Office in Washington. She maintained this position from late 1948 until illness forced her resignation in the early 1970s.

The financial burden, together with the difficulty of raising two small children as a single working parent, must have made life difficult for Elsie, especially during the first few years. The question of alimony remained a nagging, distressing issue for over eight years. Alistair suffered emotionally from Williams's withdrawal from the home: he had known his father for about five years, travelled to Trinidad with him, and must have missed him dearly. This manifested itself in aggressive behaviour, violent tantrums, and a show of toughness ("I do not need a father"[11]). He became fiercely protective of his mother. Pamela, at least outwardly, appeared to be much less affected. She was less than a year old when her father left, and for her first 20 years really only knew her mother. She was also more contemplative and reflective than her extrovert brother.

Elsie's student boarders helped to ease the financial burden, and allowed her to provide the best affordable education for her children, which eventually included private schools. She generally selected medical students, who were somewhat older and more mature, and who remained for longer periods. But she repeatedly claimed that "Eric did not take care of his responsibilities."[12] When Williams's alimony became a popular issue in Trinidad in the early 50s, James Bain, Permanent Secretary to Albert ("Bertie") Gomes, reported: "Bill told Bertie and myself that he had stopped supporting his wife because she refused to carry out his intentions for sending them to Oxford University."[13]

If Bain's recollections some 35 years later were correct, Williams's excuse was curious on many grounds, especially since in the early 1950s his children were still quite young. Of course, his wife may have told him that she would never permit her children to attend his alma mater.

Williams returned to Trinidad in June 1948, settling into his position at the Caribbean Commission. Within a few months he had befriended Soy Suilan Moyou, a typist at the Commission, and not long after began visiting the Moyou family home in Port of Spain. This large family included five girls and one boy. Soy's father had died, and her mother was the matriarch of the family.

Soy's father had arrived in Trinidad at age 30 from China, having apparently stowed away on a ship. His name was Moy-Yen-U, which was corrupted in Trinidad to Moyou.[14] His wife, Soy's mother, was of African/Portuguese/Chinese descent; she was from Princes Town and a cousin of the wife of the future Governor General Sir Solomon Hochoy.

From all the evidence, it is apparent that Williams fell deeply in love with Soy. In January 1950, after attending a Caribbean Commission meeting in the US Virgin Islands, he instituted divorce proceedings there against Elsie. She responded with an injunction restraining him from proceeding with his petition. He dropped the proceedings, and in a letter of April 1950 submitted to the jurisdiction of the District of Columbia court, agreeing to abide by its decision and be bound by an order regarding alimony.[15]

But a few months later Williams again started divorce proceedings, this time in Reno, Nevada. His haste was probably due to the fact that Soy was pregnant.

Reno, Nevada, was well known as a location for "quick divorces". Two years earlier, C. L. R. James had gone there seeking a divorce from his first wife. James had asked Williams to obtain the relevant data in Trinidad to hasten the process.[16] Since James's divorce was apparently approved, Williams assumed that his would be also.

But there were some additional factors that prompted his trip to Nevada. Throughout his life, Williams had been dogged by sinus problems and hay fever. Even in Washington he was aware that the dry, semi-desert climate of Nevada was more conducive to his health; he may have considered a permanent move.[17] At this time he was disenchanted with his position at the Commission, and was upset with the recent appointment of a Secretary General who lacked "all educational and professional qualifications for the post."[18] He wanted to settle down and write a history of the Caribbean, but the pressures of his formal position would not permit this.[19] As a resident alien of the United States, he had a legal right to return.[20] He settled for a compromise: he was due for six months' long leave, and decided to spend that time in the United States.

Williams stated in his autobiography that he "had six months' long leave at the end of 1950 which I spent in the US in various libraries."[21] But the stay was more complicated than that. He did spend an active six months in the United States, but his activities went well beyond research.

In September 1950, Williams and Soy Moyou travelled to New York, where he purchased his famous maroon Buick Dynaflow car (he eventually brought it back with him to Trinidad). It was probably the first vehicle with automatic transmission in Trinidad. He had seen a beautiful Buick owned by his friend Dr Dolly at Pointe-à-Pierre, and wanted a similar vehicle. He and Soy drove this convertible across the country to Reno, where they settled in for a six-month stay while he pursued divorce proceedings against his first wife. In Washington, Elsie became aware of these proceedings and obtained a preliminary injunction preventing her husband from making any attempt at divorce, on the grounds that he had earlier subjected himself to the jurisdiction of the District of Columbia court.[22] However, Williams filed formal proceedings for a divorce on November 24, 1950.

On December 13, Williams was ordered to appear in court, probably because he had filed for a divorce in Nevada even though he had earlier submitted himself to the District of Columbia court system. He did not appear, even though a lawyer had been assigned to him. On December 22, he was ordered to be taken into custody by a US Marshal. His lawyer in Nevada pointed out that his divorce had been granted, though a search of the court records showed no entry for a final decree. Williams had apparently met the six-week residential requirement to obtain a Nevada divorce. On January 2, 1951, he married Soy Moyou in Reno, in a ceremony performed by the Reverend Munroe Warner of First Christian Church, in the presence of Mrs D. L. Robinson and Charlotte Hunter. Their daughter Erica was born on February 12,

1951, in Reno.

Elsie Williams obtained a divorce from Eric Williams on January 20, 1951, on grounds of desertion. This was made effective on July 21, 1951, and Williams was ordered to pay the sum of $275.00 monthly as maintenance for his first wife and the two children of this marriage.

Williams himself did not return to Trinidad until his six months' leave was over, in March 1951. During those first few months of 1951 he presumably conducted research for his proposed history of the Caribbean. His wife and baby did not accompany him immediately, instead spending a few months in Antigua before returning to Trinidad.

Williams's marriage to Soy was intense and short. It lasted less than 30 months. Soy died after a four-day illness caused by rapidly advancing tuberculosis on May 25, 1953. Williams's love for Soy was deep and possessive. A relative recalled that on one occasion Soy needed to buy some clothing material but was worried that her husband would be upset if she went out alone. She called him at the Commission. He left his job, took her to the store and returned her to their home before resuming his work.[23]

Williams's love for his second wife is captured in letters that he kept until he died and which reveal much about the man behind the mask. His job at the Commission required him to be away from Trinidad fairly frequently, but he maintained contact with Soy through letters.[24] On June 20, 1952, he wrote to her, "Well, lover, tomorrow is another day, and that means one less day. Please write to me every day. I miss you." On another trip a few months later, he wrote, "Lover girl . . . if we were together now, I know from experience how you will be able to help me, as no one has been able to do and no one ever will . . . I do not understand, darling Suilan, or do not quite understand, this longing for you. I feel quite lost, quite empty. I used to be so self-contained."

Some 25 years later, Williams's warm feelings for Soy had not changed. On an official visit to Japan, he and his group sat for dinner one evening in the Imperial Hotel. As strolling violinists walked around the hall, Williams whispered to Errol Mahabir, "Could you get them to play Limelight for me, 'I'll Be Loving You Eternally'?" Mahabir was astounded at Williams's request. He had never seen this side of the Prime Minister. As the song was played, Mahabir recalled, "I saw for the first time a moment of weakness and I saw tears in Dr Williams's eye." When questioned about the significance of the tune, Williams explained that it was played the first time he danced with Erica's mother, Soy, on their first date.[25]

His daughter Erica, after years of discussion with her father about his love for Soy, summarized the significance of their relationship:

> I know that Eric Williams the man blossomed during the years when my mother was alive . . . on numerous occasions my father told me that had she lived, he would have never entered politics. She was against this, and he would have respected her wishes. I believe that when she died he made a very conscious decision to enter the political arena. The life he had shared with my mother was no more. He believed he could never have such an intensely personal relationship again, and he never did. Eric Williams the man gave way to Eric Williams the politician.[26]

Williams's close friend Halsey McShine observed, "I think this was the one woman he truly loved. I think his life would have taken a different course if she had not died."[27] But she did, quickly and tragically.

Soy, whom her brother considered to be a "delicate" person, lived with Eric in Diego Martin.[28] Because of the cool temperature, and on her doctor's recommendation, they moved into the Moyou family home on Sackville Street in Port of Spain. After completing a typing project for her husband, who was in Puerto Rico at the time, Soy apparently began to cough up blood. She was taken by ambulance to the Port of Spain General Hospital, where McShine and others debated over the course of treatment. She was then sent to the Caura Hospital, and died shortly after. Williams was contacted and arrived two days before her death.

Soy's funeral was a very sad occasion. She was still a relatively young woman, who had had a brief marriage and a baby in just over two years. One onlooker at the graveside noted that "Soy's mother was completely devastated. The only thing she did not do was to throw herself into the grave."[29] Mrs Moyou visited the gravesite for several weeks until, fearing for her mental health, her other daughters urged her to stop.

Williams's reaction to Soy's death was predictably stoic. A relative noted that he "was good at masking his feelings, but you could tell that he was very hurt. It changed him — maybe too much. He suffered in silence. He shared his grief with no one. He held it and he paid the price."[30] A sister observed that "nobody ever saw him shed a tear . . .

he was very distraught, but he tried to stay in control of everything."[31]
The day after the funeral, Williams drove to Piarco where he met a
brother-in-law who worked at the Customs office. He mentioned that
on the previous day — the day of the funeral — he and Soy had been
scheduled to leave for a trip to Europe, where he would explore job
opportunities because of his disenchantment with his position at the
Caribbean Commission.[32] But he made the trip alone. Curiously, he
had his car shipped ahead and used it to travel throughout Europe,
perhaps as part of the healing process.

Williams was now faced with the daunting task of bringing up his
baby daughter alone. By all accounts, he did an admirable job, ably
supported by the Moyou family, particularly Soy's sisters, Erica's aunts.
But while he had an overwhelming love for his daughter, his personality
still demanded firm discipline. For instance, he required her to drink
milk three times a day, even though she did not care for it. If she did
not do this, she would be spanked with a newspaper and sent to her
room.

His insistence became the source of many problems which those
around the home sought to alleviate. Even before Soy died, Eric would
sometimes prepare Erica's milk and place it before her at breakfast.
Seeing her daughter's unwillingness to drink such large amounts, Soy
developed a ruse. She would ask her husband to retrieve an item from
another room; while he was gone, she herself drank some of Erica's
milk. On his return, Eric would congratulate his daughter.[33]

A frequent visitor to the house recalled how she and Aunt Kathleen
[Moyou] tried to have Erica dressed and seated for breakfast when her
father entered the room. This was the sort of behaviour he required.
Little Erica was particularly uncooperative one morning, and when her
father arrived for breakfast she was not yet ready. He ordered her to sit
at the table and drink her milk, but she only pretended to do so.
Becoming annoyed, he smacked her and sent her to her room, ordered
her not to go to school and required everyone not to speak to her that
day. Of course, no one complied.[34]

Despite his stern demeanour, Williams tried to provide, as far as
he could, a normal childhood for his daughter. The circumstances, of
course, were difficult. After Soy's death, Williams had to be both mother
and father to his very young daughter, yet his job with the Commission

demanded extensive travel. For baby Erica, it must have seemed that she had lost both parents. Before she was five years old, Williams had organized the first major political party in the history of the country, and less than a year later he was voted in as the leader of Trinidad and Tobago. This brought a whole array of new problems for father and daughter, including many time-consuming activities, the loss of family privacy and a threat to personal security.

A lifelong friend of Erica recalled attending a birthday party at the Williams home when Erica was about six years old: "It was only a daddy and his little girl."[35] Here was Williams, trying valiantly to host a party for his daughter, including the preparation of the food, games, costumes, etc. And this was probably just the first of many such parties that Williams would organize for his daughter over the years.

Because Williams was away from Trinidad frequently during the first five years after Erica's birth, he wrote letters to her in order to stay in contact, and to demonstrate his affection. He also did this to maintain firm discipline during his absence. Thus in June 1954 he wrote "the first instruction is to play you opera and symphonies", while the second cautioned her grandmother that "you should not be given too many sweets . . . the distribution must be orderly and centralized!" That juxtaposition between "sweets" and "orderly and centralized" provides revealing insights into Williams's mind. A few months earlier, in a letter to Charlotte Hunter about the absence of a mother, he wrote, "What she lacks in feminine affection she makes up in masculine discipline."[36]

It was beyond question that Williams adored his daughter. A family friend, who herself was quite young at the time, recalled:

> I remember when Erica was maybe two or three years old . . . I remember her as being a thing so special and the relationship between Uncle Bill and Erica has always been something that fascinated me. I don't think I understood it then but it struck me that here was this father who loved his daughter so much and vice versa. They were completely taken up with each other. She seemed to be the centre of his life.[37]

Inevitably, Williams remained caught between his public and private responsibilities. For instance, because he was committed to public education, and thereby to earning political legitimacy, he was unable to devote as much time as he would have wished to bringing up his daughter. With the party less than a year old, he was propelled into national leadership of an emerging country. So the task of raising Erica fell not only to her father but also to countless relatives and close family friends.

Then there was the issue of security. Erica enjoyed playing in the park after school. Here she was attended by "Zorro", the family chauffeur. But after a threatening call was received at the family home, Williams prohibited Erica from appearing in public. She was confined to the home and visits to the homes of very trusted friends. As a child of five or six, she obviously could not understand the constraints placed on her, or the fact that she was almost always surrounded by adults. The security protection continued at school, with her teachers making special efforts to ensure her safety.

Eventually these extra precautions affected the lives of both father and daughter, and the agonizing decision was made that Erica should undertake her high school education in England. It was one of the most difficult decisions that Williams ever made. Erica was the "gold bead" of his life.[38] A close friend observed that the relationship was "very strong, very devoted. He had an adoration for her that was unreal . . . if she walked into a room and he was sitting there his whole face would just light up like a bulb . . . we used to give him jokes and say, 'She has arrived, she is here.' Erica around him was unbelievable. It was like magic."[39]

Before making this decision, Williams turned to the wives of close friends, including the Carr, Attale and Dupres families. The issue was two-fold: Erica would be leaving home even though she was still quite young; and her father would become a very lonely individual. What Williams struggled with was the difficulty of providing a "normal" life for his daughter in the conditions under which he lived. Recognizing his inability to meet her needs, he agonized: "How often can you break a promise with a child?"[40]

Erica left Trinidad for England at the age of eleven, though she returned to Trinidad each Christmas and for summer vacations. But about five years before her departure, Williams entered into his controversial and secret third marriage, to Dr Mayleen Mook Sang.

Their meeting was fortuitous. Ibbit Mosaheb was Williams's personal dentist, and attempted to serve as dentist for little Erica. But he quickly realized that a female professional would be more appropriate. He had attended dental school at McGill University with Mayleen Mook Sang, and though he was a year ahead, they had remained friends. He recommended Mook Sang as Erica's dentist; this may have been how Eric Williams met her.

Williams had been a widower since 1953, and the problem of looking after a young daughter, especially as the new political party was being formed, preoccupied the minds of some around him. A suggestion was made that he should remarry. To this, Eric replied, in all seriousness, "I don't mind. But bring me a Chinese or East Indian, don't bring me a negro woman."[41] Williams's second wife, Soy, had been part Chinese; his third was of Chinese descent, born in Guyana.

Williams and Mayleen Mook Sang were secretly married at a beach house on Caledonia Island, one of Trinidad's "Five Islands", on November 13, 1957. The ceremony was performed by the Reverend A. N. McKean of Greyfriars Presbyterian Church in Port of Spain, and was witnessed by two close political colleagues, John O'Halloran and Ulric Lee. The couple did not live together. They lived about a mile apart, he in Woodbrook and she on Frederick Street. Details of the marriage were not revealed to the public until the *Trinidad Chronicle* broke the story over a year later, on December 5, 1958.

The Cabinet had become aware of the matter a few months earlier, when a petition from Mook Sang for a marriage certificate came before the Executive Council. A copy of the marriage certificate — No. A/21/56 , Vol. 4, Folio 518 — was subsequently published in the *Trinidad Guardian*. Later efforts to locate the certificate at the Registry revealed that the relevant page had been torn from the Volume.

The marriage certificate took just over a year to arrive at the office of the Registrar General. Initially, McKean was blamed for the delay, but when he stubbornly insisted that he had submitted it properly, blame passed to the Red House. Apparently, the certificate was discovered among the office papers of Registrar Hector Deeble, who died suddenly in April 1958. Deeble's wife denied that the fault was her husband's; she claimed that he was deeply troubled a few weeks before his death, telling her, "Man, I can't do it. It is impossible." He did not explain to her what he meant by that statement.[42] By the time the marriage certificate arrived at the registry, A. A. Thompson was the new Registrar. In his view, "it was no mystery about the registration one year after it took place."[43] He was later appointed to Williams's Cabinet.

Mayleen Mook Sang was understandably upset when her very private marriage became a public spectacle, especially since her husband had made no provision for a home for her. She felt humiliated, and threatened a libel suit. She did reveal, however, that she had met Williams before he became Chief Minister, and that both had agreed to a secret wedding. She insisted that this was a personal affair. "I do not think about the future . . . I cross my bridges when I come to them."[44] More than 25 years later, after the court had accepted her as Williams's widow, she maintained her warm feelings for him. "I have nothing bad to say about Eric," she said. "In fact, all the times we spent together were very happy times; every day was better than the day before."[45]

While Williams may have spent some happy times with her, in 1956–57 he was still engaged in a fierce dispute with his first wife over the issue of alimony. The implications seriously affected him as Chief Minister.

It may be recalled that Elsie Williams had obtained a divorce from her husband in January 1951, a month after he had obtained his divorce in Reno, Nevada, and that he was required to pay alimony of $275.00 a month, beginning in July 1951. It seems unlikely that Williams paid alimony, at least until he became Chief Minister in 1956, because by that time a US court had found him in contempt. Indirectly, this may have contributed to his dismissal from the Caribbean Commission, since US representatives there were aware of the court's decision.[46]

After Williams was appointed Chief Minister, Chester Bowles, a US government official, wrote in an article in the *Wall Street Journal* that Williams would be jailed if he entered America. The Trinidad government protested to the US, which responded that freedom of the press permitted Mr Bowles to express his views. Williams was then forced to deal with the issue of alimony. Elsie Williams also brought the issue to the Trinidad courts, where she was represented by Ellis Clarke.[47] Williams turned to his "right hand man", Alan Reece.[48]

Reece and Williams had attended QRC together. Williams was a few years ahead, but the two met on the soccer field. Like so many others, Reece, who was then a senior civil servant, had attended Williams's lectures during the early 1950s. After the PNM took office in 1956, Williams promoted him, and he eventually served as Secretary to the Cabinet. He made several trips to Washington to negotiate the alimony problem with Elsie. But because Williams provided him with little flexibility, he was little more than a conduit for the exchange of positions. The issue was exacerbated when an irate Williams accused Elsie of passing information to the US government. This may have influenced his future attitude to the United States.

It is unlikely that Elsie provided the US government with information to enlarge their file on Williams. What is known is that, some years later, her US divorce attorney was revealed, in another case, as a government informant. But the accusation made the divorce negotiations even more difficult. Eventually, a settlement was reached, and Williams presumably began to make regular payments for the support of his first family.[49] But if Elsie believed that this would end her family's relationship with Williams, she was wrong.

In their teens, Alistair and Pamela expressed a desire to get to know their father. Elsie was understandingly apprehensive. Would her children become excited and enamoured about being with their Prime Minister father? She had reared them single-handedly: could she compete with a father who was a famous public figure? Would she lose her children to him? She nevertheless agreed, reasoning that after one visit her children's curiosity would be satisfied. After some negotiations, arrangements were made for a visit in the late 1960s.

Not surprisingly, Williams too was somewhat apprehensive. He naturally wanted to develop a relationship with his two first children, but was unsure of their reaction. He recruited his political secretary Diane Dupres, herself a younger woman, to look after Pamela. Alistair eventually befriended Rolf Moyou, Williams's brother-in-law and a personal assistant during those years.

To their mother's dismay, Alistair and Pamela both enjoyed their visit to Trinidad. Pamela was introduced to relatives and shown the various sights. She liked getting to know her father, and enjoyed the intellectual exchanges with him. Alistair gradually became involved with Moyou in spreading the steelband movement across the country, and seriously dated a daughter of Williams's old friend Ray Dolly. At the time of this first trip, Erica was in Geneva; sibling rivalry would develop in succeeding years.

Back in Washington, both children announced their desire to make another visit to Trinidad. Elsie feared losing her children to their father, but there was probably little she could do. Repeated visits were made in the early 70s, by which time Erica was living with her father. The three young people were eventually able to work out their relationships with each other. After Pamela entered university in California, Alistair visited Trinidad more frequently. Eventually, as a consequence of some domestic conflicts, he left Trinidad, and did not return until his father's death nine years later.

In the 1970s, Elsie developed heart problems. Her brother, now a cardiologist in London, tried to assist her, but by this time she was disappointed and disillusioned. Her children's visits to Trinidad could not have helped. She was now much more alone; she spent much time in a Washington hospital, and was then placed in a nursing home. She died in April 1975, and was buried in St Vincent.[50]

Early 1970 was a tumultuous time for Trinidad, with the "Black Power" explosion and army revolt. Williams was bunkered down at his home; from Geneva, Erica demanded to come home to be with him. She was brought in under tight security, but within two days began socializing even though the country was under a curfew.[51] With tensions subsiding, she returned to Geneva in September; but when she came home for Christmas, she decided to discontinue her studies and stay in Trinidad. She lived there until November 1973.

Because Williams had begun working mainly out of his home at the onset of the 1970 upheaval, he was now more available and had more interaction with Erica. She had left Trinidad as a youthful eleven-year-old, but had returned as a very bright 19-year-old woman. Finally, he had someone in his house with whom he could interact on a personal and daily basis. The deep bond between father and daughter, well established before Erica had left for England, was further strengthened.

There was, however, one thorny issue: his possible resignation.

Erica had returned home partly because she recognized how lonely her father was as he grew older. She began urging him to resign and to devote the remainder of his life to his first love: research and writing. He stubbornly held on for another two years, but Erica was relentless. Living at home, she was able to understand, for the first time, the constant political pressures to which he was subjected.[52] By that time,

Williams had begun to share his desire to resign with close advisers.[53] He bought a home in Goodwood Park. At the annual PNM convention in September 1973, he announced his intention to resign, and recommended that the party seek a new leader. Erica must have been ecstatic. The convention would meet again in November to select a new leader.

But when the party reconvened, a ground swell of support forced Williams to reconsider. On the Sunday afternoon of the conference, he returned to the convention hall to accept leadership of the party once more. Undoubtedly, Erica would have been sorely disappointed; her father had again placed country before family. A few weeks later, she quietly slipped out of Trinidad to settle in Florida. Both father and daughter were deeply hurt by this decision.[54]

Nevertheless, the bond between them was as intense as ever; even though there was occasional conflict, it was "among people who cared for each other." Erica admits: "His advice was always of great help and very important to me. He was a man of much wisdom and vision, and I trusted his views implicitly . . . he was really and truly my confidante."[55]

Williams was lonely after his daughter left home. One of her friends, who continued to visit him, noted: "He missed Erica terribly . . . it is difficult to express in words."[56] They remained in touch by telephone, and he encouraged her friends in Trinidad to maintain their contacts with her. For a while, Erica made return visits to Trinidad, and introduced her future husband to her father. But Williams did not attend her wedding in Florida. His representative was one of his closest confidantes, Errol Mahabir. He did, however, receive reports and wedding pictures from Erica's friends who attended the wedding.[57]

In the final years of his life, Williams was a lonely and reclusive individual. He no longer interacted with his children. He had become estranged from his son Alistair, and his daughters were preoccupied with their own lives and families. Erica strongly desired to visit him, but he did not encourage her. Outwardly, he may have rationalized this in terms of security, but privately he had cut himself off from all but a few close advisers. During the last weekend of his life, he remained very much alone.[58]

C. L. R. James was a teacher and early mentor of Eric Williams

JAMES AND
WILLIAMS

E ric Williams described himself to C. L. R. James as "your godchild!"[1] James referred to Williams as "my devoted admirer."[2] Clearly, the two men enjoyed a close relationship, at least during that period of their lives. This closeness continued for about 15 years; in 1958, Williams, then Chief Minister of Trinidad and Tobago, invited James to attend the celebrations for the recently formed West Indies Federation. Yet two years later, Williams refused to speak with James, and five years after that he had James placed under house arrest and tapped his telephone. Viewed over the entire period, then, Williams's relationship with James, like so many of his other relationships, was a somewhat chequered one.

James was born in Tunapuna in 1901, ten years before Williams, to a family "descended from the class of free coloured artisans."[3] His class background was therefore somewhat similar to that of the Williams family. He was very bright, and at the age of nine placed first in the college exhibition, which granted tuition-free high school education to the top four students. Williams achieved the same feat ten years later, by which time the number of exhibitions had been increased to ten. James entered Queen's Royal College in the year of Williams's birth.

His performance there, however, was decidedly unlike that of Williams.

James explained it best when he wrote: "When I put my foot on the steps of the college building in January 1911, I carried within me the seeds of revolt against all it formally stood for and for all that I was supposed to do."[4] He continued, "Two people lived in me: one, the rebel against all family and school discipline and order: the other, a Puritan who would have cut off a finger sooner than do anything contrary to the ethics of the game."[5] "The game" is an obvious reference to his obsession with cricket, but at another level he was also alluding to the game of life, and the quandary in which he found himself, trying to live by puritanical rules while succumbing to his growing rebellious impulses.

The problem with James was that, as a member of that tiny dark-skinned group that had been admitted to high school at the expense of the government, the path before him had been clearly outlined. As he noted, he was expected to keep his "eye on the course: exhibition, scholarship, profession, wealth, Legislative Council."[6] While one part of him accepted that direction, for the other, "cricket and English Literature . . . fed an inexhaustible passion."[7] Thus he performed poorly at QRC: as he admitted, he "did not try."

James's final year in high school was 1918. Fortunately for him, his father, who had lectured, punished and flogged him during his earlier years, decided to "accept me as I was and I became a respectable and self-respecting member of society."[8] With the support of his family, James completed his high school education. He now viewed himself as "an educated person, but I had educated myself into a member of the British middle class with literary gifts and I had done it in defiance of authority."[9] Within a few years, he returned to QRC as one of its first non-English teachers; by that time Eric Williams, a senior student at QRC, had begun his preparation for the island scholarship examination.

At QRC, Williams befriended James. Some claim that he was a student of James,[10] while others hold that James simply served as a tutor preparing Williams for the national examinations.[11] In late 1931, Williams was briefly on the staff of QRC and presumably continued his interaction with James. James recalled a chance meeting on the street near QRC shortly before he left Trinidad in early 1932; he remembered congratulating Williams on his scholarship, and expressed his pleasure at Williams's decision not to pursue law or medicine, the traditional areas of study.[12]

Some years before his trip to England, James had befriended Learie Constantine, who would emerge as one of the most famous cricketers in the pre-war Caribbean. By 1929, Constantine was spending much of the year playing cricket professionally in England. But on each of his return trips to Trinidad, according to James, "we continued our discussions and arguments about cricket as energetically as before." In 1931, Constantine professed an interest in writing a book about his experiences. James planned to travel to England "as soon as I could to write books." Constantine therefore offered to sponsor James's trip: the expectation was that he would assist Constantine in the preparation of his book. Commenting on this emerging relationship, James noted, "We didn't know it but we were making history. This transcendence of our relations as cricketers was to initiate the West Indian renaissance not only in cricket, but in politics, in history and in writing."[13]

James's primary interests were cricket and writing, but gradually he began to develop political convictions. His long discussions with Constantine contributed to this.

> Constantine had always been more political, far more than I had ever been. My sentiments were in the right place, but I was still enclosed within the mould of nineteenth-century intellectualism. Unbeknown to me, however, the shell had been cracked.[14]

Credit for cracking the shell had to go to Constantine, but also to the mass labour movement that was being built by Captain A. A. Cipriani in the late 1920s.

This growing political consciousness led James to begin a systematic study of the political history of the British Caribbean islands, especially Trinidad. He read all the available government documents and began collecting his notes. Eventually, he admitted, "my hitherto vague ideas of freedom crystallized around a political conviction: we should be free to govern ourselves."[15] It was at this point that James began to appreciate the latent power of the ordinary people. The culmination of this process was his decision to write a biography of Cipriani, who readily agreed to assist in the project. Thus, as James boarded the boat in Trinidad in March 1932, he already had a rapidly developing political philosophy.

He also carried two manuscripts in preparation: one on Constantine, the other on Cipriani.

By this time, Eric Williams, now 21 years old, had won his island scholarship, had taught briefly at QRC, and was teaching temporarily at the Government Teachers College while preparing for his departure to Oxford within a few months. He was apparently unaffected by the widespread political agitation for reform in Trinidad led by Cipriani; his focus had been on preparation for the scholarship examination. At this point, Williams had an undeveloped political consciousness which would grow slowly in England, through his interaction with James and later George Padmore, lectures at the West Indian African Students Union (WASU), and through his own studies.

The political climate in England also contributed. As James himself observed, "at no time since Chartism in 1848 was Britain in such political and intellectual turmoil as in 1933–1938"[16], years during which Williams was at Oxford. For James, the Great Depression, the success of the first Russian Five Year Plan, the rise of Nazism, the threat of Hitler, the spread of Marxism and the anti-imperialist struggle all contributed "to making England a seething cauldron of political and social ideas."[17] All this impacted on the intellectual environment of Oxford.

But the impact on Williams himself was less clear. As previously observed, Williams was a totally focused individual. He had arrived at Oxford determined to be the best. His study habits reflected this desire. He worked through the university vacations, "reading steadily in my rooms and in the college and university libraries."[18]

To emphasize the fact that he had no political connections at Oxford, he later stated that the only exception was "regular meetings of the Indian nationalist students in their club, the Majliss."[19] James himself later confirmed this point about Williams's non-connectedness, saying that he "never joined anything."[20]

In London, however, Williams did attend informal lectures at WASU with Dolly and McShine, and also spent time with James, who recalled:

> Williams used to come to my house in London and spend his vacations with me. Frequently, I used to go up to Oxford and spend some time with him. When working on *The Black Jacobins*, I went to France to do some work there ... Williams would go

with me. I knew him very well and he knew me very well . . . He used to send me his papers from Oxford on Rousseau, on Plato and on Aristotle for my comments.[21]

James also wrote that Williams's holidays "were spent in London, and in our various ways George Padmore, myself and Arthur Lewis were part of this tremendous intellectual and political training."[22]

If at Oxford Williams focused primarily on his studies, staying away from the political activity that marks the life of many university students, his interaction with his West Indian friends in London, and particularly with radical Caribbean activists like James and Padmore, certainly helped to shape his political consciousness. After Williams had completed his undergraduate degree and enrolled for his doctorate, James began to play an even more important role in influencing and shaping his political ideology.

James's own political consciousness had undergone radical transformation during the first half of the 1930s. Having gone to England "to write books", he soon obtained employment with the *Manchester Guardian*, reporting on cricket. He lived at Learie Constantine's home, working on his two manuscripts: cricket and self-government together dominated his mind. The idea that "we should be free to govern ourselves" found a prominent place in his book on Cipriani, and was later reproduced as *The Case for West Indian Self Government*. The role of the ordinary people in obtaining their liberation would be a central theme in his future writing.

As James's political transformation continued, he admitted that "literature was vanishing from my consciousness and politics was substituting itself."[23] Eventually, "fiction-writing drained out of me and was replaced by politics."[24]

By the mid 1930s, James had begun preparatory work on *The Black Jacobins*, his account of Toussaint L'Ouverture and the Haitian revolution. This involved, among other things, reading French historiography. One writer concluded that this reading

> played an important part in helping to create very definite radical political responses on James' part . . . It was instrumental in helping him to make the transition from literature to a political consciousness, and from a West Indian to a world consciousness.[25]

James's intellectual work was complemented by his efforts to find like-minded people in London. In 1935, he organized the International African Friends of Ethiopia, directed at educating the British about imperialism in Africa. He was joined by George Padmore, recently arrived from the United States. Thus between 1936 and 1938 James found himself "ideologically as well as organizationally, and was embarked upon the political course which would see him become a full-time professional Marxist theoretician."[26]

It was during this period that Williams began research for his doctorate. After spending a year in the unsuccessful pursuit of a second undergraduate degree, in late 1936 he switched programmes and began working towards his Ph.D. He chose as his theme "the very beginning of modern society in the West Indies, the abolition of the British West Indian slave system."[27] His primary thesis was that slavery was not abolished for humanitarian reasons but for very practical economic motives, arising from the diminishing importance of slavery.

What was the stimulus for this research topic? James recalled that Williams had come to him with the question: "I am to do a doctorate, what shall I write on?" James responded:

> I know exactly what you should write on. I have done the economic basis of slavery emancipation as it was in France. But that has never been done in Great Britain, and Britain is wide open for it. A lot of people think the British showed goodwill. There were lots of people who had goodwill, but it was the basis, the economic basis, that allowed the goodwill to function.[28]

According to James, not only did he suggest this subject for Williams's thesis, but "I sat down and wrote what the thesis should be with my own hand, and I gave it to him." He believed that Williams submitted this to his thesis committee at Oxford, who approved it as the subject for his research.[29]

James clearly provided guidance as Williams worked on his thesis. He had already travelled to France to conduct research for his proposed Black Jacobins, taking Williams with him.[30] He claimed: "I saw the manuscript quite often, I read it about three or four times."[31]

Around the time that Williams completed his research, in October 1938, James left for a lecture tour in the United States. Ten months later, Williams himself arrived in Washington to begin teaching at Howard University. The interaction between Williams and James intensified in Washington, and continued, by correspondence, after

Williams resigned his position at Howard in mid-1948. A major factor underpinning the relationship was that Williams had successfully completed a brilliant doctoral thesis, but remained essentially a student, in that his thesis research had exposed him to a whole new world — western imperialism. James, already a student of the subject, from a Marxist perspective, served as his teacher .

James was also able to assist in other ways. Williams arrived in Washington just two months before university classes were to begin, and immediately recognized that the reading material for his new Social Science class was inadequate. In typical manner, he set about creating his own. He called on James for assistance, recognizing the breadth of James's reading and the thoroughness of his studies. James later recalled that Williams "for his classes at Howard . . . embarked upon a project into which he roped me and to this day, I wonder at it." James recalled helping to compile the three-volume collection of extracts from world literature, including the stencilling and mimeographing of the materials.[32]

It would appear, then, that James and Williams were close friends during the latter's time in Washington. This was not surprising: one of Williams's most recognizable traits, especially during the years he considered himself to be a "learner", was the formation of close relationships with older and more established thinkers: W. D. Inniss at QRC, R. Trevor Davies and D. W. Brogan at Oxford, Alain Locke at Howard. Outside the academic world, James served as tutor, adviser and friend.

Yet one also has to look to James for his version of the relationship, for Williams provided very few insights. From 1939, the year after his arrival in the United States, until 1948, James maintained a steady correspondence with Constance Webb, his American student and lover. The publication of this correspondence provides indirect insights into the relationship with Williams, who is repeatedly referred to in the letters. James wrote to Webb in April 1939, for instance: "There is my old pupil, Dr Eric Williams, whom I taught when he was a boy and whom I have seen grow up and now is Ph.D. Oxford, my devoted admirer and a most brilliant young man."[33] By late 1939, James was in Washington, probably assisting Williams in preparation of the three-volume collection of readings — all his mail is addressed in care of Williams at Howard University.

James looked on Williams as one of the star students, especially during the period when *Capitalism and Slavery* was in preparation. He wrote:

> You know I have three special "pupils." There is Bill Williams. He is a Ph.D. from Oxford. He has already written and published some brilliant work and this fall will appear a superb book on Capitalism and Slavery . . . When you see Bill's book you will understand the quality of the work that is being done.[34]

Concerning Williams's text and his involvement in it, James wrote to Webb: "By the late fall, my friend Bill Williams's book will be out — I have read the page proofs — a masterpiece."[35] Later, James also read and commented on Williams's manuscript on education.

In general, Williams did not give credit to James for providing the subject of his thesis, or for his guidance during the research. Nor did he acknowledge James's assistance in the preparation of *Capitalism and Slavery*, though in the bibliography he did cite *The Black Jacobins* as a source.[36] Williams accepted the argument provided by James — that economic rather than humanitarian concerns lay behind the abolition of slavery, arising from the growing dominance of industrial over commercial capital — and ran with it. By doing so, he became the "first scholar to make the anti-humanitarian case in a detailed fashion and to make the case the central theme of a work written in English."[37]

When James read the page proofs of *Capitalism and Slavery* he realized that Williams had not analyzed the role that the slaves themselves had played in gaining their emancipation. In his own biography of Toussaint L'Ouverture, the slave who had led the revolution in Haiti, James had discussed this subject extensively: by this time his own theoretical development emphasized the contribution of the masses. But Williams's text had already been sent to the publishers. On June 3, 1944, Williams sent a letter to Mary Little John, his editor, suggesting that he should add a chapter to his manuscript.

> On reading over the proofs with a friend, he realizes that the section on the revolt of the slaves themselves, as a reflection of the growing economic dislocation, should be substantiated. . . . I have already begun the chapter, which is two-thirds written in draft. You can depend on it that you will have it as soon as possible. Under the circumstances, will you ask the printer not to go beyond Chapter 11 in the page proofs at this stage.[38]

Within a few days the editor responded, "We will be glad to have you add the extra chapter to your book."[39] Two weeks later, Williams completed "The Slaves and Slavery," chapter 12 of his text, which he promptly sent to his publisher. James's unacknowledged contribution to *Capitalism and Slavery* remained significant.

The close interaction between the two men continued after the publication of Williams's book. In the summer of 1945, presumably in New York, James reported to Webb that "Bill came from Washington to see me. We talked. He progresses mightily. What a good pupil to have."[40]

On another occasion, he told Webb: "I shall write Bill soon . . . I am expecting some money from him."[41] Clearly, the relationship between James and Williams was not purely intellectual. This is borne out by another letter written in August 1948 after Williams had returned to Trinidad to begin his job with the Caribbean Commission. James was in Reno, Nevada. He instructed Webb to write to Williams in Trinidad and ask him "to get my brother or one of them to get the exact dates of my marriage and cable it to you."[42] James was seeking a Reno divorce and thought that Williams could provide him with the data he needed for filing the papers. Two years later, Williams and Soy Moyou also travelled to Reno, where Williams sought a divorce from his first wife Elsie, in order to marry Soy.

James remained in the United States for another five years after Williams returned to Trinidad. But they were difficult years for him. In the early 1950s, the intensification of the Cold War gave rise to McCarthyism and a witch-hunt against apparent communists, especially within the US government. In this climate of hysteria, James was detained in 1952 for a few months, and deported to England the following year.

In Trinidad, Williams's fight with the Caribbean Commission was approaching its apex. In 1955 the Commission refused to renew his contract, and immediately Williams "let his bucket down" among the people of Trinidad and Tobago. But as the organization of the People's National Movement (PNM) progressed, Williams left in October to serve as an adviser to the International Confederation of Trade Unions on a two-month contract, then spent two weeks in England in December, consulting with James and Padmore on the programme and constitution of the PNM — returning to his political roots, as it were, before launching the new party.

James recalled that Williams came to London, sometime "before September 1956", to talk to him about the formation of the PNM. This may have been during Williams's December 1955 visit or sometime before the Trinidad and Tobago general elections of September 24, 1956. James emphasized to Williams the importance of a party newspaper, which he saw "not only as a political necessity but a commercial possibility." He arranged for Williams to meet with British journalist Basil Davidson, who offered advice on the establishment and funding of such a paper.[43]

Two years later, when James returned to Trinidad in April 1958, Williams offered him the position of editor of the PNM's paper. It was his first visit since leaving in 1932. He had been invited back as a guest of the Trinidad government at the inauguration of the West Indies federal government. But the invitation was by no means unanimous. Gerard Montano, a member of Williams's Cabinet, argued furiously against it, on the grounds that James was a communist.[44] This was a portent of James's relationship with much of the old guard of the party. Both Patrick Solomon and Arthur Robinson expressed early reservations about James's involvement with Williams, and later with the PNM.[45]

Shortly after his arrival, at Williams's suggestion, James began work on a report which would evaluate the state of the party and make recommendations for strengthening it. A devout believer in the role of the masses, he was well aware of the massive following that had emerged around the PNM in 1956. He noted that the

> political temper of the West Indian masses is at an extremely high pitch. The masses . . . are aware of a profound change in their society and are looking for new foundations. This is the key to the whole situation . . . The West Indian masses are on a broad road, and travelling fast. Everything pushes them forward . . .This is a theoretical point to be systematically and carefully developed . . . All party leaders should be kept aware of it.[46]

For James, the party was an instrument to harness the masses. This pointed to a key difference in the ways that James and Williams interpreted the forces shaping the history of the region, and provided one of the grounds for the later dispute between the two men.

Williams, with his own historical perspective and different personality, firmly believed that it was the powerful, especially the economically influential, who shaped societies. On a personal level, he also believed that because he was the educated one and acknowledged leader, the authority and power was his, to determine the direction of Trinidadian society.

James was the quintessential outsider. He was less concerned with the "is" than with the "ought". He had examined the Haitian slave revolution in detail, and appreciated the power of the masses. Like the Haitian slaves, he visualized an uprising of the Caribbean masses, which he believed had already begun to materialize in Trinidad, with the PNM. What the masses needed was organization and direction. He believed that if the PNM could achieve this in Trinidad, the process could engulf the entire region. While Williams believed that power emanated from the top, James was convinced that it arose from below. Williams was a pragmatic politician: James was guided by romantic notions.

For a brief period, Williams appeared to succumb to James's magnetism. Mahabir, recalling his first meeting with James at the home of an influential party member, observed a group gathered around an individual whom he did not recognize. "I asked my wife if she recognized him. She said she did not know his name . . . But whoever he was, that was the man whom Williams was imitating. That man was C. L. R. James . . . His manner of speech, his ideas, his mannerisms — they were all Williams magnified."[47]

Two months after his arrival in Trinidad, James addressed the Central Committee of the PNM, using his report on the re-organization of the party — which he had earlier presented to Williams — as the basis for discussion. Williams took notes furiously, as was his custom — James later remarked, "Bill should be a permanent secretary, he takes so much notes!"[48] Williams used the Report and his notes as the basis for his address to the Third Convention of the PNM in October 1958. As James noted, "almost word for word it formed the body of Dr Williams's address."[49] It was later published as one of the party's major documents, *Perspectives for our Party*.

In this address, Williams lamented the "subordination" of the party since its formation. Determined to correct this, he announced that "the Party, left to fend for itself . . . becomes automatically and necessarily the number one priority from October 1958." He continued: "We have to build our Party organization from the bottom up. We have to reorganize our system of education so that, through the Party, it penetrates into the deepest masses of the people. We have to reorganize our press on the same scale."[50] This was clearly the political thought of James, who by this time had rejected Trotskyism and the notion of the vanguard party in favour of harnessing the power of the masses.

Williams thus put fear into the minds of the old guard of the PNM. Some by this time were clearly worried about his closeness to James, which affected their previous cozy relationship with him. Elton Richardson, one of the first five members of the party, criticised some of Williams's ideas at the Convention. But, astute politician that he was, Williams used his Convention address to go over the heads of his advisers and appeal directly to his audience. He and James had already decided that James should be the editor of the reorganized party paper.[51] After reviewing the qualifications of an editor, Williams told the assembled crowd: "We have in the country today such a man, C. L. R. James." James was thus made editor of the *PNM Weekly*, and promptly changed its name to *The Nation*.

In his report to Williams in June 1958, James had noted the deplorable state of party finances, and suggested to Williams that the party "raise a fund of $100,000 for its own press, headquarters etc."[52] In his proposal for the party's development programme, Williams announced an "arbitrary figure . . . to cost $100,000 a year [for] . . . the acquisition of land for the Party Headquarters and the purchase of a linotype machine."[53]

But while Williams was quite willing to make use of James's ideas, it was not long before he became suspicious of James himself.

Recognizing that James was a very competent organizer, Williams selected a group of key party workers to attend a class at James's home to study party organization. Among these were Nicholas Simonette, then the PNM's acting secretary, Ivan Williams, an important informal adviser, Isabel Teshea, a leader of the women's wing, and Carlton Gomes, then a teacher and party organizer in the south. This group met three times a week for several months, and its members, especially Simonette, drew close to James. Since he was from south Trinidad, Simonette asked James to conduct seminars there. Eventually, Williams learned of a group meeting with James in the south and felt very threatened.[54]

Williams faced two problems. Firstly, some senior party members had been upset over James's involvement in building the party. They felt further threatened by the relationship which James, an acknowledged Marxist, had with Williams. Essentially conservative, they had serious ideological problems with James, whose closeness to Williams meant that they were frozen out of their privileged positions. Secondly, Williams was by nature a suspicious individual; he perceived threats everywhere, and was always determined that no one would threaten his leadership. He began to view James as a threat. Encouraged by James's enemies within the party, Williams took action against James and his friends from the south. He brought charges in the party against a group he termed the "Southern Regional Committee", whose activities, he claimed, were unconstitutional and subversive. These charges were eventually dismissed.

For two or three years, while James was working closely with Williams, he was very influential in shaping party and government policy. One area of great importance was the dispute over the Chaguaramas military base, west of Port of Spain.

The Chaguaramas issue arose after the Standing Federation Committee, in 1957, chose Trinidad as the site of the federal capital. After a few months, a local site committee selected the north-west peninsula, which included the US base at Chaguaramas, as their first choice. Williams was initially embarrassed by this decision, for even though the PNM was a nationalist party, it had committed itself to honouring all international obligations, which would have included the agreement establishing the US bases in Chaguaramas.

The federal government decided to press its case in London. Williams refused to participate as a member of the delegation, choosing instead to attend as an observer. But he altered his neutralist position considerably. He had begun to study the history of the bases agreement, and realized that it had been completed, some 20 years earlier, over the strenuous objections of the Trinidad Governor and the Legislative Council. His argument now was that the agreement was morally invalid. Was this a "historian's retroactive nationalistic logic", as one writer has stated, or is there another possible explanation for his abrupt reversal of position?

James was still in London when the Chaguaramas dispute began.

It is known that Williams would consult with him on a variety of issues whenever they met. While no meeting between James and Williams has been recorded at this time, it is entirely possible that Williams's change of position on the US bases in Trinidad was instigated by James. When James returned to Trinidad the following year, Williams's position hardened even further.

The struggle between Trinidad and the United States over the future of the Chaguaramas base continued for almost three years. In late 1958, James, newly appointed editor of *The Nation*, began to use the pages of the party paper to attack the United States. This continued through 1959 as his relationship with Williams deepened. Trinidad's demand, as reported in the pages of *The Nation*, was that the US must give up Chaguaramas, failing which, life would be made difficult for the occupants.

The impasse reached a climax on April 22, 1960, when the PNM staged a mass rally in Woodford Square, including among its speakers two known Marxists, Lennox Pierre of Trinidad and Janet Jagan of Guyana. This was followed by the famous march on Chaguaramas, in heavy rain, where Trinidad's demands were read to US officials. This "March in the Rain" is generally recognized as the militant high point of Trinidad nationalism.

Five weeks later, Williams abruptly turned to the right, and away from James. In a speech in San Fernando on May 30, 1960, titled "Perspectives for the West Indies", he declared:

> The world is divided into two camps; the hot war will follow the the cold. Where do we, a new nation of three million people, stand? If the Iron Curtain is the great divide separating the two camps, then it is axiomatic that we are West of the Curtain and not a part of it.[55]

This speech marked Williams's public break with James. It has been suggested that the split materialized after the United States "recognized Trinidad's right" to negotiate the issue of the Chaguaramas base.[56] But while this "West of the Curtain" statement would certainly have affected Williams's relationship with James, a convergence of factors precipitated the break. The US had let it be known that it would not work with Williams if James remained his adviser. Further, for two years Williams had seen his relationship with his close advisers deteriorate as a direct consequence of his closeness to James. By this time, too, James's doctrinaire position was beginning to conflict with Williams's more pragmatic ideas. Finally, Williams had never had a problem severing a relationship if doing so protected his own interests.

James had been threatening to resign from the party's newspaper for several months. He had sent a letter to Williams on the subject on March 26, 1960.[57] He repeated his wish to resign on March 30 and on June 27.[58] His final letter was written on July 14, when he told Williams: "You have had my resignation now a long time, Bill . . . now it is final."[59] Soon after that, James telephoned Williams, proposing a discussion. Williams responded abruptly: "There is nothing to discuss!"[60]

In 1962, before Trinidad celebrated its independence, James returned to England to continue his newspaper writing. In 1965, he visited Trinidad to cover a cricket Test series for the British press, and again became embroiled in domestic politics, identifying himself with the left and with radical trade unions. He was placed under house arrest by the Williams government and his telephone was tapped. He assisted in the formation of the Workers and Farmers Party (WFP) that contested the 1966 general elections. The WFP candidates received minimal support from the electorate, and forfeited their deposits.

At this point, James's involvement in local politics ended. His relationship with Williams had effectively ended six years earlier.

the elusive eric williams

Eric Wiliams in happier times with Winston Mahabir (left), Gerard Montano (right, behind Williams) and John O'Halloran (in background, centre). O'Halloran was to remain in favour, but Mahabir and Montano became politically exiled

POLITICAL EXILE—
THE ULTIMATE WEAPON

One persistent and disturbing characteristic of Williams's 25-year leadership of Trinidad and Tobago is what Winston Mahabir — originally one of his closest friends — chose to call the "erection-to-crucifixion" phenomenon.

Mahabir noted what most had recognized and many had actually experienced: the long "list of those whom Williams . . . lifted to high places and then destroyed."[1] For with very few exceptions, the many supporters Williams elevated from obscurity to national leadership were discarded. This led Mahabir to pose the rhetorical question: "Does Williams care at all about people apart from their value as manipulable political objects?"[2] Another early supporter, Patrick Solomon, who at one point emerged as deputy leader of the PNM but eventually suffered the fate of so many others, was even harsher about this aspect of Williams's behaviour. He said:

> No one or nothing was left untouched if he or it could serve Eric Williams's purpose. As the years rolled by, person after person was used and discarded — sometimes even destroyed, if he could not be got rid of in any other way — in Eric Williams's triumphant march to the top of the political ladder.[3]

There were several dimensions to the erection-to-crucifixion phenomenon. Some individuals were cast aside for a relatively short period, then reinstated for one reason or another. This was seen as being in Williams's "doghouse" for a while. A larger group was placed in "cold storage" for a longer period, sometimes for years, though in many cases the individuals continued to function within the party or the government; it was simply that their existence was not acknowledged by the leader. If Williams needed to communicate with them, he did so through unsigned and undated notes, or through intermediaries. In general, he made use of intermediaries to perform functions he considered distasteful.

Members of a third group were forced to resign or were simply exiled from the government. This group of the crucified had no opportunity for resurrection. Many were provided with no reasons for their dismissal. There was also a category of rare individuals like Kamaluddin Mohammed and Johnny O'Halloran. The former simply refused to acknowledge being put in the doghouse, while the latter, in spite of relentless and persistent attacks from the media and party members, lived a charmed life as far as Williams was concerned.

If there was one common thread that linked these different experiences, it was the crucial role of gossip and "news-carrying" during Williams's leadership. There were two primary reasons for this. Both activities had always been endemic to the culture. More importantly, they flourished because everyone around Williams knew that he permitted them. Many in the party were aware of Williams's penchant for gossip, and exploited it for their individual benefit. Solomon observed that Williams "was an easy prey to any schemer who chose to fill his ears with poison."[4] This gave rise to another reason for "news-carrying": it could destroy the status of an enemy, while enhancing the position of the news-carrier vis-à-vis the leader.

Williams's daughter Erica observed that her father had a "propensity for putting people in cold storage, for infractions both real and imagined." She attributed this to "news-carriers [who] would not hesitate to supply him under the guise of 'intelligence'. This was sometimes at best self-serving on their own part, and, at worst, amounted to what I am convinced was often a deliberate attempt at misinformation."[5] Sometimes the bearer of news misjudged the demeanour of the leader, or his relationship with the subject of the story. In such cases, it was entirely possible that both the news-carrier and his subject would find themselves in Williams's doghouse.

Why did Williams encourage a climate of news-carrying, a whispering campaign, to encircle him? The answer lies partly in the personality and partly in the lifestyle of the leader.

Williams was by nature a very suspicious individual. And, as most were aware, he needed to control his environment. His suspicious nature, which in later years manifested itself in paranoiac tendencies,[6] was part of his complexity. While many claimed that Williams trusted no one, others, including his daughter Erica, believed that he possessed a "blind and trusting faith, yes . . . sometimes in the wrong people."[7] Supporting this latter view, one of his primary assistants in later years said, "He kept the confidences of his colleagues so much so that for many he was the father confessor. This loyalty, even though a virtue in itself, was an attribute of his character, which could be exploited cynically, and perhaps it was often abused."[8]

So, over the years, while a few earned the trust and consequently the loyalty of Williams, he nevertheless remained distrustful of the majority with whom he was involved. Carlton Gomes, a frequent visitor to Williams's home, and for a time a personal aide until he too was placed in cold storage, recalled the point at which he learned he had earned Williams's trust. One evening, he was taken aback when the Prime Minister turned to him saying, "Carlton, it is your turn to mix the drinks today." Only very few ever earned the honour of mixing the drinks at the Prime Minister's home; as Williams told Gomes: "You cannot have anybody monkeying around with your drinks."[9]

Winston Mahabir catalogued in careful detail Williams's suspicious nature.[10] He subtitled part of his political memoir "The Worst of Williams", and cited examples such as the misperceived threats to his leadership from Patrick Solomon, Williams's fear of food poisoning, the idea of a Chinese conspiracy, and radiation from Chaguaramas. The evidence led Mahabir to conclude that Williams suffered from "gross emotional instability."[11] This meant he was perpetually concerned that others in the party were seeking to usurp his position. Thus he was quite open to members who he believed could provide him with information that would keep him one step ahead of the others.

The information that Williams received helped him to remain in control of any situation, since he knew in advance what others were planning. Max Awon, a Cabinet member, recalled his decision not to stand for re-election because of what he perceived as Williams's interference in the affairs of his ministry. He made this decision privately, yet "it became known to Williams because everything you said or whispered or thought . . . he got to know eventually."[12] Ferdie Ferreira recalled how Williams used his information system to disarm potential opposition within the party. Ferreira and others had decided to confront Williams on a particular issue one Sunday morning at a General Council meeting. Before the meeting began, Ferreira saw Williams in deep conversation with the individual who was expected to lead the confrontation. Williams had used his information system to learn of the proposed attack, and had already defused the issue, which was not even raised during the meeting. Ferreira and others were left to marvel at Williams's political skills.[13]

By permitting people to bring him information, Williams kept potential opposition within the party in a state of perpetual disarray. Ferreira concluded that while Williams "tolerated opposition in the country, he did not permit it in the party." Yet, interestingly, Ferreira was still willing to rationalize this aspect of Williams's behaviour because "he worked very hard. He generated the ideas, plans and wrote the proposals."[14]

Some have argued that Williams "always gave a good ear to people"[15] because he lived alone and was not in touch with the "news on the street". One must give some credence to this argument. Williams did live alone. He had no one to talk to at home in the evenings. If he invited someone over for a drink, conversation could easily produce some interesting news, especially if the guest was familiar with a particular area or activity.

Eventually, Williams's regular visitors became conduits of information from others. In a small society like Trinidad, anyone with an interest in getting the ear of the Prime Minister knew which individuals to approach. One frequent visitor to the Prime Minister's home recalled being asked to plead the case of someone who had been placed in cold storage. Williams listened intently without interruption or comment, then patted the visitor on the back as he walked him to the door at the end of the evening with the comment, "Don't worry about it, it is all in a day's work!"[16]

Living alone limited Williams's contacts with the broader society; and as the responsibilities of his position increased, his professional circle was restricted to close advisers and selected Cabinet members. After the 1970 upheaval, he spent more time working out of his home, going to his office not more than once or twice a week. After the 1976 elections, his lifestyle became even more reclusive. He left his home only to attend Cabinet meetings on Thursdays and parliament on Fridays. Cumulatively, this meant that his contacts with the wider community became severely limited. The private information system that he maintained became his primary means of communication. The results were largely negative, since he had few ways of checking the information provided and no one with whom he could weigh and evaluate reports — though he occasionally relied on John O'Halloran to verify information received.

Increasingly, news-carrying sources determined the kinds of information Williams received. Their own biases, prejudices and private agendas came into play. A PNM member of parliament at that time asserted:

> In my humble opinion the men around him were giving him a shaft coming and going, and the guy [Williams], I don't know if he became confused. He accepted what these fellas told him and then suddenly you are confronted with the bare facts because you hear it from the outside.[17]

Disgusted with the behaviour of his fellow PNM parliamentarians, this MP continued: "Them fellas cornered the fella [Williams], had him in a circle that he couldn't hear what was going on, feeding the man exactly what they wanted him to know."[18]

According to Patrick Solomon, Williams's

> abiding fault is his total lack of comprehension of the human animal. To him all human beings are the same; they either want to buy or have something to sell; and he has a single formula for dealing with them all — if the price is right, he will do business. He cannot imagine anyone performing a disinterested act of kindness, there must be an ulterior motive . . . he grew increasingly suspicious of anyone . . . being convinced that they merely sought an opportunity to destroy or replace him.[19]

Solomon harboured much bitterness toward Williams, the result of Williams's harsh treatment of him, and his analysis must be viewed in that light. But others who worked closely with Williams provided similar evaluations.

Nicholas Simonette, the PNM General Secretary for many years, observed that Williams had a limited understanding of the "nature and dynamic of human relationships."[20] Williams was never really aware how his relationship with one person would affect his relationships with others. For instance, he never seemed to understand why his relationship with C. L. R. James should have caused such consternation among other members of his inner circle, even though the ideology espoused by James was not accepted by the party. But Williams could publicly exploit such relationships to signal to party members who was currently in favour, and who was not. In public, he would signal his feelings by approaching individuals and greeting them warmly. His entourage would follow suit. If he avoided an individual, they were required to do the same. At public gatherings, he frequently kept party "props" around him — one or two individuals who were required to stay near him purely for the purpose of keeping others away, by pretending to be in deep conversation with him.

While Williams could be at ease in a crowd, he was widely considered to be "naïve in human relationships" on a one-to-one basis.[21] This naiveté extended to the few with whom he was especially close. One of these individuals observed: "His weakness was, if he liked you, he listened to what you had to say and believed it."[22] Inevitably, he was told half-truths, and acted on them because he trusted the bearer of the information. Thus people were relegated to the famous doghouse purely on the basis of rumour. Some careers might have been destroyed in this way. This bears out Erica's observation that her father possessed "a blind and trusting faith . . . sometimes in the wrong people."[23]

Because of this naiveté, Williams hardly thought it necessary to check the information he received. An aide observed: "He could not believe that anybody could openly and boldfacedly come and lie to him."[24] Many around him recognized this weakness, and exploited it for their personal benefit.

Williams sometimes recognized that he had acted too harshly or even incorrectly with regard to a particular individual. But he found it exceedingly difficult to express regret or admit he had made a mistake. An aide noted: "I never heard him say that he was sorry."[25] He found it equally difficult to confront an individual concerning something he may have heard. But he did sometimes manage it. Ibbit Mosaheb recalled that on one occasion Williams approached him with information he had received about a private meeting held at Mosaheb's home: he assumed that this was an attempt to form an opposition group. Mosaheb explained to Williams that his information was incorrect. Williams apparently accepted this explanation, since Mosaheb was an old and trusted friend.[26]

Only time could reverse the problem of cold storage. Occasionally the individual might receive a telephone call from Williams. One astute observer noted: "If he served you coconut ice-cream or sorrel at his home, you were assured that you were back in his favor."[27] He apparently did not share these items with many of his guests.

Williams's refusal to admit mistakes, his intense loyalty to a few and his weakness as a judge of human character all helped to explain his strange, fascinating and long-lived relationship with John O'Halloran.

A very early member of the PNM, O'Halloran was the only person constantly close to Williams from 1956 until his death in 1981. O'Halloran himself died in Canada in 1985. Kamaluddin Mohammed was the only other survivor over this lengthy period, but he did not enjoy as close a relationship with Williams as O'Halloran did. As a personal adviser for over 25 years, and the only light-skinned individual close to Williams in an overwhelmingly black party, O'Halloran faced a constant barrage of criticism, in public and in private. He would have been the subject of constant news-carrying by others hoping to supplant him. Williams would have faced constant demands to rid himself of O'Halloran, who was tainted by a steady stream of allegations of corruption, bribery and disrespect for the law, resulting in a poor public image. But through it all, O'Halloran maintained his envied status as personal aide, adviser and close friend. An understanding of this relationship requires, again, an understanding of Williams's personal characteristics and weaknesses.

Williams's "blind and trusting faith" in a chosen few inevitably led to problems.[28] A close friend observed that "if he liked you, he listened to what you say, and believed it."[29] Another noted that "Eric believed people to his detriment."[30] Simply put, Williams trusted

O'Halloran and did not believe the stories he heard over the years. And even if he did, another weakness was his inability to admit that he was wrong.

Williams's trust in O'Halloran developed gradually. O'Halloran was a major news-carrier about others in and out of the party. Williams made use of him, and probably no one else, to check stories others had told him. Another aide remembered that Williams frequently remarked: "I will have Johnny check this out."[31] So if O'Halloran was a close confidant, trusted to bring in news and trusted to check out news from others, it stands to reason that Williams would not have believed what others said about him. O'Halloran's apparent straightforwardness in his dealings with Williams further reduced reason for doubt.

O'Halloran was useful to Williams in many ways. Because of his ethnicity and his connections with the business community, both local and foreign, he was probably the PNM's primary fund-raiser. The class composition of the PNM required that party finances should be raised from varied sources, and O'Halloran was extremely important in sourcing finance for elections and party activities. He was apparently the party's primary connection with the petroleum companies operating in Trinidad, and with other US business interests in Trinidad. Since the burden of fund-raising for the PNM fell to Williams, O'Halloran could help to lighten the load, and Williams would have held him in high esteem.

Even in more informal matters, O'Halloran was important. His lifestyle, which included parties, gambling and attractive women, apparently intrigued Williams; it has been suggested that "Williams lived vicariously through O'Halloran."[32] While Williams lived a disciplined, structured and well-organized life, privately he may have admired O'Halloran's fun-loving lifestyle. O'Halloran tried to brighten Williams's dour pattern of life, and his efforts must have been appreciated.

With regard to the broader issue of cold storage, O'Halloran provides additional insights into Williams's *modus operandi*. If Williams trusted the bearer of information, not only did he find it difficult to think ill of him, but he was quite willing to use the information without verifying its accuracy. Thus many found their way into the doghouse, or longer periods in cold storage, without having the opportunity to defend themselves. Very few dared to confront Williams on such a matter. In that context, the strategy of Kamaluddin Mohammed is interesting. He simply refused to stay in the doghouse, and demanded that Williams speak to him. In the case of Simonette, his position as party secretary required him to be in constant contact with the leader, and he continued this contact even though Williams was cold with him.

In fact, the doghouse phenomenon may have had as much to do with the victims as it did with Williams.[33] According to Simonette, Williams would normally have preferred to clear the air with an individual over a particular problem, but few were prepared to initiate discussion, even though it may well have earned Williams's respect. Because he ruled the party with an iron fist, very few dared to question his actions. Even senior party members were paralyzed by fear. Recalling his own dismissal from office, Solomon noted that while the case against him was not "ironclad", and those sitting in judgement would have been aware of this, "perhaps the most shocking aspect of the whole situation [was] the grip of fear in which Williams held all those who came close to him."[34] No one spoke in defence of Solomon at a private hearing among party officials.

In the final analysis, therefore, because Williams permitted "news" to be brought to him, because he was a poor judge of human personality and because most were afraid of him, many important party members were placed in the doghouse, in cold storage, or even dismissed. Others, disgusted by the climate of conspiracy he created, simply left his group. Careers and people were destroyed, but Williams maintained control of the reins of power until his death.

the elusive eric williams

Eric Williams threw a party at his home in honour of Janelle "Penny" Commissiong
when she won the Miss Universe title in 1977. At left is Kim Sabeeny

AT HOME WITH
THE PRIME MINISTER

Many in Trinidad have tended to assume that Williams's public persona — gruff, dour, demanding, unapproachable — carried over into his private relationships and his life in general. Relatively few got to know this introverted individual intimately, but they describe him as a relaxed, warm, friendly, caring, generous individual and a gracious host. Among these favoured few were his informal advisers, children of close friends, and his nieces. For it was with young people, especially, that Williams displayed these private characteristics most freely.

It is not surprising that children held a special place in Williams's life. He had come from a family of twelve children. He adored his daughter Erica, and he developed a good relationship with his older daughter Pamela much later in life. At another level, much of Williams's political agenda concerned the future of Trinidad, and consequently its children. A few months after he considered resigning in 1973, oil prices skyrocketed, and he remarked to his daughter that he needed to stay on to secure the oil money for Trinidad's children. It was his firm conviction that the path to independence and development was through education, and he was determined that the country's children would not suffer the educational difficulties that his family had faced. The views and ideas of young people were important to him as he sought to develop his vision for the future of the society. Children met his emotional need for human contact and relationship, especially after his daughter Erica was sent to boarding school in England. These relationships were for him more genuine and sincere than those he maintained with older individuals, whose motives he tended to suspect.

Children from two families, the Dollys and the Bests, were particularly close to Williams. His friendship with Ray Dolly had lasted from elementary school through university in England; on his return to Trinidad in 1948, the Dollys, now living in Pointe-à-Pierre, were one of the few families he socialized with. Mrs Dolly had emerged as one of the founders of the League of Women Voters, so she and Williams had common interests, though she remained neutral with regard to local politics. The young daughters of the family, Joan and Hilary, soon began to look upon Williams as a much-favoured uncle.

Williams also befriended the Best family in the early 1950s in Point Fortin, where the father was an educator. Like many other educators, Wilfred Best was anxious for change in an oppressive, religion-dominated educational system, and began to regard Williams as a liberator. He helped to organize Williams's lectures in the area, and a warm friendship soon developed. Williams visited the Best home, where he met Lucille and Barbara, two young daughters of the family.

When the Best children began their high school education, they resided with Olive and Frankie Solomon in San Fernando. The Solomons were important members of the PNM and close friends of the Dupres family, who were among Williams's chief assistants in the early years of the party. When he lectured in San Fernando, Williams usually visited the Solomon home, maintaining his contact with Lucille and Barbara.

Both sets of young people, the Dollys and the Bests, fondly recall Williams's many visits. They were still in their pre-teen years, and he obviously had a powerful impact on them — many years later, they could still recall their meetings with him. This was not because he was a politician or national leader. Joan wistfully recalled: "I remember being always very excited when he was coming. There was always something very special about him. He would take us on his knee and talk to us, I do not remember about what, but he loved us. He loved us as children and I think we loved him."[1] Williams seemed to be part of her family:

> I knew him as an uncle. We spent a lot of time with him . . . when he came it was special. He took us for drives in his convertible, letting us do anything we wanted, playing with the buttons in the car . . . it was a lot of fun. This is how I remember him . . . as somebody who was warm and kind and very loving.[2]

Lucille also remembers Williams's visits, even as a child, and also being taken to his political meetings:

> I was very much in awe and admiration of Dr Williams . . . I developed a very keen interest in the man Eric Williams because he was a very fascinating person. He was very short but very dynamic. He did not play with little children but he always had some attention for you. He always showed some interest.[3]

When the daughters were teenagers, the Best family moved to Port of Spain, and the family interacted even more closely with Williams, who constantly sought ideas from young people. As one Best sister recalled, "He always wanted to know what young people thought about certain things."[4] He provided his unlisted telephone number so that the sisters could talk to him when particular issues arose. "We were I guess in a way privileged, even more so than our parents. We would get invited to his home for dinner, or to come over and have tea with him. He liked young people. He wanted the views of the young people."[5]

By this time, Williams's own daughter Erica, a few years younger than the Best sisters, had left Trinidad for school in England, so the visits of the Best sisters served to fill a void in his life. He saw in them, and in the Dolly sisters, what he projected for Trinidad's future. They were intelligent, upwardly mobile and professionally oriented. He nurtured this, as he did for children in the wider society.

After the Best sisters left Trinidad for university studies in England, Williams's concern for their welfare and academic progress continued. He contacted them during official visits, and occasionally invited them to dinner at his hotel. When the two sisters returned to Trinidad on vacation, the interaction continued, leading to a surprising incident. Williams often made fun of what he believed was their pampered lifestyle, including their inability to cook and generally to look after themselves. In response, the sisters dared him to have supper with them at their flat on his next visit to London. They did not believe that the leader of their country would really take time from his busy schedule to dine with them. To their amazement, a few months later, Williams sent word that he would be soon dining with them at their London flat. The sisters and their flatmate were in a state of panic. What would the menu be, were the utensils appropriate, what wine should be served? Williams had always chided them about their inability to cook rice, but fortunately, the flatmate was good at that task.

The British security services were equally amazed. Why should a Prime Minister visit a student's apartment? Would he be safe? They checked the neighbourhood thoroughly and closed off the street on the evening of Williams's visit. Williams himself was highly amused, complimenting the students on their preparations, and especially on their choice of wine. His ultimate compliment to them was: "I will now inform your mother that you are able to cook rice!"[6] This side of Williams's personality was known only to a few: a man who was warm and caring, capable of interacting with state leaders but quite comfortable with young people in a relaxed atmosphere.

After this incident, Williams asked the Best sisters to reach out and befriend Erica, who was also in England but somewhat lonely. Perhaps he felt guilty about his inability to be fully available to his daughter. The sisters responded, and interacted frequently with Erica, who spent some weekends with them. On one occasion they took Erica on the river in Cambridge in a rowboat; being unfamiliar with boats, they had much difficulty navigating, and feared that the Prime Minister's daughter might drown.[7] It is unlikely that Williams was ever informed of this incident.

Williams sometimes dined at the Bests' home. While the sisters were teenagers, and during their vacations in Trinidad, they had occasionally invited the Prime Minister to dinner with their parents at home. His stipulation was that only the family should be present. Pleasant and lengthy non-political discussion usually continued after dinner. One sister remarked that

> the side that my sister and I saw of Eric Williams was of a very eminent, scholarly gentleman who was deeply interested in young people. He always wanted to try to understand what made young people tick. He was interested from the educational

point of view, but also from the developmental perspective and what was the direction that young people of our country were going."[8]

The warm, friendly and loving side of the private Williams was also evident when he had supper at the Dollys' home. One daughter remembered:

> He was very easy to love and to have fun with. I looked forward to those special times when he came. Even when he became Chief Minister (and later Prime Minister) on an odd occasion we got a call from his office saying that he was dropping by for dinner at our home . . . From the time he walked through the doors all the trappings fell away. The person I saw out there in the public light was a completely different person from the moment he walked through our door.[9]

Williams was also generous, even a "soft touch". He easily succumbed to individuals who told him stories of hardship, especially if they lived in his constituency. One young lady wanted to attend classes at a commercial school but claimed she could not pay for the textbooks; Williams's assistants did not believe that her case was particularly strong — it was one of many requests for assistance — but Williams insisted on purchasing the books. The young woman dropped out of classes after two days![10] A junior minister once described Williams as "one of the most generous men I have met in my life", recalling the many times he gave money to people who brought him "sob stories".[11]

Williams was particularly touched by stories of hardship from young people, especially when they could not finance their education. This, of course, would have reminded him of his own childhood experiences and the extreme necessity of winning scholarships. He assisted a young lady and a young man who had performed extremely well in high school, but were unable to afford their medical studies.[12] He paid the high-school tuition fees for some children of families in his constituency.[13]

He was as caring with his friends as he was generous. An unofficial adviser and medical consultant developed a warm relationship with Williams over the years and eventually began to look upon him as a father figure. On one occasion this doctor became quite ill; Williams showed genuine concern for his well-being over a lengthy period, repeatedly calling to inquire about the state of his health.[14] Another family friend recalled that on the death of her father, a personal assistant and close friend of Williams, he wrote a detailed letter to her mother with an offer of very generous assistance.[15] Yet another friend, later a Cabinet member, reported that Williams provided financial support to his mother's family after the sudden death of his father, an old friend and a minister in the government.[16] Williams was generally known to be tough and even somewhat ruthless in his political relationships, but this was clearly counterbalanced in his personal relationships.

At home, Williams was a hospitable host. For much of his life as a political leader, he lived alone, first at his home on Mary Street and later at the official residence in St Ann's. Until 1962 his daughter Erica lived with him as a pre-teen, though she spent much time at the homes of various relatives in the city. After 1962 she was at school in England, and later in Geneva. She returned home each Christmas and during summer vacation, and lived in Trinidad from April to September 1970, during the "Black Power" uprising, and again from the end of 1970 until November 1973. But for the last eight years of his life, Williams was emotionally alone.

He was never entirely neglected, however. From 1961 to 1981, two nieces of his sister Flora Gittens, Peggy and Patsy, slept at his home each evening, so that he would not be alone. Since at first they were still attending school, and later on were employed, they usually arrived late in the evening and left early in the morning. Thus for days they would have no direct contact with their uncle. A system of cards ("Peggy is in", "Patsy is out") was organized to track movement in and out of the house, with the cards strategically placed. Occasionally, they would all meet in the kitchen late in the evening, either by arrangement or by accident. The sisters were sometimes apprehensive about these meetings, not because they did not want to meet their uncle, but because his discussions with them could last for hours, which affected their need to rise early in the morning.[17]

Williams clearly looked forward to these encounters, and the nieces suspected that his conversations with them broke the monotony of quiet evenings, especially during his last years. He told them lengthy stories about their family history, problems, etc.

In addition to the advisers who saw Williams individually at his home on a regular basis — including Ken Julien, Errol Mahabir, Francis Prevatt and John O'Halloran — two unstructured groups were regular visitors. The first were unofficial advisers and contacts from the wider community. This "bar" group — those who sat around his bar — included Ivan Williams, Ferdie Ferreira, Carlton Gomes, and others who joined the group less regularly. By the mid-1970s, most of this group had been placed in Williams's famous "cold storage" or dismissed. The second group, a number of couples from the Moyou family, met weekly in members' homes for dinner and to play cards. Since meeting sites rotated each week, they met at Williams's home about once a month, providing him with an important social outlet. A third group, the so-called "Kitchen Cabinet", was composed of senior women officials of the PNM, chaired by Marilyn Gordon. They met infrequently with Williams, largely because they held private meetings among themselves.

The bar group had began even before independence, and was important to Williams because it provided him with a sounding board outside the formal Cabinet. Its members were all personally committed to Williams and probably wanted nothing more than the personal satisfaction of advising him, even though unofficially. They discussed current issues and provided input about possible public reaction to policies, projects and, importantly, appointments. The meetings were held in an atmosphere of true conviviality, with Williams serving as a gracious host, preparing a multiplicity of drinks. One participant noted of him: "He drank a lot, none of us could outdrink him."[18]

Possibly Williams's happiest moments at home were at his bar preparing drinks and socializing with his guests. He was very careful about who mixed the drinks. In most cases he fixed them himself. Only a few who had earned his trust were allowed to take over. He was deeply suspicious about people "monkeying around" with the drinks — "They can poison them!"[19]

When Williams had no one to socialize with, he spent his evenings alone. Occasionally, he would invite someone for a chat, which might indirectly provide him with an opportunity to obtain information on a particular issue. But for at least the last five years of his life, solitude was the general pattern. His maids worked in the house from about 8.00 a.m. to about 4.00 p.m. Generally he was served his breakfast in his room. He ate his lunch at home; dinner was prepared by the maids before they left, and placed in the refrigerator. He heated his evening meal himself and sat alone at the kitchen table to eat it.

While his daughter Erica lived with him from December 1970 for almost three years, she prepared some of his evening meals. But he soon stopped this when he realized that he was gaining too much weight.[20] Erica sometimes had friends visiting while her father ate his dinner. One vividly recalled:

> At nights, he would sit down very simply having dinner in his kitchen. Somebody who does not know him would not be able to imagine the Prime Minister . . . sitting in a kitchen. There was nobody there but Erica and her friends. We would sit on the table sometimes not even on a chair and this great man is having his dinner and thoroughly enjoying the fact that we are all around . . . he is eating his dinner without any pomp or glory. He was a very simple person when it comes to things like that.[21]

For the last few years before he died, Williams was visited on Tuesday afternoons by his old friend, now one of his personal physicians, Dr Halsey McShine. Each week McShine gave Williams a brief medical checkup, taking his blood pressure and occasionally a blood sample for testing. This was sent to the Port of Spain hospital under an assumed name because of Williams's demand for secrecy. After the checkup, the two old friends sat at the bar having supper, prepared by the maid Claudia and heated up by Williams. But a few months before he died, Williams abruptly ended these regular get-togethers with a curt note which he had his security deliver to McShine: "I will call you when I need you!"[22] McShine did not meet with him again.

Williams's relationships with doctors were somewhat unusual. In general, he was distrustful of them. McShine remained a constant presence, but more because he was a friend from childhood than because he was a doctor. And since he was a surgeon, Williams needed other doctors to look after him as well. For a while, Dr Courtney Bartholomew served that purpose, and later Dr Winston Ince, who was called in during the last minutes of Williams's life. One reason for Williams's distrust was his belief that any publicity about possible illness could have serious negative political implications.

Perhaps Williams held this tough position because of his own belief in his invincibility. A charismatic leader had to be viewed — and had to view himself — as no mere mortal; illness could be viewed as a sign of weakness and mortality. Williams scheduled his longer and more detailed medical visits when he was outside Trinidad. England, and even Japan, were the sites of his most thorough medical examinations. If tests were conducted in Trinidad, a fictitious name was used.

But Williams was also distrustful because he believed he did not have to succumb to illness. To that extent, he did not believe that he really needed doctors. By all accounts, he was an extremely strong-willed individual. This accounted for his enormous capacity for work, and possibly too for his ability to get by — reputedly — on less than five hours of sleep each night. On more than a few occasions, one of his senior Cabinet ministers (Solomon in the early days, Prevatt later on) would announce before a Cabinet meeting that "Williams is ill, he will not be attending the meeting today", only to have Williams walk in just before the meeting began and take over the proceedings without explanation. He simply willed himself to attend the meeting. On one occasion at his home, Williams apparently lost consciousness for a moment; in a panic, the adviser who was with him called for Dr McShine, but was later harshly scolded by Williams for doing so.[23] Williams believed he could cure himself. On another occasion, an adviser sat with him in his bedroom upstairs because he complained of feeling unwell. After they had shared a drink, Williams began to discuss an article he was preparing on education. The adviser protested: "But you are not well!" Williams responded: "Carlton, the will does it!"[24]

It is possible that Williams's particular spiritual convictions led him to believe that the material world was the world of the weak and the superficial. In general, he displayed little interest in material things. Sickness and grief were part of the material world and did not reflect reality and truth, which resided in the spiritual world. If sickness arose from the mind, then the mind could be conditioned by determination and a powerful will to reject it. Only then could reality and truth be achieved. This philosophy could dispense with doctors since the individual has the power to cure himself.[25]

Sadly for Williams, his distrust of doctors was well known to his circle of advisers, some of whom had previous experience of Williams's wrath on this issue. This is possibly the primary reason why doctors were not called in until it was too late on his last Sunday evening.

Williams's aversion to doctors was matched by other dislikes, including an all-consuming distaste for flies. If he heard a fly buzzing around him, all activity stopped until he was able to get rid of the offending creature. In this regard, his behaviour was undoubtedly "obsessive compulsive". He sometimes placed a fly-swatter next to him before he sat down for his meal. It is possible that his hearing aid magnified the sounds of the fly and irritated him. A more complex explanation might be that the fly invaded his space and therefore needed to be controlled.

This preoccupation with flies caused an amusing incident. Williams and his elections committee interviewed all prospective candidates before elections. Late one evening, a Mr Richards from the Point Fortin area was being interviewed for a seat on the local County Council. Williams was impatient. Both he and his committee were tired, and wanted prompt and precise answers. Asked why he wanted to become a County Councillor, Richards unhesitatingly answered, "Because I want to get rid of the flies!" The committee was mildly amused. O'Halloran asked a follow-up question: "If you got rid of the flies in the first two years, what would you do in the third year?" Richards retorted: "What is wrong with this man, you think it is two flies I am talking about? We have plenty of flies!" Williams related the story at a Woodford Square meeting shortly afterwards, but added a new twist: he claimed that there was indeed a fly problem in south Trinidad. And, he continued, "the fly menace has come from Venezuela!" He proceeded to support his argument with statistics.[26]

That Williams was a most unusual individual would hardly be debated. The few who came to know him closely admit that he was the most "unforgettable individual they had met in their lives."[27] Even now, two other aspects of his personality — his appreciation of some of the finer aspects of life, including music, and his tastes in perfumes, toiletries, crystals etc. — are not generally known.

Williams's liking for music, art and literature was developed while he was a student in England with the opportunity to travel to Europe, where he spent much time in museums and art galleries. His taste in music was eclectic, including classical, opera, jazz and pop. He particularly enjoyed classical music and introduced it to his daughter Erica while she was quite young, even prescribing "opera and symphonies" for her while he was away travelling.[28] He introduced jazz to some of his close friends, including the work of jazz violinist Stéphane Grappelli from the Hot Club d'France.[29]

Whenever his friends travelled, he would ask them to bring him particular kinds of music, literature and even toiletries, items that were unavailable at home. In return he was very generous with his close friends, giving them tastefully-selected Christmas gifts and special items from his foreign travels. His secretaries assisted with the selection and purchase of some gifts, but he selected Christmas gifts himself with the assistance of Sheila and Hans Stecher at their store in Port of Spain or their outlet at the Hilton Hotel.

Williams was as organized and meticulous in his gift-giving as he was in other aspects of his life. He generally met with Mrs Stecher at her Hilton store after it closed, because of his desire for privacy. He arrived with a list of names and gift ideas. Mrs Stecher maintained records of what gifts had been given to each individual in previous years. The Stechers were always impressed by his "amazing knowledge of the finest merchandise in the world" and his familiarity with "all the great names in crystal, china, jewellery and watches."[30] Together, Williams and Mrs Stecher selected his Christmas gifts and others that he needed during the year. Williams began this practice around 1958 and continued it until Christmas 1979. For over 20 years, his close friends experienced his generosity and good taste; many of them provided him with an important social outlet, through their involvement in his card club.

Most of Williams's political relationships were with the black sector of Trinidad society, but his personal and social relationships were primarily with those of Chinese and French Creole ancestry. The card club was an informal gathering, comprising members of the Moyou family, their spouses and close friends. About nine or ten couples met weekly to play poker and ramole. Williams participated in the ramole, and approached the game as he did everything else, in a deliberate and organized manner. He did not enjoy losing.

The meeting place rotated among the homes of the different participants. The games began about 7.00 p.m. on Saturday evenings, and were interrupted for a sumptuous supper provided by that weekend's host, after which they continued until about midnight. Williams served as a host according to rotation, with the supper prepared by his housekeeper or catered by the Hilton Hotel. During long weekends, a second gathering was sometimes held on the Monday, usually at Williams's home, to which the entire families were invited. The children would have access to his swimming pool, and all the families contributed to the meals.

This group provided Williams with an important outlet for relaxation beyond the pressures of his office, away from those seeking to further their private interests. Williams looked upon this group as a family. No one used it to obtain special favours. In fact, in this context, many saw Williams as a warm, caring friend, not their prime minister.[31] Williams took an active part in this gathering for at least 16 years, from about 1962 to 1978: in it, he found individuals whose company he enjoyed, and more importantly, whom he could trust. Given his inherently suspicious nature, this is much to the credit of its participants.

But despite this long involvement, Williams abruptly terminated the relationship, about two years before he died. In his final years[32] he lived a reclusive life. He severed relationships with almost all his friends and informal advisers. He simply stopped seeing the former, while the latter were all in cold storage. He was surrounded only by a small, tight circle of professional and political advisers. Some observers thought he was being shielded from an intrusive public, others that he was being force-fed the ideas and interests of a few. Under these conditions, his ability to distinguish between myth and reality, exacerbated by declining health, must have been questionable.

Trinidad Express headlines tell the story of the 1970 upheaval

CHAPTER THIRTEEN
THE 1970 REVOLUTION
AND ITS AFTERMATH

When Williams came to power in 1956, he did so on a platform of black nationalism and a promise to liberate the poor black masses from centuries of colonial oppression. Ten years later this had materialized as black control of the political system and key decision-making positions in the state. Business, however, was still dominated by the European minority, with some involvement from the East Indian community. This situation persisted some six years after Williams's "Massa Day Done" declaration in Woodford Square, directed at the business community.

It was in this setting that Finance Minister A. N. R. Robinson introduced the Finance Bill of 1966, which laid bare the smouldering confrontation between the business sector and the PNM. Business leaders felt that the government's nationalistic stance, and the harsh rhetoric of its leader, were not conducive to business; they were not mollified by the Industrial Stabilization Act, hastily approved the previous year. There were divisions of opinion even inside Williams's Cabinet. Robinson viewed the Bill as "a major technique of reform", but he was well aware that "business members in the Cabinet were opposed to it."[1] The Bill itself "basically proposed a more modern system of taxation, including the introduction of withholding taxes."[2] But local companies, believing that they had some support within the Cabinet, prepared for a confrontation.

According to Robinson, the US government was also aware that the Cabinet was divided over the proposed legislation. A team of government technicians travelled to the US, but the American authorities saw no point in discussion, knowing that the Trinidad and Tobago government itself was not united on the issue.[3] Under pressure domestically and internationally, Williams eventually became "ambivalent over the Act" and sought to resolve the issue privately.[4]

He organized a private evening meeting between leading representatives of the business community and himself, without the participation of his Minister of Finance. The *Trinidad Guardian* learned about it, and a reporter and a cameraman stood in the shadows observing the procession of businessmen arriving at Mary Street.[5] Williams was photographed as he alighted from his car. He exploded: "Who the hell are you?" The frightened photographer identified himself, and Williams snarled, "You tell your editor, I say, if he publish that picture or write any story, he will be on the first boat back to England in the morning!"[6] Both reporter and cameraman promptly returned to the office and related the story to their foreign-born editor, who at first decided to publish the story and picture. But he was overruled by the Canadian-born publisher, himself apparently threatened by the Prime Minister's reaction.

Within a few months the Finance Bill was withdrawn, and Williams assumed responsibility for the Ministry of Finance, transferring Robinson to External Affairs. As Robinson observed, this encouraged those in the party "who saw me as a reformist, the reactionary element, to rise up."[7] In effect it marked the beginning of the end for Robinson in the PNM, even though it had been generally assumed that he would be Williams's successor.

Williams's stance on the Finance Bill was an important turning point for the PNM. Until then, the party's commitment to black nationalism and its identification with the masses had remained relatively intact. But the Industrial Stabilization Act of 1965 severely circumscribed workers' right to strike, and with the failure of the Finance Bill, questions began to arise about the party's identity, interest and loyalty. This provided fertile ground for the "Black Power" movement to exploit four years later.

Gordon Rohlehr has suggested that another schism was developing between the PNM and the population.[8] Williams's position was that the intelligentsia must provide leadership, since "the masses at the grass roots . . . were incapable of generating from within their ranks leaders who were adequate and relevant."[9] Williams could thus manipulate "culture" to meet political needs. Rohlehr continued: "'Culture' as perceived by Williams as 'commandant' of the intellectual ruling class became a manipulable lever in an elaborate machinery of patronage on the part of the controlling elite and clientism on the part of the common folk."[10] The cultural forms promoted through Williams's Best Village competitions "involved the recovery and rehabilitation of the steadily waning pastoral folk culture which had declined . . . during the last quarter of the 19th century." The main flaw in this programme, Rohlehr argued, "was that it had not moved beyond the agenda of the 1940s . . . Critics pointed to the vast gap between nostalgically resuscitated pastoral folk forms and the urgencies of the world in which the post-Independence generation moved."[11]

Williams's supporters would have vehemently disagreed with this interpretation. The coordinator of the Best Village programme subsequently wrote:

> Best Village became a platform, a wellspring of talent was being unearthed each year. It caused an awakening of cultural consciousness in the people on a national level. It is time that Williams received the recognition that is due to him for having the foresight to institute such a programme.[12]

According to Rohlehr, however, as the euphoria of independence wore off,

> the gap between an exhumed pastoral culture and the fluid, dynamic, unpredictable but intensively alive "counter-culture" of post-Independence youth became immediately obvious . . . The 1970 "revolution" was simply a projection of the cultural gap separating the generation of the 1920s and 1930s from that of the 1950s and 1960s. It signalled the presence of a gulf within Creole society.[13]

To support his argument Rohlehr quoted from Derek Walcott, who in 1971 had commented on the cultural dimension of the Black Power movement:

> One of the most dangerous signs of cultural fascism is the assimilation of folk culture in the policy of the state. This goes under the image of national identity and it manifests itself in folk parades, folk circuses, folk costume . . . But it is the people who choose their image, not the state, and if the folk image of another generation is now Afro, Afros and dashikis, then it is the right image, and it cannot be intimidated or challenged by the state's insistence on the folk image . . . To obstruct that force politically is also to try to obstruct the flow of culture . . . There was political obstruction last year, and I doubt whether there would have been so much violence if the cultural direction of a large part of the country was recognized.[14]

So by the late 1960s, Williams had severely moderated his original position on black nationalism and the upliftment of the ordinary people, and had acquiesced to pressures from the business sector. He firmly believed that it was up to him to determine cultural direction, and that he knew what was best for the society. A clash with the now politically-conscious masses — educated largely by his own public lectures — was now almost inevitable. His primary challenger from the grass roots would be Geddes Granger.

Granger was born and grew up in Laventille, "one of the most rabidly pro-PNM" areas of Trinidad. By the early 1960s he had experienced an "interesting transformation from young, aspiring middle-class black boy from Laventille to passionate Black Power advocate and activist."[15] A natural organizer and leader, he organised Pegasus in the early 1960s, a club that emphasized cultural programmes. In 1966, Pegasus initiated "Project Independence", a celebration of the achievement of major cultural personalities. The Vice-President of the Senate agreed to preside at the function, to be held at the Public Library on Woodford Square.

The PNM, which had always used Woodford Square as its major rallying ground, organized its own event there for the same evening. An embittered Granger was forced to cancel his celebration, convinced that the PNM had deliberately destroyed it. He interpreted this as a personal threat, and he promised to "bring Williams to his knees".[16] Rightly or wrongly, Granger interpreted future problems with the state as a personal attack directed by Williams.

Granger began attending classes at the university and was soon elected to head the student organization. In early 1969, shortly after West Indian students at Sir George Williams University in Canada had embarked on protest demonstrations, the Governor General of

Canada arrived in Trinidad for a state visit. When he attempted to enter the university campus at St Augustine, his motorcade was blocked by students, much to the embarrassment of the government. Later that evening, students, intoxicated with their victory and instigated by Granger, organized the National Joint Action Committee (NJAC), which would serve as the vehicle to launch the Black Power demonstrations a year later.

Williams did not ignore the crisis involving West Indian students in Canada. He despatched a one-man Commission "to enquire into racial discrimination in Canada." Trinidad and Tobago's ambassador to Canada, Donald Granado, was horrified. He promptly wrote Williams enquiring what right Trinidad had to interfere in Canadian affairs. Williams later conceded to Granado that he had not "thought through the matter very carefully." He admitted that "he had made a mistake", but also anticipated that "nothing would come of it."[17]

The crisis at Sir George Williams University came on the heels of a confrontation in Jamaica over the Guyanese radical Walter Rodney, and served to fan the flames of discontent spreading throughout the Caribbean. From Jamaica in October 1968, the crisis spread to Trinidad in February 1969, and by Christmas that year was affecting the country's army. During the traditional Christmas dinner, when enlisted men were traditionally served by officers, there was a near riot. A subsequent investigation concluded that there was a "subversive" element within the army which should be dismissed. Nothing was done, and four months later there was an army revolt.

By that time, popular demonstrations had been criss-crossing Port of Spain for almost two months. They began on Thursday February 26, when a relatively small group of university students, led by Granger and Dave Darbeau, staged a march in front of the Canadian High Commission on South Quay to protest the trial of West Indian students in Canada, arising from the Sir George Williams incident a year earlier. Growing in size, the march moved on to the Royal Bank of Canada, and after the cry of "Let we go to the church!" entered the Cathedral of the Immaculate Conception on Independence Square.

The original target of "white racism" in Canada now extended to the "white power structure" and anything which appeared to represent white domination of the society. Granger himself had written earlier:

> We were raped of our culture, of our manhood, of our dignity, our sense of brotherhood and justice, and forced to accept a twisted, capitalistic view of life in which everything is meaningless except in terms of survival, power, wealth: the complete domination of one class over another.[18]

Dave Darbeau had commented:

> We are guilty of the same self-contempt, self-despisement and servility to the whites (all stemming from the white values which dominate the society) which led the Williams band to hold cocktail parties at the Country Club and trample the interests of the Black Community.[19]

The ultimate aim of the Black Power movement was to bring economic power to the ordinary people, Darbeau argued, and this process began with an "awareness not just that problems exist, but an awareness of the roots of the problems." He continued:

> When we understand ourselves in this way we can build a genuine brotherhood . . . a sense of pride . . . and the confidence and courage to tackle our problems. The development of this consciousness on a national scale will allow us to take control of our economy and so our lives. Then the chains will be burst.[20]

A few weeks later, when Williams finally spoke out on the demonstrations, he startled much of Trinidad's middle class by agreeing with some of the ideas expressed by Darbeau. He noted that a fundamental feature of the movement was

> the insistence on Black dignity, the manifestation of Black dignity, the manifestation of Black consciousness, and the demand for Black economic power. The entire population must understand that these demands are perfectly legitimate and are entirely in the interest of the community as a whole. If this is Black Power, then I am for Black Power![21]

Yet for a month before this, the Black Power demonstrations had continued and an anxious population had not heard from its Prime Minister. The state had unwittingly provided an extra impetus for the protests by arresting eight Black Power leaders for "disorderly behaviour in a place of worship" the night after the occupation of the Cathedral. As word of these arrests spread, a crowd of hundreds gathered outside the court where the accused were due to appear, shouting "Freedom!"

and "Power!"

The following Monday, hundreds gathered at Woodford Square to listen to Geddes Granger and the seven other defendants, now free on bail. Within two days a mass movement was born, and Trinidad watched in amazement as a crowd of over 10,000 assembled at Woodford Square and marched peacefully to the symbolic centre of Trinidad's downtrodden: "shantytown". The *Express* headlined the event next day: "BLACK POWER STUNS THE CITY".

Before this mammoth march began, Granger lectured to the assembled thousands. The focal point was no longer Canadian racism but the "black puppet government" which had been manipulated by the "local white power structure". Granger held Williams responsible for the depressed condition of the ordinary people and "for not allowing the African and Indian population their true place in this land of ours."[22] Granger had clearly developed a deep mistrust of Williams. Growing up in depressed Laventille, he would have remembered Williams from his childhood days, and may even have been stirred by Williams's promises to uplift the black man. The adults around him would have placed their hopes in Williams as their liberator.

One of the devices Williams used to gain the trust of the black lower class was the steelband.

> Williams thoroughly understood the function and symbolic value of the steelband in communities and established firm relations with the steelband movement in order to elicit and maintain grassroots support . . . Soon after the PNM won the elections, Williams developed a particularly close relationship with Desperadoes and Laventille, a predominantly grass roots African neighborhood, that was currently plagued by steel-band related gang warfare.[23]

A Laventille community leader and captain of the Desperadoes steelband, George Yeates, recalled Williams's offer of assistance to the area:

> When Williams came up Laventille Hill and spoke to us, that was one of the proposals that we put to him . . . there were too many young people that were idle . . . we thought if the government could put aside some money . . . we in the village [could] see areas that needed repair . . . the whole thing became a national idea employing thousands of people.[24]

The PNM incorporated the steelband movement into its campaigns. Williams used members of the Desperadoes for security protection, especially after threats were made to kidnap his daughter. The Laventille panmen became known as a PNM band. Bertie Marshall recalled:

> We were called the PNM band simply because we played at everything the PNM had in Laventille. Granado [the area representative] . . . announced that he was giving us a cheque to buy a pair of cymbals . . . I never got those cymbals as I never got any of the things promised me by members of government over the last 15 or 16 years. Still we played as the PNM band.[25]

It would appear from the observations of these two Laventille community leaders that, while the PNM used the steelband as an important means of establishing a connection to the grass roots during the initial stages of party building, once in office, the party shifted its focus towards the middle class. The early practical support given to the grass roots, as in Laventille, simply dissipated in the 1960s.

It was during the early 60s that Granger organized the Pegasus cultural club in Laventille. He began to view the state, and Williams, as an obstacle to its progress. Later, he went a step further: Williams was not merely an obstacle, he was a "puppet" of the "white power structure". The hasty passage of the Industrial Stabilization Act and the fiasco over the Finance Bill contributed to this perception. Thus on March 4, 1970, Trinidad witnessed a public demonstration against the government, the size of which it had never seen.

Granger believed that the demonstration would bring down the PNM government. But Williams, at least outwardly, appeared unruffled. His Cabinet and his personal advisers pleaded with him to take decisive action, but he remained serene. The problem was not simply weakness, or inability to take a firm decision. For Williams, timing was the essence of politics. As one of his primary advisers later observed, "He was a master of timing" and a "supreme strategist."[26] His daughter, reflecting on his political strategy, said, "My father always viewed most things in life with the precision and strategy worthy of a military campaign . . . He always enjoyed using a French proverb, *reculer pour mieux sauter*, which means 'Retreat in order to advance.'"[27] Mahabir remembered Williams saying in his meetings, "Gentlemen, do not shoot until you see the whites of their eyes."[28] So the demonstrations continued, and Williams made no public response for another three weeks.

The demonstrations in Trinidad sparked similar activity outside the country's High Commission in London, which soon heard that Abdul Malik, the infamous Michael X, wanted to arrange a meeting with High Commissioner Granado. Because of his "love for that boy, Eric, he wanted to go to Trinidad to help resolve the problems there." When informed that as a national he could visit whenever he wished, his response was, "If Eric invites me, the people will see that I have a special reason for being in Trinidad."[29] Malik, of course, received no formal invitation, but did arrive in Trinidad and participated in the demonstrations.

In a move designed to blunt criticism that the Black Power movement was essentially anti-East Indian, Granger announced a march to Caroni, under the banner "INDIANS AND AFRICANS UNITE". Bhadase Maraj, the ostensible leader of the Indians in Caroni, first declared his support for the demonstrations, but within a few hours changed his mind, calling the marchers "a bunch of Black Power radicals" — possibly after receiving a call from the Prime Minister himself.[30] Williams was undoubtedly unnerved by this demonstration, since his political strategy required a division of the two major ethnic groups. The largely black marchers were generally well received by the East Indians in Caroni; but again Williams displayed no outward emotion.

By this time, the Movement had been infiltrated by state security and daily reports were being forwarded to Williams. Some of his private advisers literally begged him to take decisive action to head off the demonstrations. His response was "Burn, baby, burn." He observed that taxes would need to be increased to repair the damage caused by the almost nightly fires.[31]

Finally, on March 23, Williams addressed the nation — his first public response to the crisis. Typically, he began his speech by placing the demonstrations in an international context. Such events occurred regularly across the world, he said; citizens should not be unduly perturbed. He suggested it was simply part of "a worldwide revolt against authority and traditional institutions and values", especially foreign investment. The events pitted "black people against the growing indignities to which they have been subjected", but his "government has fully appreciated all these world currents and its whole policy has been directed toward a restructuring of the society which we inherited."[32]

Williams conceded that, in Trinidad, "unemployment fanned the flames." But, delineating the goals and the achievements of his government, he argued, "We consciously sought to promote a multiracial society with emphasis on the economic and social upliftment of the two major disadvantaged groups. Our goal has always been Afro-Asian solidarity. We have consciously sought to promote black economic power."[33] After listing the job opportunities created for black small farmers, the introduction of free secondary education and job training, and the government's overall contribution to alleviating unemployment, he concluded:

> The demonstrations, however, suggested that neither the policy of the Government, nor the measures taken . . . are sufficiently known . . . I get the feeling also that there is not sufficient awareness of our deliberate policy to control land allocation to foreigners . . . this lack of awareness by the people is a worldwide problem.[34]

He willingly conceded that

> the pace of change has been and is too slow . . . the Government must be more forceful in implementing its policies. I am myself frequently infuriated by the delays we encounter of one sort of another at various turns. But the population must understand that there are some basic difficulties. Most important is the parliamentary system which we are trying to promote and maintain . . . Administrative procedures are also slow and bureaucratic.[35]

On the assumption that the Black Power demonstrations were motivated by the need for jobs, Williams outlined the solution proposed by his government:

> Cabinet has therefore decided to impose, as from 1 January 1970, a special levy of 5 per cent on the chargeable income of all companies paying corporation tax . . . On individuals the levy will be 5 per cent on the excess of the chargeable income over $10,000. I anticipate that this levy will yield $10 million in the first year.[36]

The response from the Black Power movement was entirely negative. Williams's argument concerning the international dimensions of the protest movement was dismissed:

> Williams is insensitive to one major reason for our revolt. That reason is Williams himself. Had it not been for Williams' sellout to the white imperialists, had it not been for the PNM's political bankruptcy, had it not been for his racial politics, had

it not been for his alliance with clowns . . . had it not been for his rejection of respected black leaders like James and Carmichael . . . the black people of this island would not have been out on the hot streets.[37]

The recommended solution to the crisis — a five per cent levy on corporations and the more affluent — was "completely meaningless", NJAC's pamphlet continued.

Taxes backdated . . . to raise money for the unemployed cannot solve the problem when we operate in a society which is dominated by capitalistic whites who have no loyalty . . . his [Williams's] short-term measures are completely meaningless. We do not want crumbs taken from businessmen . . . [we] want the whole bread with butter . . . We cannot afford stopgap measures, taking from the rich to give to the poor as Williams says he will do . . . we can see that Williams is merely trying to fool us . . . Williams' electioneering on Monday night shows he does not know what black people . . . are trying to achieve . . . He has played the fool too long, and now he is fooling himself.[38]

The response of the Black Power movement to Williams's address clearly showed that by this time the Movement viewed him as the source of the problem, ostensibly because he had acquiesced to the white business elite in Trinidad. A re-activated crash programme meant that he did not understand the roots of the discontent — the demand for black dignity and respect in a society whose majority was dark-skinned. Williams was seen as a true "Afro-Saxon", in effect selling out a movement that he himself had initiated 15 years earlier. This signalled a hardening of positions on both sides. Violence was imminent.

By this time, radical trade union leader George Weekes had begun speaking on the Black Power platform. Soon the Tapia House movement declared that "the regime is dead. It is power to the people."[39] Divisions began to appear in the police force and the army. The National Steelband Association, long associated with the PNM, declared its support for NJAC. Williams remained closeted with his advisers.

A group of unofficial advisers met regularly with Williams at his home. Among them were Ivan Williams, Ferdie Ferreira, Carlton Gomes, Bertie Ballantyne and Irwin Merritt. Sometimes Rolf Moyou, Williams's brother-in-law, and Carl Tull were present. This group discussed the security reports and evaluated different strategies.

In early May, Mahalia Jackson arrived in Trinidad for some pre-arranged concerts, and Williams saw that she could be used to blunt the force of the Movement. He said: "Let us give the sister to the Black Power boys." In a hastily arranged supper meeting, Williams offered her three additional public concerts, with the additional fees to be paid by the government.[40] This would demonstrate that the government encouraged black culture.

Ironically, NJAC also sought political mileage from Mahalia's visit. The Black Power movement had just gained its first martyr, when the police shot and killed a 21-year-old unknown black activist, Basil Davis, near Woodford Square. Davis's parents handed the body of their son over to NJAC, which organized a "state" funeral. The Black Power leaders asked Mahalia Jackson to sing at Davis's funeral. Her response to one of Williams's advisers was, "What fee should I charge?" When told that she was expected to perform at the funeral without a fee, her response was, "But I did not get this voice for free!"[41] Not only did she not sing at Davis's funeral, but she antagonized some of the Movement's leadership by recommending that they "cool it" with regard to their demonstrations.[42]

Having made his public statement, and with Mahalia Jackson entertaining the crowds at government expense, Williams continued with the normal affairs of the state, assuming that the crisis was largely resolved and the demonstrations would eventually fizzle out. At a Cabinet meeting on Thursday April 10, it was agreed that Williams and Kamaluddin Mohammed, Minister of West Indian Affairs, would represent Trinidad that weekend at a CARIFTA meeting in Jamaica. On Friday, Williams met with the Prime Ministers of Guyana and Suriname in Trinidad, seeking to resolve their border disputes. But while Mahalia Jackson sang to thousands at the Queen's Park Savannah on Saturday evening, Williams, nearby in St Ann's, received security reports which prompted him to postpone his trip to Jamaica on the Sunday. Mohammed left without him.

Early on Monday morning, April 13, A. N. R. Robinson, who had been upset with Williams for four years, ever since the fiasco over the Finance Bill, launched a scathing attack on him in a speech to the Seamen and Waterfront Workers' Trade Union. He later explained that "it was time to take action; to recognize the criticism being made, the dissatisfaction being expressed."[43] He ended his speech by announcing his resignation, accusing the government of not making "a sufficiently serious attempt . . . to remove the underlying causes of the present situation."[44] This increased the pressure on Williams; some believed that the government would collapse.

Tension increased significantly when that weekend's issue of the *Vanguard*, the weekly newspaper of Weekes's Oilfield Workers Trade Union, declared in a front-page article that the government could not rely on the loyalty of its 800-man Regiment. A disastrous fire in San Juan that same weekend took the lives of four East Indian teenagers. Arson was suspected. Some pointed to Black Power followers as the likely culprits.[45]

On Sunday morning, April 19, a special meeting of the General Council of the PNM was convened. After Williams summarized the current situation, the Council gave him complete support; the following evening he advised the Governor General to declare a State of Emergency.

During the night of April 20, state security rounded up the leaders of the Black Power Movement. Granger himself was not located until April 23. But by the morning of Tuesday 21, chaos reigned at Williams's home. Most of his Cabinet Ministers were in a state of panic. Some feared that they were going to be killed, others sought ways to leave the country. But Williams remained "cool and calm, like a general in control."[46] Kamaluddin Mohammed was also calm; he claimed to have remained at Williams's home for the first three days of the State of Emergency.[47] Later that day Cabinet members and their families, ostensibly for security reasons, were moved to the Hilton Hotel. But Williams adamantly refused to leave his home, even though a rebellion in the army greatly exacerbated the situation.

During the first few days of the crisis, Williams met constantly with his official security advisers, including the Commissioner of Police. Each evening he and a small loyal group of political advisers, together with Carlton Gomes, met at his home from about six o'clock, sometimes till after midnight. Williams arranged official passes so that they could travel at night, though occasionally they were required to stay overnight if travelling was thought to be too dangerous. This continued for four or five months.

The members of this group had been serving Williams and the PNM since around 1955. They were deeply devoted and totally loyal. Some, to the dismay of their families, spent more time with Williams than at their homes. They were his eyes and ears; they felt obliged to support him. They provided a forum, in a relaxed environment, in which to discuss and synthesize information and suggest policy. This was Williams's "Kitchen Cabinet" during the crisis, while many of his formal advisers were locked away in the relative safety of the Hilton Hotel.

Every night Williams gave informal lectures to this small group, placing the Trinidad situation in the context of world history. He was particularly attracted to the Haitian revolution of the late 18th century; his early mentor C. L. R. James had written definitively on the subject. The irony, probably lost on this small audience, was that the Haitian revolution was stimulated by black slaves seeking their freedom: was there not a rough parallel to the situation being played out in Trinidad? Williams's supporters, though, apparently sat in awe as they listened. As one later observed, "We no longer belonged to that period, he overtrained us!"[48]

Williams clearly trusted this small loyal group; eventually he allowed each member to prepare drinks. Dinner was catered at a nearby Chinese restaurant, though a problem erupted when the restaurant management complained about not being paid, in spite of Williams's nightly provision of funds (which had apparently been used by a relative for other purposes). Williams provided an additional cheque. Occasionally, he took his group to the Hotel Normandie for a more sumptuous supper.

One evening, early in the crisis, security at the gate announced the arrival of A. C. Alexis, a member of parliament and Williams's brother-in-law. Alexis had been sent as an emissary by the other PNM parliamentarians at the Hilton, bearing a note for Williams. Since he was a relative, they thought Williams would see him. Williams sent an aide to the door to inquire why he was there. Alexis waited while the note was taken inside, but Williams decided he did not want to meet. An excuse was hastily concocted.[49]

But Williams soon had to deal with another relative, his daughter Erica, who returned to Trinidad to be with her father. He was naturally apprehensive, with the obvious dangers involved. But she rationalized: "If he was to go out, we would go out together."[50] Erica flew from Geneva, where she was a student, to Barbados, and was met by her uncle, Rolf Moyou, and Sergeant Harvey. Both were armed, and accompanied her to Trinidad.

In the midst of the State of Emergency, and just a few days after her arrival in Trinidad, 19-year-old Erica decided to attend a party at Fort George. The sound of guns was heard, and Erica was hustled home safely. Lieutenant Jack Williams and the police discreetly provided security on her future trips outside the home.

Erica's desire to participate in the 1971 Carnival caused renewed fears for her safety. Jack Williams, a family friend in the Coast Guard, was a member of Edmund Hart's band, and it was decided that Erica could participate if adequate security arrangements were in place. Jack Williams and a number of male and female police officers, all armed, paraded in costumes around her. It was only when the handbag of one of the female officers fell noisily to the ground that other masqueraders realized there were armed police around them — there was a weapon in the purse.[51]

With the jailing of the Black Power leaders, the focus shifted to the army revolt. The government organized a negotiating team consisting of Attorney General Karl Hudson-Phillips, Dodderidge Alleyne, Head of the Public Service, and former Regiment commander Joffre Serrette. After a week Serrette persuaded the rebel leaders, Lieutenants Raffique Shah and Rex Lassalle, to accompany him to Port of Spain "for questioning." At Police Headquarters they were arrested. From Williams's perspective, the immediate crisis was now over, permitting him to make another address to the nation on Sunday May 3.

On this occasion, Williams began by painting a very broad picture of a conspiracy against his government, which necessitated a State of Emergency. He said that for some years now

> we have been aware of dissident elements in the society, especially among a minority of trade unions, seeking to displace the government . . . they tried to do so by the electoral process . . . when that failed they turned to unconstitutional means and armed revolution . . . During the weekend before the declaration of the State of Emergency . . . a new factor was introduced . . . the total repudiation by certain workers . . . of all recognized trade union practices . . . This was in the context of public statements . . . that the sugar workers and the workers in other services were to march on 21st April to link up with transport workers . . . The Cabinet decided the time had come for action.[52]

Williams claimed that he could not act earlier, as many had urged him to do, because he felt the general population would have been sceptical about his accusations. He claimed: "You had to be made to put your finger in the wound in order to believe." He had acted only when the "total breakdown of the trade union movement was imminent."[53]

Williams repeated his previous views concerning the constructive aspects of the Black Power movement. "Let me make no bones about it: I identify myself fully with its constructive aspect. I wish you all to understand that the claims of black people to social justice, economic dignity . . . will be . . . supported and positively encouraged by my government."[54] He called for a reconsideration of the role of the Defence Force; a re-organization of the government machinery and the Public Service; and the appointment of an Ombudsman. He cautioned, however, that the emergency was not yet over. Indeed, it continued in a modified form for some months.

Williams's leadership in the next decade was markedly influenced by the Black Power rebellion. It affected his behaviour toward his party and the country in general. After introducing the State of Emergency, he shifted his base of operations from his office in Whitehall to his home, a practical decision based on security considerations. But after the emergency ended, he did not return to his office. His secretaries were required to work at his home, and Cabinet officials and others made daily treks there to meet with him.

Thus Williams became even more disconnected from the lives of ordinary citizens. At Whitehall he had had limited opportunities to meet with constituency representatives, but this too was terminated when he began to work at home. During the decade of the 1970s, his primary contacts with the party and the country were through Cabinet officials and advisers.

When in 1973 he tendered his resignation, many factors lay behind his decision. They included his sense of the ingratitude of one sector of the population, evidenced by the Black Power uprising; his lack of trust in the reliability of those around him, partly stemming from their behaviour during the crisis; the sense that his vision of the society was increasingly rejected; his desire to return to academic life; and the influence exerted by his daughter, who was urging him to return to private life.

Williams entertains Andrew Young, US Ambassador to the United Nations. Young visited Trinidad and Tobago in August 1977

THE DIFFICULT
LAST YEARS

On Friday September 28, 1973, Eric Williams delivered a long and rambling address to the 15th Annual Convention of the PNM in which he stated his desire not to seek re-election as the party's political leader. "The time has come for me to return to private life and to take no further part in political activity."[1] He launched into a 35-page explanation, and in familiar Williams style began by presenting the broad parameters that shaped his decision.

At the top of his list of reasons was the state of Caribbean integration. "It is now clear beyond any possibility of doubt," he declared, "that Caribbean integration will not be achieved in the foreseeable future and that the reality is continued Caribbean disunity and even perhaps the reaffirmation of colonialism."[2] Presumably, as an early and ardent supporter of regional integration, Williams could not accept what he saw as increasing fragmentation among regional states, renewed external domination by the US, and even the creeping influence of Venezuela and Cuba.

He identified three additional economic issues which, in his view, appeared insoluble for the region. The first was domination by multinational corporations, whose sheer size overwhelmed tiny Caribbean states. As a rationale for disgust, even resignation, this was a curious argument. When the PNM rose to power in 1956, Trinidad and Tobago had already been dominated for many years by multinational corporations, particularly Texaco in oil and Tate and Lyle in sugar. Yet 17 years later, Williams was well on the way, *de facto*, to building a socialist state. The Black Power movement had pushed him further in the direction of state control over the economy. How then could the multinational corporation still be as serious a problem as it was earlier?

The second issue, as Williams explained it, was the Caribbean's "virtual obsession with tourism". He declared: "It is not only the vice and crime increasingly associated with tourism . . . It is also the economic effects and dislocation itself."[3] In the case of Trinidad, this argument was also odd, since tourism had never been an important contributor to the economy. But Williams asked, "What doth it profit a man if he gains the industrial world and loses his soul and identity?"[4]

The European Economic Community (EEC) (as it then was) was Williams's third concern. He conceded that the Caribbean's "association with the European Economic Community could well include active encouragement rather than positive prohibition of industrial development and the provision of employment opportunities at home."[5] Nevertheless he saw the EEC as a problem. He did not explain, but turned to domestic reasons for his decision to resign.

Here, the first argument was one that he had repeated for many years: his distaste for rampant individualism. "Today, seventeen years [after the formation of the PNM], the disease of individualism is more pronounced than ever before, and such national movement as there is does not go beyond the increased participation in Carnival and the general desire to migrate."[6] This had resulted in a society immersed in petty complaints reflecting individual desires, and a preoccupation with the so-called guerilla movement in Trinidad at that time.

Williams complained that this "peculiar national psychology" was reflected in popular attitudes to government economic policy. He cited "economic confusion" with respect to policy on oil and gas, with some calling for nationalization and others demanding that the companies should be left alone.[7] Things were even worse "in relation to the question of national planning", with "all sorts of requests for this, that and the other" and total disregard for existing plans.[8]

Then he turned to problems within the party, and listed the need to declare individual assets, the difficulty of selecting appropriate election candidates given the constraints of the party's constitution, and his refusal to nominate a successor. He also discussed a personal problem.

> As I return to private life, I find myself with no place of my own to go to, and of equal importance no place for my collection of books and research documents . . . My daughter and I have decided to proceed jointly to secure an appropriate home and the transaction is now being finalized.[9]

He was indeed negotiating to buy a home in Goodwood Park, where he planned to return to his research and writing.

Williams was clearly caught between different forces as he ended his resignation speech.

> I have spoken to you tonight without bitterness . . . as objectively and as unemotionally as can be expected; if any slight edge of disappointment has showed itself, please attribute it to fatigue. I have decided, with the full support of my daughter (whose only complaint is that it comes three years too late), that I shall not seek re-election as your Political Leader . . . the time has come for me to return to private life.[10]

In this final statement Williams provided a broad hint of one of the real reasons for his resignation: disappointment. He shrugged this off as "fatigue". But by 1973 Williams had indeed become disappointed: in his Cabinet, for not standing up with him during the 1970 crisis, and more generally for no longer sharing his vision for Trinidad; and in his party. He felt that he alone was carrying the burden of fund-raising, administration, and the party newspaper. He also felt disappointed in the general population, for the ingratitude expressed in the 1970 demonstrations, and for its individualism, its constant preoccupation with individual interest. He was disappointed because he had failed to alter the political culture at all three levels, as he had set out to do.

This was not a rash, impulsive decision on Williams's part. He had threatened to resign for many years, and had discussed it on many occasions with his private advisers.[11] When he finally decided, many of them did not believe he was serious — they had heard it before.

What they did not understand was that Erica, who had now been at home with him for almost three years, was an important contributor to this decision.

When Erica Williams returned to Trinidad in the midst of the Black Power upheaval, she saw the enormous stress which her father was under, and the threat to both their lives. She noted the absence of Cabinet colleagues and the hostility to Williams in a sector of the population. It is hardly surprising that, as his daughter and his only true confidante, she encouraged him to resign.

Between 1971 and 1973 the country's economic condition and social environment deteriorated further. The government was in the somewhat embarrassing position of operating without an opposition, after a no-vote campaign in the 1971 elections. Williams was working at home, emerging only for special meetings. His isolation and disillusion were growing. Erica, living at home, "quarrelled with him all the time" as she tried to persuade him to resign, according to one observer.[12] Eventually, she succeeded.

A new book was already under consideration. In March 1973 Williams had proposed to his publisher Andre Deutsch that he convert his published article "The Blackest Thing About Slavery is Not the Black Man" into a book.[13] Deutsch had responded with enthusiasm.[14] The two men met in Trinidad in September, and in December Deutsch offered a book contract.

Not everyone was convinced, however, that Williams was serious about resigning. Errol Mahabir, one of his closest associates, later observed: "I never in my mind felt that Williams had any intention of going anywhere. Dr Williams made that announcement so that crabs could cover their holes."[15] At that point, the Attorney-General, Karl Hudson-Phillips, was the major threat to Williams's leadership. Some, like Mahabir, speculated that the resignation was a way of learning who was loyal and who supported Hudson-Phillips.

But another of Williams's close associates — Dodderidge Alleyne, at that time Permanent Secretary to the Prime Minister and "very close" to him — disagreed. After the resignation was announced,

> I said to him, "Why are you leaving now?" "What do you mean, why am I leaving now?" So I said to him, "What do you think history would say if you left now?" He said, "You do not understand, Dod, what you have to understand is what history

would say if I do not go now."[16]

Alleyne tried to explain to Williams that, though the treasury never seemed to have enough money to implement all the projects planned by the government, it eventually would, with significant oil price increases ahead.

This was certainly a factor in Williams's thinking. In October 1973, the month after the resignation announcement, war broke out between Israel and the Arab states, and there was a dramatic escalation in the price of oil — by December it had quadrupled. Trinidad and Tobago, an oil producer, albeit a small one, stood to reap enormous benefits. The party had not yet reconvened to select a new leader; various groups were bringing pressure on Williams to rescind his resignation. Probably from fear — a sense that only Williams could hold the social fabric together — broad sectors of the population bombarded him with petitions. These were gathered into huge files at his office, and came, broadly, from three sectors of the population: PNM constituency groups, over 100 mostly handwritten letters from citizens, and private organizations.[17]

While 25 party groups asked the Prime Minister to reconsider his decision, even more appealing, perhaps, were the detailed and urgent letters from ordinary people.[18] One wrote, "Why are you resigning Sir, some of our people have no thanks. I beg you Sir, do not resign." An eleven-year-old said, "I have never felt so sad in my life since you announced your retirement." From PT in Cumana came this plea: "With tears blinding my eyes . . . please, please stay with us a little longer." Williams's old friend and Cabinet member Kamaluddin Mohammed warned that "the consequences of your withdrawal . . . can be fatal to the Party, can cause disintegration of the community." Then there were petitions from community and trade organizations including the Taxi Drivers Association, the Market Vendors, and the Chinese and Syrian-Lebanese groups.[19]

Some of the most effective pleas came from the country's women, particularly those representing PNM grass roots support, who were well organized. Regular prayer vigils were held, and a representative was sent to Williams's home each morning to report on these activities. Many of the women involved were known to Williams's house staff and his guards, and were permitted to enter the grounds. They knew when and where he had his breakfast — on a small open patio. There, each stood and recited the latest efforts to keep him in office. He did not generally respond.[20]

The women personalized their appeal. To them, he was not merely the Prime Minister but the father of the nation. Since the father had led his children out of bondage into independence, they argued, how could he abandon them to pursue his own interests? It was an approach that resonated with Williams. They let him know that they were holding nightly prayer meetings to encourage him to reconsider his decision. Some wrote lengthy letters to him, and those who knew him best made repeated telephone calls to his home.

The Inter-Religious Organization (IRO) was also instrumental in persuading Williams to stay in office.[21] The initiative came from President Clarke, who invited the IRO to meet him while he was vacationing in Tobago and strongly suggested that it should write to Williams urging him to stay on.[22] This was done, and the group subsequently met with Williams in early November. Kamaluddin Mohammed met with Williams a week later and came away with the impression that he would return to office.[23] But Archbishop Anthony Pantin summarized the IRO's role this way: "IRO or no IRO, if Eric Williams did not want to return to office, he would not have done so." According to the Archbishop, "oil gave new life to the Prime Minister."[24] Erica, seeing her father very tired late one evening after the oil boom had begun, said, "Daddy, why don't you get out of politics?" To which he replied, "I have got to stay on a little longer and secure the oil money for Trinidad's children."[25]

During the brief period of indecision over the future of Williams's leadership, two men — Hudson-Phillips and Kamaluddin Mohammed — emerged as major contenders for the succession. With the party in obvious confusion, Williams's personal advisers repeatedly sought his advice about its future direction, but he refused to give any.[26] Some saw a clue to his thinking when his daughter Erica reportedly seconded the nomination of Mohammed at a meeting of Party Group Number One of the Port of Spain Central constituency,[27] at about the time that Williams had his meeting with the IRO. Mohammed, who claimed that he did not seek the nomination and wanted Williams to stay on, met with the Prime Minister shortly afterwards. Realizing that Williams had decided to return, he "never canvassed nor signed any consent forms."[28]

In mid-November, Williams signalled his intention to return to head the party. The General Council of the PNM met on Sunday November 18 to consider nominations for a new leader. Responses were received from 299 party groups, of which 224 supported Hudson-Phillips. But at the reconvened PNM Convention on Sunday December 2, it was proposed to send a delegation to Williams to ask him to reconsider his decision to resign. The vote on the resolution was 348 in favour, 61 against, with 14 abstentions. The forces rallying for Hudson-Phillips could not contain the groundswell of support for Williams, who made his triumphant return later that evening. He told the Convention that he was willing to defer his "retirement from public life at least until all the necessary steps have been taken to implement the proposed new Constitution."[29] In fact, Williams remained in office until his death, over seven years later. But he also told his audience:

> On the basis of my announcement to you on 28 September, I have already arranged my personal plans and work programme. I have no desire to hold on to what is called power . . . Your resolution that I continue in office and the representations from so many . . . will disrupt my plans and interrupt my personal work. But I recognize my obligations both to the nation and to the Party, to subordinate personal interests to the public well-being.[30]

Later that month, Erica quietly left Trinidad to settle in the United States. She subsequently visited her father only occasionally, and not at all after her marriage. Williams had chosen Trinidad over his daughter. The consequences for him were enormous. With her departure, he was left very much alone, and soon lost other close relationships.

Ivan Williams and Ferdie Ferreira had been like Eric Williams's shadows since 1956. They had endured all his crises with him. They were unpaid by the party and held no high office in it, but were totally loyal. After Williams resigned, they asked him whom they should support, but he refused to guide them. Both gravitated toward Hudson-Phillips. In Williams's eyes, this was perceived as disloyalty. Ivan Williams was the subject of constant whispering campaigns. By late

1973 the Prime Minister had begun to listen to these whisperings. Both Ivan Williams, and Ferdie Ferreira by association, were placed in permanent cold storage after a dispute at Williams's home one Sunday morning. Both believed that domestic factors contributed to their dismissal. Not long after, Carlton Gomes suffered a similar fate.

Williams lost much of his emotional support. The technicians and the formal advisers remained, but their relationship with him was primarily intellectual. Only Errol Mahabir and John O'Halloran maintained a relatively close personal relationship with him. In 1978, he abruptly terminated his long relationship with his friends in the weekly card club, an activity which he had thoroughly enjoyed.

The 1976 election was a source of further aggravation for Williams. Since 1971, he had felt that the calibre of his government needed to be improved, but he was constrained by the requirements of the PNM constitution. Nominees were first approved at the constituency level, then presented to the screening committee. Williams chaired this committee, and signed off on the candidates before the names were forwarded to the Central Executive of the party. He was determined to have "new blood" for the 1976 election. He had complained bitterly about the party's selection process in his September 1973 resignation address, but the system had not been changed. Before the 1976 election, he named five of his Cabinet ministers as being unworthy to represent the party again: Brensley Barrow, Victor Campbell, Carlton Gomes, Sham Mohammed and Lionel Robinson. He publicly branded them "millstones". Ironically, all five were approved by their constituency groups and were presented to the screening committee. Williams refused to sign off on their nomination papers, hoping that the Central Executive would not support their candidatures. But all five were approved at this level. Williams's only recourse was to refuse to speak on their campaign platforms. But all five won their seats, though they languished as backbenchers for the next five years.

Williams also demanded that all candidates provide him with an undated letter of resignation. The background to this was the "crossing of the floor" by two PNM representatives, Roy Richardson and Horace Charles, during the 1971–76 Parliament, and his inability to stop them. Of equal importance was the independent stance assumed by Karl Hudson-Phillips, who had resigned as Attorney General to challenge

Williams for the leadership of the PNM in December 1973 and had remained a thorn in Williams's side, not least by publicly refusing to sign the undated letter. The "millstones" had initially adopted a similar position, but then changed their minds. After the election, Carlton Gomes demanded that Williams return his letter; Williams refused, and the issue was taken to court.[31] Gomes (represented by Hudson-Phillips) eventually lost his case, and was ordered to pay costs. He apparently did not pay the full amount, since the issue later resurfaced in Williams's will.

As well as "new blood" for the 1976 election, Williams wanted greater gender equity: the male bias of the government had become painfully obvious. The search led, among others, to Marilyn Gordon, a college graduate and high school teacher. Williams recommended her as the PNM candidate in a constituency along the East/West corridor, but again the relative autonomy of constituency groups and the constraints of the party's constitution prevented this. The day after the PNM's election victory, Williams, undeterred, invited Gordon to join his government as a Senator, and appointed her Parliamentary Secretary in the Ministry of Education. Impressed with her competence, he later asked her to chair his famous "Kitchen Cabinet," which comprised, among others, the five female representatives in the government. This group had special access to Williams, and met with him at his home, to the chagrin of older and more established male counterparts.[32]

During his final five years in office, Williams's circle of advisers shrank significantly. They included a few old political advisers and an even smaller number of technocrats, some of whom only joined his team after the 1970 uprising. There was almost no one left with whom he could have a warm, friendly chat. He had even broken with his long-serving party secretary Nicholas Simonette over nominations for the elections. He had heaped all the blame on Simonette, who had fought back in the screening committee while the council members sat quietly. Simonette remained in office until 1978, but his relationship with Williams effectively ended in 1976[33], and he was not re-appointed to the Senate.

Yet while Williams shed himself of his close associates during the final years of his life, he did develop at least one new and curious relationship, with reporter John Babb, then with the *Trinidad Guardian*. He had never had a cordial relationship with the media, but was always keenly aware of their reporting, and especially of Babb's work. In 1974, with the oil price boom taking hold, Babb requested and was eventually granted an interview on oil policy. It was conducted at Williams's home in the presence of a government media official, and was published as a two-part series. Williams was apparently pleased, because he agreed to a second interview. Again, a government official was present. A third interview was conducted in private, indicating that Williams now trusted Babb. Thereafter a warm friendship developed. From 1974 until Williams's death in 1981, Babb met with him frequently, sometimes every week. On some occasions formal interviews were conducted, but more frequently the two simply socialised. Babb had difficulty using the resulting information in formal articles. But he was one of the rare private individuals to remain in close contact with the Prime Minister in his last years, and could appreciate the Prime Minister's human side, as well as his slow physical deterioration.

Williams would often ask about his visitor's family. Babb recalled:

> Seeing [Williams] at his bar with a drink in his hand, he becomes people. He was an ordinary down-to-earth man, you would not think that was the Prime Minister sitting there . . . Once he was with his close friends he would do things for himself. He would get the glasses out, he would pour the drinks and chat. It was normal. Sometimes he would say things I wonder what direction he was coming from.[34]

Williams kept more keys in his pocket than he did before, and installed a "one-way mirror" at his home: he was becoming more suspicious and distrustful, probably even a little paranoid. Babb ventured the opinion that in his latter years Williams "got cornered or stuck into this government bureaucracy . . . people told him what they thought that he wanted to hear."[35]

Since in his final years the number of party and government officials who interacted with him was steadily reduced, Williams clearly lost touch with the views and sentiments of the broader community. Some believe that those around him deliberately kept him isolated and thus a hostage to their advice. It has even been suggested that they tried to convert him into a figurehead.[36] One parliamentarian who was close to the Prime Minister in his final five years was very critical of the way Williams was treated by his advisers. "Them fellas cornered [Williams], had him in a circle so that he could not hear what was going on. They were feeding the man exactly what they wanted him to know. That is what was going on and I think that is what killed the man."[37] If accurate, this represents an extremely harsh indictment of at least some who were around Williams during his final years.

Williams's physical condition, and to some extent his mental condition, deteriorated steadily during this time. One aide described him "with shoulder drooping, an air of resignation, an air of 'why could this have happened?'[38] A Cabinet official noted that Williams was "spending a lot of time at his home" and commented:

> Trinidad is a hard country. Trinidad is an uncaring country. I think toward the end he must have asked himself, "Why did I do this?" I think he saw himself as a carrier of a battle which should have been taken from him and carried on. He did not see anyone willing to take on the battle. I think he might have gotten exhausted and disappointed.[39]

But while Williams became increasingly disillusioned, some around him "felt that they were entrenched like nobody could put them out."[40] In this context, it is not hard to understand how Williams could have been manipulated in the interest of personal agendas. In his last days, he had few true friends.

But he did have his "first mistress", his research and writing. When he announced his resignation in September 1973, he was planning a new book with the publisher he had worked with since 1963, and in December 1973 had received a book contract.[41] Probably because of brief periods of illness, problems over the nomination of candidates for the 1976 elections, and the election campaign itself, he had made little progress with this project.

In April 1978, he wrote a detailed letter to Deutsch, explaining the delay.[42] He reported: "I am seeking to fight off what is probably no more than staleness and fatigue, but may be a touch of the flu." He assured Deutsch that he had been working on the project "for the past eighteen months," though interrupted "by flu", and continued:

> I began again in September 1977 and have continued unremittedly with only a break for the 1978 budget . . .   In this period I have been in total hibernation giving up all but the most essential official responsibilities, and getting on an average over the past eight months, four hours per day on the project . . . I shall keep in touch with you, as I can force myself to take time out even to write letters.[43]

That Williams was willing to admit that he had given up "all but the most essential official responsibilities", even in a private letter to a friend in England, is remarkable. Many years earlier he had written in similar terms to his close friend and adviser, Norman Manley[44], after growing disillusioned with his position at the Caribbean Commission.

Throughout 1978, Williams worked assiduously on the manuscript. Later that year he informed Deutsch, "I have began to organize the material."[45] In April 1979, he was optimistic, and "hoped to have something worthwhile by August, 1979."[46] Increasingly disillusioned with affairs of state, he focused much of his energy and attention on academic research. A few months later, he was "proud of the progress" of his writing.[47]

Yet the following year the project stalled again. A number of factors were involved. The year 1980 would be the last full year of Williams's life. And he had been distracted by another book project that was probably more meaningful to him at that stage in his life than the work he had been doing for Andre Deutsch. This was a proposal to collect his speeches in book form. Williams was excited by the idea: it was the only kind of memorial that he would have wanted for himself[48], and he believed that sales of this book could establish a scholarship fund to support the education of the children of party members.[49]

Williams established a three-member Cabinet committee to work out the details with the publisher, Longman Caribbean. Three versions were agreed on: a regular paperback; a library edition; and a special leatherbound edition which would fund the scholarship programme. The party apparently agreed to support the project fully. Williams began the work of selecting and editing his speeches. But he died before the project was completed. The party displayed little interest in the book when it eventually appeared, and the publisher incurred a large financial loss.[50]

Williams never informed Deutsch that he was involved in producing another book with another publisher. But late in 1980 Deutsch learnt of the project through Ellis Clarke, and wrote a letter of complaint to Williams.[51] Williams replied with a brief hand-written note, but did not respond to Deutsch's specific complaint.[52] On the last day of 1980 Deutsch wrote to Williams, "You have not answered my letter on your volume of speeches. I am very unhappy that this has gone to Longman's."[53] There is no evidence that Williams responded to this letter. He apparently ended his relationship with Deutsch at about the same time as that with his oldest friend, Halsey McShine, just a few months before his death.

McShine was not only Williams's personal friend, he was also one of his doctors. Throughout 1980, he visited the Prime Minister's home regularly, both to do brief medical checks, at Williams's request, and also to socialize — the two old friends sat at the bar and had supper. Williams enjoyed steaks and rich sugary desserts. McShine claimed he was never aware that Williams was a diabetic.[54]

By this time, McShine was a widower. On Christmas Eve, 1980, he attempted to visit Williams to exchange season's greetings. He rang the doorbell, having been previously informed by the guards on duty that Williams was at home. He suspected that Williams may have seen him — the "one-way mirror" had been installed — but Williams, who always warmly greeted visitors himself, did not come to the door. McShine never saw him again. He received a note the following week, which stated: "I will call you when I need you!"[55] But in the three months before he died, Williams did not call.

Crowds file past the casket lying in state in the Red House, Port of Spain

DEATH AND
CONTROVERSY

On Friday morning, March 27, 1981, President Ellis Clarke received an unusual request from his staff: would he explain his duties to them? Somewhat astonished, President Clarke employed an analogy. His job, he explained, was somewhat similar to that of a fire brigade; he always had to be prepared and ready in case of an emergency. He offered an illustration: "Suppose the cherubim and seraphim decided that their circle would be completed by the presence of their brother Eric, then the President must be ready to act in such an occurrence."[1] The staff were mystified by this analogy, and asked for further explanation. Suppose — the President explained — that Prime Minister Williams did not come downstairs to have breakfast one morning, causing his staff to go to his room, only to find him dead in his bed. The staff finally understood his point, though they suggested that his illustration was somewhat unrealistic. To which Clarke responded, "We must all die some time."

President Clarke had no idea that the Prime Minister was indeed very ill that morning. He could hardly know: he was one of the many with whom Williams had severely reduced contact, preferring to interact with the President through Errol Mahabir. After speaking to his staff, the President prepared a note informing Williams that he was about to take his wife on a shopping trip to Miami. He thought the timing was appropriate, since there was "nothing on the horizon that could cause a problem."[2] He could not conceive that within two days the country would be plunged into one of the deepest crises in its short history.

This chapter will survey the events of the final weekend of Williams's life, his death, the resulting controversies, and the legal difficulties over his estate. It will demonstrate that it was fear of Williams that incapacitated his advisers and prevented them from acting decisively. It will show how Williams became a victim of his reclusive lifestyle and his deliberate estrangement from those who could have been of crucial assistance when most needed, especially his doctors. It will also concede that Williams may have wanted it that way.

That Friday evening, President Clarke attended a function at the Hilton Hotel, where in the crowded room he was informed by John Donaldson that the Prime Minister was unwell. Clarke arranged to meet with Donaldson on Saturday morning, when he learned that Williams's condition had not improved. He became extremely apprehensive, recalling the hypothetical illustration he had used to his staff the previous morning, and the "wild references" that some might draw from it. At horse races later that day, he was relieved to find that Errol Mahabir was not "unduly perturbed", believing that Williams's medical condition had improved.

But the President's apprehension was reflected by a group of secretaries who worked in the Prime Minister's office. Williams came to his office only on Thursdays to chair meetings of the Cabinet, and on Fridays for meetings of parliament. On Thursday March 26, Williams had arrived late for a brief Cabinet meeting. He was usually on time. According to Kamaluddin Mohammed, when Williams

> sat down he looked distressed and started to perspire. During the short Cabinet meeting which lasted only forty minutes he left the room three times . . . All members of the Cabinet knew something was not right. When the Cabinet meeting ended, [Francis] Prevatt and [Mervyn] de Souza went into his office.[3]

Normally Williams met with several ministers after a Cabinet meeting, and then would return home for lunch. But on this occasion he held no meetings. He promptly left, accompanied by Mervyn de

Souza. Observing the Prime Minister's entry and hasty departure, a group of his secretaries concluded that he "was not looking well". They walked over to the private chapel in the home of the Archbishop, located next door to Whitehall, and requested that a special Mass be said for him. The attending priest was surprised, but agreed. "We all came back to Whitehall," one noted, "and I felt good."[4]

March had been a difficult month for the Prime Minister. A public opinion poll had been published with dire predictions for him and the PNM; there were labour demonstrations across the country, and accusations of bribery and corruption were being made by the opposition in parliament. The poll results had appeared in the middle of the month: 50% of those surveyed expressed the view that the Prime Minister should resign, an 8% increase from a year earlier. Further, 29% said they would vote for the new Organization for National Reconstruction (ONR), against 28% for the ruling PNM. Very few believed that the government was telling all that it knew about bribery and corruption among its members.[5] The figures were very discouraging for Williams and his party after almost 25 years in office; they also reflected rising antagonism from within the labour movement.

The industrial protests had begun at the Port of Spain and San Fernando public hospitals, where nurses focused on the "general breakdown" in the health services, and spread to other health workers, including doctors, ward maids and attendants, and to district hospitals and clinics. The nurses were particularly vociferous, with placard demonstrations, "go-slows" at the hospitals and refusal to eat the meals provided.

On Thursday March 26, the day of the Cabinet meeting, a broad array of disgruntled workers joined the nurses in noisy demonstrations around the Red House in Port of Spain. They included sugar workers who were concerned about retrenchment, shift workers from Federated Chemicals (Fedchem) who had been on strike over a wage dispute since December 1980, and small groups of teachers. Many of the demonstrators viewed the occasion as the sixth anniversary of the "Bloody Tuesday" crisis when there was a violent confrontation with striking workers in San Fernando; their noisy protests forced some employees in the Red House to flee their jobs. During an earlier demonstration, Williams himself was reported to have "sneaked out of the back door [of the Red House] into a hastily provided ambulance."[6]

The next day, Friday 27, the government assured sugar workers that there would be no retrenchment, but issued new regulations concerning demonstrations around the Red House, the seat of parliament. In response to two ominous fires at the state-owned telephone company, the Prime Minister named an investigation team that was required to report to him in 72 hours.

While another 400 nurses demonstrated in Port of Spain, the government was confronted with equally vociferous attacks from within the parliament.[7] Williams, who rarely addressed the parliament in his final years, had made his last statement on Monday March 23, on the Chattel House Bill. Without calling names, he took the opportunity to criticize Karl Hudson-Phillips, his former Attorney General and now the leader of a new opposition party, the Organization for National Reconstruction (ONR). He told the House of Representatives that in 1972 Hudson-Phillips had claimed that a draft of the Chattel House Bill would be ready in a few months, but the legislation had taken another eight years (Hudson Phillips was not the Attorney General for the 1976–81 Parliament, so could not be blamed for any delays during that period). The Bill was approved later that day and the House was adjourned.

When it met again, on Friday March 27, it was consumed with explosive charges about the so-called "McDonnell Douglas Affair". The opposition claimed that McDonnell Douglas had bribed government officials in the amount of US$500,000 to buy three DC-9 aircraft for the national airline BWIA, and that the government had engaged in a massive cover-up. Opposition leader Basdeo Panday tabled a motion on the issue. There were further corruption charges against the government concerning the Caroni Racing Complex.

This Friday, Williams's last day in parliament, was thus a difficult time for him and his government. Whether he was aware of the torrent of abuse both inside and outside the parliament is unclear. He had arrived on time and, accompanied by Kamaluddin Mohammed, went to the Attorney General's office to await the start of the session.[8] He had complained to Errol Mahabir that some tablets which he took for his allergy problems were beginning to affect his health, and asked

Mahabir to check on their side-effects. When the parliamentary session began, Mahabir slipped him a note explaining that the tablets could cause drowsiness. Williams may thus have assumed that his symptoms were caused by the allergy tablets he was taking.

As Mahabir was about to speak on a Private Members' Bill before the House, he saw that Williams's condition had begun to worsen. He passed a note to Senator Mervyn de Souza, asking him to take Williams out of the Chamber. By this time Williams was perspiring profusely. Parts of his suit coat were soaked through with sweat. On the pretext of wanting to discuss a financial problem, de Souza led Williams to the Attorney General's office nearby. John Donaldson recognized what was going on, and sent a note to Mahabir suggesting that Erica Williams-Connell be informed of her father's health problems and advised to come to Trinidad.

Mahabir had represented Williams at Erica's wedding, and was well aware that he would oppose a visit to Trinidad by his daughter. Erica had not been home for over two years; she was anxious to visit her father, but he had discouraged her. As one friend observed, his "reasons were always irrelevant and sometimes foolish . . . but they showed how paranoid he was in later years. He actually had fears that she would be kidnapped."[9]

After completing his presentation in parliament, Mahabir joined de Souza and Williams in the Attorney General's office. Mohammed arrived as they were seeking to persuade Williams to leave. Mohammed said to him, "Bill, you had better go home." Williams became upset: "Kamal, I know my feelings, I also know my rights and responsibilities." Mohammed was accustomed to being submissive to Williams, but the Prime Minister was still perspiring profusely and seemed to be "weakening by the minute". So he persisted, saying, "Bill, you are not looking well, you must go home." Williams replied, "But what about the Attorney General's Bill?" The Bill had already been approved; clearly, the Prime Minister was not fully in control of his faculties. At this point he relented, and with the support of de Souza walked down the stairs to his car and was taken home. No one except de Souza, Mahabir, Donaldson, Ken Julien and his maids would see him alive again.

That evening, he was visited by de Souza, Donaldson and Mahabir, who asked whether Erica should be asked to come home. He replied, "Not yet." Mahabir did not pursue the issue further. Possibly, he did not yet comprehend the seriousness of Williams's condition. Donaldson, meeting President Clarke at the Hilton, reported that Williams's condition "was more serious than others had thought."[10]

It is possible that all the individuals immediately involved with Williams that fateful weekend, including Williams himself, misread the seriousness of the situation. Williams had apparently been very ill in a similar manner about a month earlier, and had recovered without the assistance of doctors. Throughout his life, he had portrayed himself as someone who could overcome adversity. Thus, on that last weekend, it would have been easy to assume that he had done it before, and would do it again. There was also his very well-known distaste for doctors. When in the past doctors had occasionally been summoned, the culprit had faced Williams's wrath later. Thus the hope may have been that Williams's famous will-power would see him through yet again.

On the morning of Saturday March 28, as we have seen, Donaldson reported to President Clarke that Williams's condition had not improved. But when the President spoke to Mahabir later that day at the races, where they were seated in adjoining boxes, he felt somewhat relieved. Both Williams's previous doctors were also at the races that day — Courtney Bartholomew and Halsey McShine. Bartholomew no longer attended Williams because — according to him — the Prime Minister refused to maintain the medication prescribed for his heart.[11] Mahabir was aware of the break between Williams and Bartholomew, so he did not mention Williams's illness. Clarke was aware that McShine was no longer Williams's doctor. Bartholomew mentioned Williams's illness to McShine, who repeated the information to Clarke.[12] The President advised McShine to stand aside, but to be ready to assist if he was called upon.[13] Throughout Saturday and into Sunday, McShine debated with himself whether he should visit Williams's home; but as he played over in his mind Williams's last curt note to him — "I will call you when I need you" — he hesitated, until he was called by Claudia, Williams's maid, early on Sunday evening. By then it was too late.[14]

Another close adviser who might have helped that weekend was preoccupied with other responsibilities. Dr Kenneth Julien had worked with Williams from the early 1970s, advising him in the areas of industrial and energy policy, and over the ten-year period had developed a close professional relationship. During what turned out to be the final few months of Williams's life, Julien visited him every Saturday morning to review the activities of the week and to plan the following week.

Saturday March 28 was the final Saturday before local students would write the "eleven-plus examination" for entry into secondary school. Julien had a son who was writing this examination, and it was a tradition of the school he was attending that candidates went on an outing that day. Fathers were expected to take part. Julien telephoned Williams's home to say he would visit on Sunday morning instead. The message would have been taken by one of Williams's maids. However, the outing was completed earlier than expected, and Julien wondered about making the visit after all. But he was accompanied by his son, and decided not to. If he had visited, he would have seen Williams's deteriorating condition, and might have been able to persuade him to consult a doctor.[15] But he was totally unaware that the Prime Minister's health had deteriorated so rapidly over the last two days. He had visited earlier "during that week and [Williams] was fine."[16]

For the rest of that Saturday, de Souza and Donaldson watched over Williams. His fever seemed to have abated, and he appeared in somewhat better spirits.[17] That night one of his nieces slept over upstairs, and apparently so did a maid and her son. But by Sunday morning his condition had again worsened. Donaldson saw him at 6.30 a.m. and telephoned Mahabir; together with de Souza, they agreed to meet at the Prime Minister's house at 10.00 a.m. to review their options. Williams was in his study downstairs, where he had spent the night. His maid helped him to a chair. His condition was worse. He was almost incoherent. He tried to speak to Mahabir, but could only manage the word "Errol". Mahabir hurried outside to call Dr Julien, but the telephone was not working. Williams was apparently able to tell de Souza that "Mahabir and Donaldson were conspiring to get him to see a doctor." De Souza asked Williams if he would be willing to see a foreign doctor; Williams nodded his head in assent.[18]

While Claudia attempted to feed him some eggnog, de Souza and Mahabir headed for de Souza's office, hoping to find a functioning telephone. There, Mahabir asked Julien to try and find a foreign doctor; Julien felt that would take a day or two. With Donaldson and Claudia at Williams's home and Julien on his way, Mahabir and de Souza parted company: "one went to lunch with friends in Couva, the other to go to his home."[19]

The President had been told of Williams's condition early on Sunday. He spent that morning at the home of a friend. Francis Prevatt, the PNM Chairman, was also there; apparently there was no discussion of Williams's condition. President Clarke heard no more details of the situation until de Souza rushed into his home at about 7.00 p.m. crying loudly that "the boss is dying!"[20]

When he arrived around midday on Sunday, Julien was shocked to see the Prime Minister's condition. He called de Souza back to the house, explaining that he thought Williams was not merely sleeping, but was in a coma. For the next few hours, those at Williams's home — Mahabir arrived in mid-afternoon — frantically searched for a doctor. De Souza and Mahabir had agreed on the phone that they would bring in a local doctor "even should Williams decide to have our skins for this when he recovers."[21]

But why did Williams's aides wait until it was too late to call a doctor? The answer probably lay in their deep fear of the man, and in their belief that since he had willed himself to recover in the past, he was quite capable of doing so again. They all knew of his aversion to doctors, especially local doctors, and of his legendary will-power. In the minds of Williams's aides, he was a colossus. The king could never die.

McShine was the logical choice to attend to Williams, since he was most familiar with the overall medical history; but no one took the initiative to call him. Williams, after all, had refused to see him the previous Christmas.[22] A few hours later, the maid Claudia, apparently on her own initiative, made a private call to McShine; but by the time he arrived, after Dr Ince, Williams, still sitting in his chair, had already died.[23] McShine asked the maid why he was not called earlier; she replied that she had made a pledge to the Prime Minister that she would not call a doctor if he fell ill. She was afraid of losing her job if Williams recovered. The fear factor, then, was as much evident with the maid as it was with aides.

Before McShine arrived, Julien and Mahabir continued their search for a doctor locally. Mahabir sought out a specialist from the south, but he was not at home. They then agreed to call in Dr Winston Ince, a heart specialist, believing that Williams may have suffered from a heart attack. He too was not at home, but was located on a tennis court. It was now at least 6.30 p.m. Ince arrived at the Prime Minister's home about 30 minutes later.[24] But there was little to be done: "his condition when I examined him was beyond recovery." McShine, when he arrived and entered the study, heard Ince say, "I can't feel his pulse."[25]

The circumstances of Williams's death have been the cause of much speculation: did he, in fact, contribute to his own demise? Did he wish to die? Did he, in effect, commit suicide? While these questions can never be conclusively answered, it seems that Williams had "put his affairs in order." He had apparently paid off most of his house staff, keeping a few on a month-to-month basis. He had inventoried his household effects, indicating which were personally his and which were the property of the state. He had made arrangements with two Cabinet officials to collect and distribute some of his books.[26] This would tend to suggest that Williams had made preparations for his death. Further, he was a more deeply spiritual person than was generally recognized, though he regarded his religious convictions very much as a private matter.

It was well known that Williams displayed little interest in material things, believing that reality and truth were spiritual. To that extent, he may have believed that the physical world encompassed the weak and the superficial. It would follow that, since the body is the epitome of the physical, the death of the body would be merely a transition from one stage to another. If Williams had a death wish, he may have viewed death in this way, as a journey from the superficial to the real.

But if Williams's death was shrouded in mystery, the events immediately following were even more so. Soon after de Souza left the President's home, Clarke received a call from McShine at the Prime Minister's home to tell him that "Bill has just died of a heart attack." McShine tried to telephone Erica in Miami and Williams's sisters in Woodbrook. Donaldson, who was present at that time, was adamant that security arrangements needed to be put in place before the public was informed of Williams's death; he feared that the phone could cause a security breach, and ordered McShine not to use the it.[27] McShine left Donaldson alone at the Prime Minister's home and set out to locate Williams's relatives, whom he knew quite well, in Woodbrook. It was now quite dark and he was understandably confused. Williams's relatives lived on Alberto Street, but McShine drove to Alfredo Street. Unable to locate them, he returned home but, recalling Donaldson's admonition, did not use his telephone.

As had been their custom for 19 years, Peggy and Patsy Gittens were driven to the Prime Minister's home that Sunday evening, but they arrived later than usual, at around 10.00 p.m. While they were on their way, a phone call was made to their home by Winnie Joseph, a close family friend, who reported that Williams had died. It is not known how she obtained this information. But the Gittens family was unaware that the Prime Minister had been ill that weekend, and found it difficult to believe what they were told. Another daughter, Eunice, had driven Peggy and Patsy to Williams's home, and they assumed she would find out what had happened.

But Eunice was unable to confirm what Winnie Joseph had reported, because she had seen nothing unusual when she had dropped off her sisters. A few hours later, another family friend, Aldwyn Parris, called the Gittens family with the same information about Williams. But without proof, the family refused to believe that he was dead. By this time, Williams's body was locked in his TV/study room downstairs; his aides had all congregated at the President's home.[28]

Because Peggy and Patsy had arrived late, they went directly to their room on the second floor. They noticed a peculiar odour in the house, and agreed it was not one of Williams's perfumes. They also thought that many more lights were on than was usual (the last occupants of the house that evening had been unaware of the location of the light switches). The only functioning telephone in the Prime Minister's home was in the kitchen downstairs, but because of the air-conditioning no one would have heard it ring. Thus the two sisters slept the entire night in their upstairs bedroom, completely unaware that their uncle Eric was laid out dead on the day bed in the room downstairs.[29]

By 11.00 p.m. that evening, the worst fears of Eric's sisters in Woodbrook were confirmed. Erica called from Miami to say she had just heard that her father had died. She was in total disbelief that her two cousins were sleeping in the house without knowing that he lay dead downstairs. Erica had been told by Kimi Christopher, who was working at the Trinidad Tourist Office in New York; Kimi had apparently heard of Williams's death from the Clarke family. Erica asked her aunts to represent her until she arrived the next day. Meanwhile, the sisters were now aware of Williams's death; one of them called the St Clair police station, where the shocked superintendent was asked to go to the Prime Minister's home and tell Peggy and Patsy that Erica was trying to speak to them on the telephone. No one had been able to contact the sisters that evening.[30]

After Erica spoke to her aunts, they and other relatives went to Williams's home to try and contact Peggy and Patsy. This was around midnight; the sisters were asleep. The family even threw stones at their window, but could not attract their attention. But they did meet Ian Anthony, a PNM parliamentarian, who took them over to the home of the President. By this time, senior PNM party members were meeting with President Clarke; no one came out to speak to the family. However, they had slipped a note under the door of Williams's home, asking Peggy and Patsy to call home urgently. At about 5.30 a.m. next morning, Patsy, the first to go downstairs, found the note, and immediately thought that her father, Hugh, had died. The two sisters were deeply shaken to learn that not only was their uncle Eric dead, but they had slept all night without any idea that he was in the same house, not many feet away from them.

At 6.00 a.m. on Monday March 30, members of the Gittens family and one of Williams's brothers returned to the Prime Minister's home, where they met Peggy and Patsy and tried to enter the breakfast room, which led to the TV/study room. The door was locked. A police inspector was now on the scene; they told him that they were members of the Williams family and wanted to view the body, which they believed was still in the TV room. The inspector at first refused to open the door. Peggy, somewhat hysterical, demanded that he open the door or she would break it down. The inspector opened the door, the family entered the TV room and saw the body of

Uncle Eric lying on a day bed. He was wearing an African robe and covered with a blanket and he looked just like his mother. He looked as though he may have been biting his lip just before he succumbed. There was some dried blood at the side of his nose and his hands were across his body.[31]

When McShine arrived at the Prime Minister's home about twelve hours earlier, Williams was already dead, but was still seated in a chair. Donaldson was present. Later, Williams had been laid out on the day bed and wrapped in an African robe. The symbolism was perplexing. Why an African robe? Was there a political message, or was it the only cloth immediately available? What was even more perplexing, and what disgusted the family, was that no one from the government had made any attempt to inform them of their brother's death. Nor did there seem to be any explanation for why the body had been left for more than twelve hours without being taken to a mortuary.

Initially, there was undoubtedly a need for some degree of secrecy to allow a successful transfer of leadership. This may have led to some confusion between the President and Mervyn de Souza, who had first told him of Williams's death. De Souza claimed that the President instructed him to "cap the news." Later the President denied giving these instructions.[32] Additionally, security arrangements had to be put in place, since some senior government officials appeared to believe that a public announcement of Williams's death could precipitate violence. Marilyn Gordon, for instance, was instructed on Sunday evening to "leave my home and go to a safe place with my family."[33]

In retrospect, however, the emphasis on secrecy and security was greatly exaggerated. The society's penchant for news-spreading and gossip quickly made secrecy irrelevant, while the security problem existed primarily in the minds of the party leadership. Did all this justify the failure to inform family members and Williams's children? Further, literally everyone in the government was aware of Williams's close relationship to his third child Erica, even though there was some degree of coldness between them at that crucial time; there can be no justification for McShine being ordered not to make a telephone call to Erica. It was unconscionable that she should have received the news of her father's death in the roundabout manner that she did. Then there was the problem of Williams's body being locked in a room for more than twelve hours, when everyone involved must have been fully aware of the prospect of its deterioration.

The absence of dignity and respect for the body of the Prime Minister was addressed by one of Williams's brothers. "What manner of men would leave a corpse covered with a thick blanket for thirteen hours before turning over the body to a mortician? When I saw his body at the funeral parlour I felt sick. His stomach was puffed . . . Many members of my family could verify this."[34] Was this callous treatment another consequence of the instinct for secrecy? Since a formal announcement was scheduled for 8.00 a.m. on the Monday morning, was it was necessary, both literally and figuratively, to keep Williams's body "under wraps" until that time? Or was it that, since the Prime Minister "dun dead", the priority of the party leadership was to protect their individual interests? Events in the days immediately following Williams's death tend to give some credibility to the latter idea.

Erica and her husband arrived in Trinidad on the Monday evening and went directly to the funeral home to view the body of her father. By this time it appeared that the Cabinet had already taken a decision to provide a state funeral for the late Prime Minister.[35] What the Cabinet had overlooked was Williams's own instructions concerning the handling of his death. In his address to the 20th Annual Convention of the PNM in 1978, he had stated:

> I wish, and never have wished, no honour, no tribute, no commendation, no commemoration of any sort, no official or public ceremonies when the time comes. I have asked my daughter, who agrees with my decision, to ensure compliance and plead for your good will and your respect of what is a deeply personal wish, aimed at nobody, critical of no policy.

Williams repeated his wish when he formulated his will a year later, stating: "It is my sincere wish that a state funeral be not given me but a simple cremation ceremony and that my ashes be thrown into the sea."[36]

While she was still at the funeral home, senior government officials argued with Erica over the holding of a state funeral for her father. The Cabinet had already agreed on it. But Erica was adamant. She was well aware of her father's wishes. Forcefully, she told them: "You had him for twenty-five years . . . that is enough . . . It will be a private family affair. That is how he wanted it . . . no awards . . . no ceremony . . . no monuments."[37]

Under pressure from many sides, Erica did agree to a compromise. Williams's body was permitted to lie in state in the Rotunda of the Red House from 10.00 a.m. on Thursday April 2 until 6.00 a.m. on Saturday April 4. During this time, an estimated 200,000 people filed past the closed mahogany casket with its bronze handles. Yet by Thursday evening another problem had developed: some mourners demanded to see the face of their leader.

The crowds had moved ten to twelve deep through the Abercromby Street entrance, passing in single file on each side of the bier. As they emerged into St Vincent Street, some began to give vent to their disappointment at not being able to see the face of the Prime Minister. A few began to shout, "We want to see the face!" As the size of the group grew, the chant became "No face, no votes!" Riot police were called out, but did not go into action. John Donaldson, then Senate President Dr Wahid Ali, appealed through megaphones for calm and order. In response, the crowd began calling for Erica.

Later that evening, as government ministers tried unsuccessfully to persuade the Williams family to open the casket, Erica made a formal public statement.[38] Responding to the demands of the crowd and the private pressure brought upon her by Cabinet officials, she explained that "my father's express wish was that there should be no public viewing of his body." She continued: "Since I was, to my eternal regret, unable to be with him in his final moment, I consider it not only my duty, but my responsibility as one who loved him perhaps more than life itself, to ensure that his final wishes are carried out to the letter." She pleaded with the population to "permit my beloved father to rest in peace [and] . . . respect his desire for privacy." She admitted, "It was I who made the concession to allow you to pay your last respects, since from the numerous condolences that I have received, I realize that it would have been unfair to deny you your right to make one last private gesture."[39]

President Clarke also tried to persuade Erica to permit a state funeral for her father. But, though the President's home is located quite close to that of the Prime Minister, he chose not to offer his condolences and his request for a state funeral personally. Instead, he did so in a telephone call, which only served to increase the aggravation of the Williams family[40] — though many were aware that Williams, in the years before his death, had displayed a certain coldness toward the President.

For a while, the confusion over funeral arrangements was overshadowed by controversy over the published cause of Williams's death. While McShine in his brief and hurried call to the President on Sunday night had expressed the view that Williams had suffered a heart attack, on reflection he considered that a post-mortem was needed to establish the precise cause of death. The President, on the advice of Cabinet officials, apparently intended to state the cause of death as a heart attack when he made his formal announcement on Monday morning.[41] But at 7.00 a.m. that morning, Dr Ince visited McShine to discuss the problem. He suspected that death was caused by a diabetic coma. Both doctors agreed that a post-mortem was appropriate.[42] McShine hurried to the television station and met with President Clarke, encouraging him not to specify the cause of death in his formal statement.[43] The President complied, simply stating, "My fellow citizens, it is with the deepest regret that I have to inform you that the Prime Minister, Dr Eric Williams, died at about 8 o'clock last night. May his soul rest in peace."[44]

Later on Monday afternoon however, when the Public Relations Division of the Prime Minister's Office issued a press release on Williams's death, the President's text read, "My fellow citizens, it is with the deepest regret that I have to inform you that about 8 o'clock last night Dr Eric Williams died from acute heart failure. May his soul rest in peace."[45] By this time, a post-mortem had been completed at Battoo's Funeral Parlour. It was undertaken by Senior Pathologist Dr Neville Jankey, assisted by Ince and McShine. Urine from Williams's bladder was found to be "loaded with sugar." Blood from his heart showed ten times the normal level of sugar, or about 1600mg, proving conclusively that death had resulted from a diabetic coma.[46]

Dr Williams's body was returned from the Rotunda of the Red House early on Saturday April 4 to the funeral home. From there, it was supposed to have been taken to a private service and cremation at Chaguaramas. But because of technical problems with the hastily imported equipment, the service and cremation were postponed until early on Sunday morning. After a private service conducted by Fr Garfield Rochard and restricted to family members, with neither the

President nor the new Prime Minister invited, Williams's body was placed into the crematorium at about 8.00 a.m. Erica placed in her father's hands a rosary which the Pope had presented to her. The gas-fuelled cremation lasted about four hours, after which the family took the ashes to the Staubles Bay headquarters of the Trinidad and Tobago Coast Guard. Here members of the family boarded the *M.V. Barracuda* and the Prime Minister's ashes were scattered in the Gulf of Paria, in accordance with his wishes.[47]

The National Commercial Bank became the executor of Williams's will, assisted by close friends John O'Halloran, Halsey McShine and lawyer Inskip Julien. At the time of his death, Williams's estate had an estimated value of TT$1,614,867. It comprised a property at 23 Windsor Road, Goodwood Park, valued at $625,000; cash in the National Commercial Bank, $37,000; gratuity from government, $337,000; royalties and sales from books, of uncertain value; books, papers, jewellery, crystal and gifts valued at $445,000; and a Toyota Super Saloon, $40,000.[48] There were three insurance policies with a total value of about $40,000, to be shared equally among his three children. He also owned shares in the PNM Co-operative, the People's Co-operative Bank and the Workers Bank Ltd. Monies were due to him under the National Insurance Scheme.[49] Finally, the estate included costs due from a suit in the High Court action between Williams and Carlton Gomes[50], and government bonds and money, presumably salary due. An annuity, apparently from his years at Howard University, was left to his American children Alastair and Pamela. Small cash donations were reserved for his three maids, Claudia Rohim, Inez Tessar and Clarita Cameron. Slightly larger amounts were bequeathed to his two nieces Margaret (Patsy) and Patricia (Peggy) Gittens, who had overnighted with him for many years. Erica was given all his books, and the will stated: "Unto my daughter Erica and her children alive at the time of my death I bequeath all property (real and personal) of which I may subsequently become entitled."[51]

But it was the final paragraph of the will that was to cause controversy. Firstly, there was the expressed wish for a "simple cremation ceremony." Secondly, Williams himself raised the issue of his third marriage. Admitting only in death that he had married for a third time, Williams wrote: "I make no provision for my wife Mayleen

Williams as she is well provided for and because we have been separated and living apart from each other from the day of our marriage and I have never supported her."[52] It was the first time he had publicly admitted or discussed his third marriage, which had taken place in 1957. Yet by referring to Mayleen Mook Sang as "my wife Mayleen Williams", he unwittingly opened a legal controversy which continued for more than three years after his death.

Just over a month after Williams died, the government announced a one-time payment of $337,000, representing the gratuity payment, plus a monthly pension of $4,500, to Williams's widow, as long as she did not remarry.[53] This decision was based on Section 5 of The Prime Minister's Pension Act of 1976, which read:

> Where a person dies while he is entitled to receive a Prime Minister's pension and leaves a widow, the widow shall . . . be paid a pension at the annual rate equivalent to two-thirds of the Prime Minister's pension that would have been payable to him had he otherwise ceased to hold office on the date of his death.[54]

The gratuity payment, too, was in accordance with the provisions of the Act. But almost immediately, debate began over whether Mook Sang was legally Williams's widow. The legal debate was not settled until December 1984.

The problem stemmed from the status of Williams's divorce from his first wife, Elsie, which took place in Reno, Nevada, in January 1951. Before the marriage laws of Trinidad and Tobago were amended in 1972, the only foreign divorces recognized in the country were those where both parties to the divorce were residents of the country in which the divorce was granted. If it could be demonstrated that Williams was not truly a resident of the United States when his divorce was granted, then he remained married to his first wife. Obviously then, both his second and third marriages could not be considered legal according to the legislation in effect at the time. Consequently, Mook Sang could not claim to be Williams's widow. According to this argument, she would have no claim on the estate, and Erica would become the primary beneficiary.

Probably because of speculation in the local media over the legality of her marriage, Mayleen Mook Sang filed a legal claim to the gratuity and pension in June 1981 with the firm of Gopiesingh, Martineau and

Edwards. She also filed a claim with the National Insurance Board concerning monies owed to Williams.

The Ministry of Legal Affairs responded to Mook Sang's claim three months later. While the government's legal opinion did not categorically deny that Mook Sang had a right to the money, it indicated that her marriage to Williams was not recognized by the laws of Trinidad and Tobago at that time. It further requested Mook Sang's solicitors "to produce documentary evidence to refute the findings in the legal opinion."[55] Both the National Commercial Bank and Erica Williams-Connell indicated that they wished to have "the matter settled as soon as possible."[56]

Rather than produce the documentary evidence demanded by the government, Mook Sang's solicitors filed suit against the Attorney General in late September for $405,000 gratuity and $60,000 annually in pension benefits. The writ stated:

> The defendant [Attorney General] is sued on behalf of Trinidad and Tobago for pension and gratuity monies due and owing to her as widow of the deceased Prime Minister . . . Dr Eric Eustace Williams, under the provision of The Prime Minister's Pension Act, Ch. 2, No. 51.[57]

Clearly, Mook Sang continued to insist that she was legally the widow of Eric Williams. The executor requested a legal opinion as to "whether the deceased (Williams) died leaving a widow" according to the laws of Trinidad and Tobago.[58] The opinion was prepared by Inskip Julien.

To declare that Mook Sang was Williams's widow, Julien had first to determine whether Williams's divorce from his first wife Elsie was legally valid, and thus whether Williams was legally a resident of the US when he obtained it. After a study of "the facts and history" supplied to him, Julien concluded that:

> Dr Eric Eustace Williams never lost his domicile of origin (Trinidad, where he was born). The mere fact that he resided for a number of years in the United States is not sufficient to change his domicile of origin . . . judging from his conduct and behaviour as a whole . . . he had always a genuine intention to return to reside permanently in the country in which he was hitherto domiciled (Trinidad and Tobago).[59]

Julien continued:

Trinidad and Tobago being Dr Williams' domicile, the Courts of Trinidad and Tobago would not have been able to recognize his Nevada foreign decree of divorce obtained in 1950 . . . The result would be that his second marriage would have been regarded as bigamous."[60]

He concluded that for these reasons:

It is my opinion that Dr Eric Eustace Williams died on the 29th day of March 1981 without leaving a widow with him surviving, so that his gratuity due to him under The Prime Minister's Pensions Ordinance 1969 as amended in 1976 should be paid to his legal personal representatives on account of his personal estate.[61]

In effect, it was Julien's conclusion that Erica Williams-Connell should inherit the estate under dispute.

Julien filed this defence on behalf of the executor to the High Court on July 18, 1984. The executor contended that:

Prior to the coming into force in the year 1973 of the Matrimonial Proceedings and Property Act No. 2 of 1972 . . . the deceased . . . went through a form of marriage with the plaintiff but that purported marriage was null and void and of no effect (for) . . . on that date, the deceased's marriage with his first wife Elsie Williams was still existing and she was alive.[62]

The executor emphasized Julien's opinion that Erica Williams-Cornell was "the person lawfully entitled to the gratuity and pension", since she was appointed by her father in his will as his "residuary devisee and legatee."[63]

Just before Christmas 1984, lawyers for the Attorney General and Mook Sang announced a surprising decision: the government agreed to pay $637,000, representing gratuity and arrears of pension, and an annual pension of $54,000 to Mook Sang. The National Insurance Board was ordered to pay the Survivor's Benefit due, with interest from January 1, 1983.[64]

Thus, almost four years after the death of the Prime Minister, the legal dispute over a significant portion of his estate came to an abrupt and unexpected conclusion, just as the case was called before Justice McMillan. The mystery of Williams's third marriage was resolved, at least legally. But the puzzle continued. Why did the lawyers for the executor settle in the way they did? Many thought that Julien had developed a strong case.

Eric Williams on the hustings, the platform decorated with balisier, the

symbol of the PNM

CONCLUSION

A t the end of his autobiography *Inward Hunger*, Eric Williams wrote that, like Dante's Ulysses, he was determined to prove that he could conquer his inward hunger "to master earth's experience, and to attain / Knowledge of man's mind, both good and bad." Could it be said, at the end of it all, that he had "mastered earth's experience"? Many would agree that to a large degree he did, though, like the rest of humankind, this mastery was accompanied by some serious weaknesses. When Williams wrote his autobiography, he had already served as Trinidad and Tobago's leader for almost 15 years, and despite his performance, the "inward hunger" was still unquenched. He did master much that he set out to achieve, but he probably did not master himself, for until the end he remained a driven individual. Such was the enigma that was Eric Williams.

Williams's mastery of earth's experience was achieved in the face of formidable challenges and obstacles, some of which existed primarily in his mind. The challenges began at birth. His father, despite economic constraints, was determined that "what he had never been given the opportunity to achieve with his brains, he might with his loins."[1] An island scholarship for his son became the dream "of his life."[2] As his son would observe, "Greatness, Trinidad style, was thrust upon me from the cradle."[3] Young Eric endured sustained pressure from his father through high school, manfully accepting the challenge of earning the coveted scholarship.

Other challenges persisted along the way. Trinidad's education system was dictated by, and oriented towards, the colonizer, with a curriculum more appropriate to the British school system than to the colony. Family resources were very limited, and had to be shared with many siblings: the "daily problem of making both ends meet dogged the family as a whole."[4] The rigid Catholic principles practised by both parents placed additional constraints upon the family. The family home was dominated more by firm discipline than by love. Family relationships were not helped by a cold, imperious mother, for whom financial constraints in no way matched her perception of her social status, itself arising from her French Creole heritage. Fortunately for Eric, he was the favourite of both parents: he was the first-born, the most brilliant, and his parents' hope for improved economic and social status.

Eric's achievements continued during his eight years in England, where he performed excellently at Oxford despite his perception of colour and race discrimination and his constant financial problems. He did undoubtedly face serious discrimination, though this may have been magnified in his mind by his father's experience and family situation. But at the end of this period, he could declare: "I had come, seen and conquered — at Oxford."[5]

At Howard University in Washington, Williams was equally successful in his professional life, if not in his personal life. With his huge capacity for work, he did double duty, maintaining various positions at the Caribbean Commission. Although he was no less productive and successful, here too he believed that he was persecuted because of his race and colour, and again the primary enemy was the British.

Relinquishing his position at Howard, and leaving his first wife and two young children in Washington, he moved with the Caribbean Commission to Trinidad and spent seven turbulent and productive years there. His perception of discrimination and persecution persisted, as he confessed in an agonizing letter to his friend and adviser, Norman

Manley.[6]

With great skill, Williams converted his conflict with the Caribbean Commission into a springboard to political office, serving as Chief Minister and then Prime Minister from 1956 until his death in 1981. Here too he was largely successful: he led the fight for constitutional reform which culminated in independence, introduced some measure of order to an archaic political system, employed education as an instrument of liberation, and significantly improved living standards. Leadership nonetheless came with a price. It took the form of alienation, involving the loss of almost all his close relationships with friends and family, with political stalwarts who had stood with him for many years, and, in the last decade of his life, with the small tight band of informal advisers with whom he enjoyed socializing.

While the loss of relationships must have hurt, it was almost inevitable as a consequence of Williams's leadership style and his other weaknesses. Because he was determined to be the all-powerful conqueror, his pathway to power was strewn with the bodies of the vanquished. His penchant for gossip, and his weakness as a judge of human character, meant that others were cast aside on the basis of little or no formal evidence. His suspicious nature made it difficult for him to separate truth from fiction; he was easy prey for those intent on destroying others. By trusting no one, he indirectly trusted everyone, giving rise to the observation that he "trusted to a fault."

He obviously enjoyed life at the top, but found this position exceedingly lonely, especially during the last five years of his life. He filled much of this loneliness by returning to his "first mistress", his research and his writing, and at the end he was in the process of completing two book-length projects. One, a collection of his speeches, was completed and published after his death. While his party appeared enthusiastic about this project while he worked on it, interest dissipated entirely after he died. The other book simply died with him.

Not only was Williams lonely toward the end: he was also disillusioned. He had endeavoured for almost 25 years to alter the political culture of the society, but towards the end he understood that its basic nature had not changed. Self-interest was an even more powerful motivator than before. To that extent, his educational campaign did not produce the fruit he desired, though that was partly because he engaged in so many political compromises.

In one sense, Williams was successful in producing change in Trinidad: the achievement of political independence, the introduction of organized party politics, the promotion of political freedoms, the elevation of the status of education. But in another sense he was unsuccessful. He fought for 25 years against what he saw as frivolity and rampant individualism. But, especially with the impact of the oil boom during the last eight years of his life, the society he had worked so hard to reshape remained true to its unsteady roots.

Williams too had his priorities. Of primary importance to him was the protection of personal power, which required him to make crucial compromises. The most capable had to be pushed aside, or not even invited to participate, since they might be a threat to his control. He exploited the religious differences between East Indians to divide the opposition and broaden his political base. Political patronage assumed precedence over personal growth. A society formerly dependent on colonial government was now encouraged to transfer its dependence to a national leader. As a result, personal development, a prerequisite for national development, was not truly achieved. To that extent, Williams's desire to alter the political culture of the society was in serious conflict with his determination to maintain control.

The same observation could be made with regard to culture. Many would agree that there is an important link between culture and national development. It is debatable whether Williams truly understood this, or whether political expediency required the manipulation of cultural activity. For while the Williams years were replete with community development activities — including the Prime Minister's Best Village programme, a strategic but superficial alliance with elements of the steelband movement, and the promotion of folk culture — they did not reflect the realities of the life of ordinary people in the post-independence years. They neglected the traditions of a large sector of the population, and in general were viewed as being promoted by the state for reasons of political expediency.

In summary, when Williams assumed office in 1956, he did so in a dependent political system characterized by elite domination. The twin bases of the economic system were foreign-owned petroleum and sugar, with minimal diversification. The social system had marginalized the majority black and East Indian populations. When Williams died in 1981, having ruled continuously for 25 years, Trinidad and Tobago by most indicators could be considered among the most progressive of emerging states. While the country's politics remained largely dominated by the racial factor, and some of the blame for this could be attributed to Williams, the political system was relatively stable. Economically, living standards had skyrocketed, especially during the oil boom, though the oil windfall could have been better managed. Williams's firm hand had guided progress during the entire period. The country was much better off under his tutelage. But whether he ever satisfied his inward hunger remains debatable.

the elusive eric williams

NOTES

CHAPTER ONE

1. G. Lewis, *The Growth of the Modern West Indies*. New York: Monthly Review Press, 1968: 205.

2. J. Millette, "The Party of '56: Eric Williams and Party Politics in Trinidad and Tobago". *Caribbean Issues, Vol. VIII, No. 1*. Port of Spain, 1998: 97.

3. B. Brereton, *A History of Modern Trinidad, 1783-1962*. Kingston: Heinemann, 1981: 139.

4. The comments of Sir Hilary Blood are quoted in Millette, op. cit.: 98.

5. Chamberlain's statement is reported in B. Brereton, op. cit.: 146–147.

6. Ibid.

7. S. Ryan, *Race and Nationalism in Trinidad and Tobago*. Toronto: University of Toronto Press, 1972: 26.

8. B. Brereton, op. cit.: 148.

9. Ibid.: 149.

10. G. Lewis, op. cit.: 200.

11. The Commission's Report is quoted in E. Williams, *History of the People of Trinidad and Tobago*. London: Andre Deutsch, 1964: 61.

12. E. Williams, *Inward Hunger: The Education of a Prime Minister*. London: Andre Deutsch, 1969: 15.

13. The observations of Charles Kingsley are recorded in P. E. T. O'Connor, *Some Trinidad Yesterdays*. Port of Spain: Inprint Caribbean, 1978: 71.

14. Ibid.: 64. De Gannes was the maternal grandfather of O'Connor.

15. Ibid.: 86.

16. C. L. R. James, *Beyond a Boundary*. New York: Pantheon Books, 1983: 40.

17. Ibid.

18. Ibid.: 55.

19. Ibid.: 56.

20. Ibid.

21. Ibid.: 59. This very honest observation typifies the personal turmoil that James experienced at that time.

22. Ibid.: 37.

23. E. Williams, *Inward Hunger*, op. cit.: 30.

CHAPTER TWO

1. Data drawn from the Williams family tree, supplied by sisters of Eric Williams.

2. A. M. Jones, *Eric Williams and His Publics*. Pamphlet. Port of Spain: Educo Press, 1983: 6.

3. E. Williams, *Inward Hunger*. London: Andre Deutsch, 1969: 27.

4   P. E. T. O'Connor, *Some Trinidad Yesterdays*. Port of Spain: Inprint Caribbean, 1978. It is worth pointing out that O'Connor's salary of $40.00 per month was paid nine years after Henry Williams was earning $56.00 per month. It is difficult to decide how comparable these positions were.

5   E. Williams, op. cit.: 27.

6   Interview with two sisters of Dr Williams, Port of Spain, July 22 and December 2, 1997. Since the children were required to clean the cutlery every weekend, we must assume that it was silver cutlery.

7   E. Williams, op. cit.: 27.

8   Interview with Archbishop Anthony Pantin, Miami, Florida, September 27, 1999.

9   V. Hudson, "Birth Order and The Personal Characteristics of World Leaders", in E. Singer and V. Hudson, ed., *Political Psychology and Foreign Policy*. Boulder: Westview, 1992: 135.

10 Ibid.: 136.

11 Ibid.: 138.

12 Ibid.: 138–139.

13 Interviews with sisters, op. cit.

14 Ibid. This, of course, referred to the threat or the use of physical punishment.

15 Ibid.

16 Ibid.

17 Ibid.

18 E. Williams, op. cit.: 26.

19 Ibid.: 30.

20 Interviews with sisters, op. cit.

21 E. Williams, op. cit.: 30.

22 V. Stollmeyer, "Queen's Royal College 1926-1934". Unpublished manuscript, 1996: 44.

23 Interview with sisters of Eric Williams, op. cit. It is therefore obvious that the parents were quite willing to administer corporal punishment to their children.

24 Ibid. It is clear that the children lived in fear of their mother.

25 E. Williams, op. cit.: 27.

26 Ibid.: 39. This trip to Trinidad, the first since leaving in 1932, resulted from field work on behalf of the Caribbean Commission, including attendance at the first West Indian Conference in Barbados in early 1944. On this occasion, Williams conducted two public lectures. See ibid.: 92 for more details.

27 T. Millon, *Disorders of Personality*. DSM-111: Axis II. New York: John Wiley, 1981: 4.

28 E. Williams, op. cit.: 30.

29 Interviews with family friends who visited the Prime Minister's home on various occasions.

CHAPTER THREE

[1] E. Williams, *Inward Hunger*. London: Andre Deutsch, 1969: 30.

[2] Ibid.: 31–32.

[3] Ibid.: 36. By the 1950s, as many more young people completed high school education, the pupil-teacher system was terminated. Yet many, directly out of high school, were appointed as teachers without any teacher training classes, and were given complete responsibility for a class.

[4] Ibid.: 31. At the time of writing, over 60 years later, "private lessons" remain an important part of the education culture, especially at the primary level.

[5] Interview with Dr and Mrs Dolly and daughter Hilary, at Pointe-à-Pierre, July 27, 1997.

[6] Interview with Dr Halsey McShine in Port of Spain, July 24, 1997, and March 22, 1998.

[7] E. Williams, op. cit.: 31.

[8] Ibid.

[9] Ibid.: 33.

[10] V. Stollmeyer, *Queen's Royal College 1926–1934*. Unpublished manuscript,1996: 2.

[11] Ibid.: 4–5.

[12] E. Williams, op. cit.: 35. This system of teaching, much more about Europe than about the Caribbean, would continue until independence in 1962.

[13] Ibid.

[14] Ibid.: 32.

[15] Ibid.: 36.

[16] Ibid.

[17] V. Stollmeyer, op. cit.: 12 and 15.

[18] E. Williams, op. cit.: 37.

[19] V. Stollmeyer, op. cit.: 44.

[20] Ibid.: 42.

[21] Ibid.: 45.

[22] E. Williams, op. cit.: 33.

[23] Speech by George Edwards, Executive Director, Trinidad and Tobago National Council on Alcoholism, on the 15th anniversary of Dr Williams's death, March 29, 1996: 3. Mr Edwards died three months later.

[24] Ibid.: 4.

[25] Ibid.: 2.

[26] E. Williams, op. cit.: 31. This represents an excellent yet unfortunate example of the enormous pressure Henry Williams placed upon his son.

[27] Ibid.: 33.

[28] Interview with two sisters of Eric Williams, Port of Spain, July 22, 1997.

29   E. Williams, op. cit.: 38.

30   Williams's statement on the BBC is quoted in I. Oxaal, *Black Intellectuals Come to Power*. Cambridge, Mass.: Schenkman Publishing Company, 1968: 65.

31   E. Williams, op. cit.: 39.

32   Eric Williams Memorial Collection, University of the West Indies, Trinidad, microfilm reel no. 001-051. C. S. Doorly, n.d. 1932, R. Cambridge 7 January, 1932.

33   E. Williams, op. cit.

34   G. Beckles, op. cit.:.6.

CHAPTER FOUR

1   Interviews with two sisters of Dr Williams, Port of Spain, July 22 and December 2, 1997.

2   E. Williams, Inward Hunger. London: Andre Deutsch, 1969: 40.

3   Ibid.: 41

4   Ibid.

5   Ibid.: 42

6   Ibid.: 41

7   Ibid.

8   Ibid.: 42

9   Ibid.: 47. Such incidents were clearly etched in Williams's memory, and could be recalled some 30 years later.

10   Interview with Dr Halsey McShine, Port of Spain, March 3, 1998.

11   Interview with Dr Halsey McShine, Port of Spain, July 24, 1997.

12   Interview with Dr and Mrs Dolly and daughter Hilary, Pointe-à-Pierre, July 27, 1997.

13   I. Oxaal, *Black Intellectuals Come to Power*. Cambridge, Mass.: Schenkman Publishing Company, 1968: 66.

14   C. L. R. James, *Party Politics in the West Indies*. Port of Spain: Vedic Enterprises, n.d.: 158

15   E. Williams, "My Relations with the Caribbean Commission; 1943-1955". A pamphlet published by Dr Williams, July 5, 1955: 33-34.

16   E. Williams, "A Colonial at Oxford". The Nation Christmas Annual, 1959: 89.

17   E. Williams, *Inward Hunger*, op. cit.: 43

18   Ibid.

19   Letter from J. K. Brook to the Government of Trinidad. Eric Williams Memorial Collection (hereafter EWMC), University of the West Indies, Trinidad: microfilm reel no. 001-051.

20   Letter from Williams to Cutteridge, June 28, 1935. EWMC, ibid.

21   Cutteridge to Williams, July 16, 1935. Ibid.

22   Cutteridge to Williams, September 10, 1935. Ibid.

23   E. Williams, Inward Hunger, op. cit.: 45.

24   Ibid.: 45. This startling statement was probably meant to contrast the deep traditions at All Souls. Dr Williams's close friends would disagree with his own evaluation, in that they found him gracious, gentlemanly and appreciative of the finer things of life.

25   Ibid.: 46.

26   Ibid.

27   Ibid.: 49.

28   Letter from Dean Thomson to Williams, April 29, 1939. EWMC: microfilm reel no. B.

29   L. Haywood, "Eric Williams: The Howard Years, 1939–1948". *Caribbean Issues*, Vol. VIII, No. 1. Port of Spain: March 1998: 16.

30   E. Williams, Inward Hunger, op. cit.: 50.

31   E. Williams, *Capitalism and Slavery*. London: Andre Deutsch, 1969: 268.

32   The relationship between James and Williams is analyzed in detail in Chapter 10.

33   L. Heywood, op. cit.: 17.

34   E. Williams, *Inward Hunger*, op. cit.: 51.

35   Interview with Dr Halsey McShine, op. cit.

36   For details of the Williams-Ribeiro marriage, see chapter 9.

37   Interview with Dr Ray Dolly, op. cit.

38   Interview with Dr Halsey McShine, op. cit.

39   Letter from Williams to Japanese Ambassador, January 26, 1938. EWMC microfilm reel no. B.

40   Williams to Siamese Legation, January 31, 1938. EWMC, ibid. Siam is the former name of Thailand.

41   Williams to Sir S. Radakrishnan, January 1938. EWMC, ibid.

42   Williams to Pres. S. Nelson, May 25, 1938. EWMC, ibid. Dilliard University is in New Orleans, USA. Williams requested an annual salary of $2,400.

CHAPTER FIVE

1   Williams, E. Inward Hunger. London: Andre Deutsch, 1969: 52.

2   Letter from E. Williams to N. Manley, 17 June, 1954. Eric Williams Memorial Collection (hereafter EWMC), University of the West Indies, Trinidad. File 039. On this rare occasion, Williams expresses his deep resentment of the British and the other metropolitan powers at the Caribbean Commission.

3   Information on Williams's job search was summarized from EMWC microfilm 001–051 and from E. Williams, op. cit.: 52.

4   Ibid.

5   Interview with a sister of Eric Williams, Port of Spain, July 22, 1997.

[6]   L. Heywood, "Eric Williams: The Howard Years, 1939–1948". *Caribbean Issues*, Vol. VIII, No. 1, March 1998: 16.

[7]   Ibid.

[8]   Williams's correspondence with Bunche: The Schomburg Library, Ralph J Bunche Papers, MB 290; quoted in ibid.: 16-17.

[9]   L. Heywood, op. cit.: 16.

[10]   Howard University, Manuscripts Division. Alain Locke Papers 164-93. Williams to Locke, November 6, 1938.

[11]   Williams to Locke, July 2, 1938.

[12]   Williams to Locke, December 11, 1938.

[13]   Williams to Locke, March 30, 1939.

[14]   Williams to Locke, June 2, 1939.

[15]   Ibid.

[16]   For details of Williams's marriages, see chapter 9.

[17]   Op. cit., Williams to Locke, October 6, 1938.

[18]   Williams to Locke, March 30, 1939.

[19]   Williams to Locke, October 1, 1940.

[20]   EWMC, microfilm roll 001-051.

[21]   E. Williams, op. cit.: 58. It is clear that Williams was given the freedom to organize this new required course as he deemed necessary, and approached this assignment with characteristic thoroughness and completeness.

[22]   Ibid.: 60.

[23]   *Documents Illustrating the Development of Civilization*. Compiled and edited by E. Williams. Washington: Kaufman Press, 1948. This limited edition was on sale to Howard University students only.

[24]   Williams, E. "Social Science Survey" in Howard University *Annual Reports*. College of Liberal Arts 1944–1947.

[25]   Interview with Dr Ibbit Mosaheb, Port of Spain, Trinidad, December 7, 1997. Dr Mosaheb was a student in Williams's first class in Fall 1939. He developed a very close friendship with Williams from that time.

[26]   Interview with Eustace Seignoret, Port of Spain, Trinidad, March 20, 1998.

[27]   Interview with Ibbit Mosaheb, op. cit.

[28]   E. Williams, op. cit.: 62.

[29]   Ibid.: 61.

[30]   As told to L. Heywood, op. cit.: 22.

[31]   E. Williams, op. cit.: 62.

[32]   Op. cit., Williams to Locke, April 26, 1946.

[33]   EWMC, Williams to Dean, 11 March, 1944: microfilm reel no. 25. Williams was paid a salary of $4,100 at the Commission: reel no. 28.

[34]   Bunche's response to Williams, April 29, 1944, no. 23.

[35] Ibid.

[36] Williams to Dean Price, April 26, 1944: ibid.

[37] Bunche's response to Williams, op. cit.

[38] Ibid.

[39] Williams to Dean Price, July 1, 1946. Ibid. No. 25.

[40] Ibid. Williams to Locke, May 11, 1943. Locke was apparently in Haiti at that time.

[41] Ibid. Locke to Williams, May 23, 1948.

[42] L. Heywood, op. cit.: 20.

[43] Op. cit., Williams to Locke, January 27, 1948.

[44] E. Williams, op. cit.: 63. Williams's work at the Caribbean Commission is the subject of chapter 6.

[45] Ibid.: 68.

[46] Ibid.: 69.

[47] Ibid.

[48] W. Darrity, "Eric Williams and Slavery: A West Indian Viewpoint?" in S. Pouchet Paquet, ed., *Callaloo*, Vol. 20, No.4. Baltimore: Johns Hopkins Press, Fall 1997: 808.

[49] E. Williams, op. cit.: 70.

[50] W. Darrity, op. cit.: 808.

[51] Ibid.: 809.

[52] E. Williams, *Capitalism and Slavery*. London: Andre Deutsch, 1964: 268.

[53] W. Darrity, op. cit.: 809–810.

[54] Ibid.: 812.

[55] E. Williams, *Capitalism and Slavery*, op. cit.: 268.

[56] W. Darrity, op. cit.: 803.

[57] James makes this claim in *KAS-KAS, Interviews with Three Caribbean Writers in Texas*. Occasional Publication of the African and Afro-American Research Institute. Austin: University of Texas, 1972: 36. The relationship between James and Williams is the subject of chapter 10.

[58] This note is reproduced in S. Cudjoe, ed., *Eric Williams Speaks: Essays on Colonialism and Independence*. Wellesley, Massachusetts: Calaloux Publications, 1993: 327.

[59] Op. cit., Williams to Locke, July 2, 1938.

[60] E. Williams and F. Fraizier, eds., *The Economic Future of the Caribbean* Washington: Howard University Press, 1944: 83-84.

[61] E. Williams, *Inward Hunger*, op. cit.: 73.

[62] For details see S. Cudjoe, op. cit.: 127.

[63] Op. cit., Williams to Locke, n.d.

[64] E. Williams, *Inward Hunger*, op. cit.: 97.

[65] S. Cudjoe, op. cit.: 127.

[66] Ibid.: 113.

[67] Ibid.: 114. Williams did not return to Howard, but extended his leave of absence. When he did return, in Fall 1946, he was offered an Associate Professorship at an annual salary of $3,970. EWMC, microfilm reel no. 25.

CHAPTER SIX

[1] As reported in E. Williams, *History of the People of Trinidad and Tobago*. London, Andre Deutsch, 1964: 267.

[2] Letter from the President to the Secretary of State, January 11, 1941, quoted in ibid.: 267–268.

[3] For detailed analysis see Ken Post, *Strike the Iron. A Colony at War: Jamaica, 1939–1945*. New Jersey: Humanities Press, 1981. Vol. 1: 138–140.

[4] The communiqué is quoted in C. Beauregard, "The Story of International Cooperation in the Caribbean", in R. Prieswek, ed., *Documents on International Relations in the Caribbean*. Port of Spain, Institute of International Relations, 1970: 228 (hereafter referred to as *Documents*).

[5] J. Pearce, *Under the Eagle: US Intervention in Central America and the Caribbean*. Boston: South End Press, 1982: 24.

[6] E. Williams, *Inward Hunger: The Education of a Prime Minister*. London, Andre Deutsch 1969: 81.

[7] Eric Williams Memorial Collection (hereafter EWMC), University of the West Indies, Trinidad. Microfilm reel 001–051, no. 28.

[8] Williams to Brogan, October 19, 1942. Ibid.

[9] Williams to J. Huggins, 28 October, 1942. Ibid.

[10] E. Williams, "My Relations with the Caribbean Commission, 1943–1955." A public lecture at Woodford Square, Port of Spain, June 21, 1955. Port of Spain: PNM Publishing Co., 1955: 32. Hereafter referred to as "Public Lecture".

[11] Ibid.: 33.

[12] E. Williams, *Inward Hunger,* op. cit.: 82.

[13] E. Williams, Public Lecture, op. cit.: 5.

[14] E. Williams, *Inward Hunger,* op. cit.: 90.

[15] Ibid.: 92.

[16] *Documents,* op. cit.: 230.

[17] E. Williams, *Inward Hunger,* op. cit.: 93.

[18] Ibid.: 93–94.

[19] Ibid.: 68.

[20] Again Williams expresses his sense of ongoing persecution by the British, which had begun while he was a student at Oxford University. Ibid.: 90–91.

[21] EWMC. Williams to Dean, July 8, 1946. No. 25.

[22] Ibid. Dean to Williams, July 16, 1946.

[23] Ibid. Williams to Dr Arndt, August 6, 1946.

24 Ibid. Williams to President Johnson, August 10, 1946.

25 Ibid. Dean to Williams, October 8, 1946.

26 E. Williams, Public Lecture, op. cit.: 34.

27 EWMC. Williams to Dean Price, June 4, 1948. No. 25.

28 Williams of course was anti-colonialist and a nationalist. He was not a leftist. Public Lecture, op. cit.: 36.

29 Ibid.

30 EWMC. Letter of Appointment, June 21, 1949. No. 59.

31 E. Williams, Public Lecture, op. cit.: 40.

32 EWMC. Williams to Robbins. File no. 54.

33 Ibid. Williams to Secretary General, April 27, 1953.

34 Ibid. "Status and Responsibilities of the Deputy Chair", 26pp.

35 Ibid. May 8, 1953.

36 Interview with Mr Eustace Seignoret in Port of Spain, March 20, 1998. Mr Seignoret later became one of the senior diplomats in the Trinidad and Tobago Foreign Service.

37 Interview with Mr John Woodstock in Miami, June 8, 1998. Mr Woodstock, a Jamaican, served as an assistant statistician. Williams held Woodstock in high regard, encouraged the Jamaican government to keep him at the Commission, and sought a salary increase for him. EWMC. File no. 49.

38 Ibid.

39 Ibid.

40 Ibid.

41 EWMC. File 054, no. 5.

42 Ibid. Secretary General to Williams, April 22, 1954.

43 Ibid. Williams to Secretary General, April 28, 1954.

44 Ibid.

45 Williams to Commission. Ibid. May 12, 1954.

46 Co-Chairmen to Williams. Ibid. May 22, 1954.

47 Williams to Manley, June 17, 1954. File no. 039 (F).

48 Ibid.

49 Williams to Commission, November 24, 1954. File no. 039 (G).

50 Co-Chairmen to Williams, December 3, 1954. Ibid (H).

51 David Nelson was born in St Kitts. When he befriended Williams, he was, in Williams's view, "Trinidad's top political reporter." Letter introducing Nelson, Williams to Manley, January 19, 1955. File no. 039 (F).

52 Williams to Manley, January 18, 1955. Hand delivered by D. Nelson. Ibid.

53 Confidential Report by E. Williams on G. Cabrera. Cabrera, an employee of the Commission, was seeking a Fulbright Scholarship to study "Economic Development in Pakistan". File no. 049.

[54] Williams to Manley, January 18, 1955, op. cit.

[55] E. Williams, *Inward Hunger*, op. cit.:127.

CHAPTER SEVEN

[1] Interview with Ibbit Mosaheb, Port of Spain, Trinidad, March 18, 1998. Mosaheb's close friendship lasted from 1939 to 1965 when he left with his family to reside in Canada. Unlike most of the others who broke with Williams, he continued to visit the Prime Minister on his return trips to Trinidad.

[2] Eric Williams Memorial Collection (hereafter EWMC). Williams to Mahabir, April 16, 1945. Microfilm reel 001+0051, no. 9.

[3] W. Mahabir, *In and Out of Politics.* Port of Spain, Inprint, 1978: 17. Other members of this study group included Elton Richardson, Donald Granado, Eustace Seignoret, Norman Girwar, Telford Georges, Dr Wattley, Claire Sloane-Seales, Gerard Montano and Dennis Mahabir. Williams had apparently dated Sloane-Seales before his second marriage to Soy Moyou. There is much symbolism attached to the name Bachacs. These little ants work meticulously, and as a team, to accomplish large tasks; they can also inflict a nasty bite if you step on them.

[4] Ibid.: 20.

[5] E. Richardson, *Revolution or Evolution.* Port of Spain, Inprint, 1984: 27.

[6] EWMC. Williams to Manley, June 17, 1954. File no. 039 (F). Williams appeared to have assisted in preparing a manifesto for the ILP. See File no. 541.

[7] E. Richardson, op. cit.: 27.

[8] S. Ryan, *Race and Nationalism in Trinidad and Tobago.* Toronto, University of Toronto Press, 1972: 108. Ryan suggests in footnote 7, p. 108, that some of Williams's friends, including Manley, "sought to discourage him from entering political life."

[9] For details of my interviews with Erica Williams-Connell, see K. Boodhoo, *Eric Williams: The Man and the Leader.* Lanham, University Press of America, 1986: 3-12.

[10] E. Williams, *Inward Hunger.* London: Andre Deutsch, 1969: 108.

[11] Ibid.: 126.

[12] EWMC. Williams to Caribbean Commission, November 24, 1954. File no. 039 (G).

[13] E. Williams, op. cit.: 138.

[14] EWMC. Williams to Manley, January 18, 1955. File no. 039.

[15] E. Richardson, op. cit.: 25. It is unlikely that Richardson was the only person Williams consulted on this issue. This was not Williams's style. Yet he remains the only one recorded.

[16] G. Rohlehr, "The Culture of Williams: Content, Performance, Legacy" in *Callaloo,* Vol. 20, No. 4. Baltimore: The Johns Hopkins University Press, Fall 97: 851.

[17] Interview with Sir Ellis Clarke, Port of Spain, Trinidad, September 25, 1998.

[18] P. Solomon, *Solomon, An Autobiography.* Port of Spain, Inprint Caribbean, 1981: 137.

[19] E. Williams, op. cit.: 126.

[20] Reported in I. Oxaal, *Black Intellectuals Come to Power.* Cambridge: Schenkman Publishing Company, 1968: 106

[21] For further details of these lectures see E. Williams, op. cit.: 114–117.

[22] W. Mahabir, op. cit.: 18. Mahabir, of course, is a psychiatrist.

[23] Interviews with Mosaheb, op. cit.

[24] As reported in W. Mahabir, op. cit.: 19.

[25] Nelson was later excluded because it was charged that he was taking information back, possibly to Albert Gomes, by then believed by Williams to be one of his major foes.

[26] E. Richardson, op. cit.: 28.

[27] E. Williams, op. cit.: 131. The reason for this attitude is obvious: Williams was unwilling to share the spotlight with anyone.

[28] Ibid.: 131–132.

[29] I. Oxaal, op. cit.: 110. Williams's methods of leadership are analyzed in the following chapter.

[30] For details of Mahabir's reservations as recorded by Richardson, see E. Richardson, op. cit.: 26–28.

[31] W. Mahabir, op. cit.: 23. Mahabir believes that he was not Williams's first choice for the San Fernando West constituency. That honour had fallen to Dr Ada Date-Camps, who refused Williams's invitation.

[32] D. Granado, *An Autobiography*. Unpublished manuscript: Port of Spain, 1987: 9. Also interview with D. Granado, Trincity, March 18, 1998.

[33] For full details see the Granado interview in ibid.

[34] Summarized from I. Oxaal, op. cit.: 140.

[35] Ibid.

[36] EWMC. Minutes of PEG Meeting, December 3, 1955. File no. 542.

[37] D. Granado, op. cit.: 12.

[38] EWMC. Minutes of PEG meeting, July 28, 1955. File no. 542.

[39] D. Granado, op. cit.: 12–13.

[40] Interview with Victor Stollmeyer, Maraval, Port of Spain, March 21, 1998.

[41] V. Stollmeyer, letter to the editor of the *Port of Spain Gazette*, June 15, 1956.

[42] Ibid.

[43] Letter from London to Victor Stollmeyer, April 15, 1955.

[44] Ibid.

[45] "For Catholic Voters", a pamphlet printed by Ben Durham Printing Works for Mr Stephen J. Scott. While the pamphlet is undated, it quotes from the *Catholic News*, August 25, 1956. The elections were to be held on September 24, 1956.

[46] People's National Movement, *Election Manifesto*. Port of Spain, College Press, n.d.: 8.

[47] Ibid.: 10.

[48] "For Catholic Voters", op. cit.

CHAPTER EIGHT

[1] G. DiRenzo, *Personality, Power and Politics*. Indiana: University of Notre Dame Press, 1967: 19. See also F. Greenstein, *Personality and Politics*. Princeton: Princeton University Press, 1987.

[2] Ibid.

[3] Ibid.: 20.

[4] D. Byrne, *An Introduction to Personality: Research, Theory, and Applications*. New Jersey: Prentice Hall, 1974: 86. The classic work on authoritarianism is T. Adorno et al., *The Authoritarian Personality*. New York: Harper, 1950.

[5] G. DiRenzo, op. cit.: 25.

[6] D. K. Simonton, "Personality and Politics", in L. A. Pervin, ed., *Handbook of Personality Theory and Research*. New York: Guildford, 1990: 672.

[7] Interview with Ken Gordon, Port of Spain, Trinidad, July 23, 1997.

[8] Interview with Ferdie Ferreira, Port of Spain, September 21, 1998. Over 20 years after he was put into Williams's famed "doghouse", Ferreira was unable to give an explanation, though he believes that his close association with Ivan Williams, considered to be Eric Williams's right hand man, contributed. When Ivan Williams was dumped by the Prime Minister, Ferreira, it would appear, suffered from "guilt by association".

[9] Interview with Donald Granado, Trincity, September 18, 1998. See also D. Granado, *An Autobiography*. Unpublished manuscript, University of the West Indies, St Augustine, 1987. Other early members of the party agree that Granado's relationship with Williams was unusual in that it was based on mutual respect.

[10] Ibid. It is worth pointing out that the practice of having Williams present his speeches in private before doing so in public continued only for a relatively short period.

[11] Ibid.

[12] Ibid. Fifth and seventh standard refers to senior levels in elementary school education.

[13] Ibid.

[14] Ferreira interview, op. cit.

[15] Harold Laswell, *Power and Personality*. New York: W. W. Norton, 1948: 39.

[16] For details of the case study of Woodrow Wilson, see Alexander George, "Power as a Compensatory Value for Political Leaders", in *Journal of Social Issues*, Vol. XXIV, No. 3, 1968: 29–49.

[17] This relationship is analyzed in detail in chapter 2.

[18] Interview with a sister of Dr Eric Williams, Port of Spain, Trinidad, July 22, 1997.

[19] E. Williams, *Inward Hunger: The Education of a Prime Minister*. London: Andre Deutsch, 1969: 30.

[20] Ibid.: 39.

[21] Interview with Dr Halsey McShine, Port of Spain, Trinidad, July 24, 1997. McShine advised Eric of his father's illness, three weeks before Henry's death. Eric claimed to be "too busy" with his work at the Caribbean Commission.

[22] For a more detailed discussion of the family's economic condition, see chapter 2. See also E. Williams, op. cit., chapter 2, "Life with Father": 26-29.

[23] Ibid.: 26

[24] The work of Freud (1950) and Fenichel (1945) are summarized in A. George, op. cit.: 37.

[25] W. Mahabir, op. cit.: 201. For details of Mahabir's analysis of Dr Williams's personality see also 67–72.

[26] See footnote 8.

[27] Interview with Diane Dupres, Palmiste, San Fernando, September 19, 1998. Ms Dupres was political secretary to Williams for about 20 years.

[28] Interview with George John, St Joseph, March 18, 1998. John served in the Williams government from 1970 to 1976.

[29] Interview with Eldon Warner, Port of Spain, September 22, 1998. He was adamant in his view that Williams was very open to advice and consultation.

[30] Interview with Dr Kenneth Julien, Port of Spain, December 5, 1997. Dr Julien served as an adviser from mid-1970 until Williams's death on March 29, 1981.

[31] Interview with J. O'Neil Lewis, Port of Spain, July 21, 1997.

[32] George John, op. cit.

[33] Interview with Madge Lee Fook, Diego Martin, July 23, 1997. Ms Lee Fook served as personal secretary from 1961 to 1981.

[34] Interview with Olga Bland, Port of Spain, December 5, 1997. Ms Bland, a devoted party member, served as assistant to the political secretary.

[35] D. Dupres, op. cit. This interview was conducted on March 22, 1998.

[36] Ibid.

[37] C. Lindholm, *Charisma*. Cambridge: Basil Blackwell, 1990: 24.

[38] Ibid.: 25.

[39] Max Weber's definition of charisma was recorded in ibid.

[40] G. Geyer, *Guerrilla Prince: The Untold Story of Fidel Castro*. Boston: Little Brown, 1991: 204.

[41] I. Oxaal, *Black Intellectuals Come to Power*. Cambridge: Schenkman Publishing Company, 1968: 98.

[42] As quoted in ibid.: 100.

[43] Interview with Ferdie Ferreira, Port of Spain, July 20, 1997.

[44] Ibid.

[45] For details of the Williams-Matthews debate, see previous chapter.

[46] Interview with C. Gomes, Trincity, September 1998.

[47] P. Solomon, *Solomon: An Autobiography*. Port of Spain: Inprint Caribbean, 1981: 131. This particular issue is analyzed in detail in chapter 12.

[48] Dr W. Mahabir, *In and Out of Politics*. Port of Spain: Inprint Caribbean, 1978: 69 and 71.

[49] Mahabir, op. cit.: 69.

[50] For details of this personality type, see Y. Vertzberger, *The World in Their Minds*. Stanford: Stanford University Press, 1990: 174-175. Also D. Sue etal., *Understanding Abnormal Behavior*. Boston: Houghton Mifflin Company, 1994: 53.

[51] G. Vier, "Analyzing Fidel". *Journal of Human Behavior*, July 1975: 70.

[52] Interviews with Nicholas Simonette, Diego Martin, July 23, 1997 and September 22, 1998.

[53] As quoted in ibid.: 70.

CHAPTER NINE

[1] Interview with a sister of Eric Williams, Port of Spain, July 25, 1997.

[2] Interview with Dr Halsey McShine, Port of Spain, March 22, 1998.

[3] Ibid.

[4] Interview with Dr Ray Dolly and family, Pointe-à-Pierre, Trinidad, July 27, 1997.

[5] Williams to Locke, June 2, 1939. Alain Locke Papers, Howard University Library.

[6] Interview with sister, op. cit.

[7] Interview with Ibbit Mosaheb, Port of Spain, Trinidad, March 18, 1998. Later Mosaheb and his student group hosted a lecture by Williams at McGill University, after the university rejected a request to host the visit. By this time, Williams's *Capitalism and Slavery* had been published, making him a somewhat controversial figure.

[8] Williams to Locke, May 11, 1943, op. cit.

[9] Interview with sister, Port of Spain, July 22, 1997. Williams resided with this sister during his brief visits on behalf of the Caribbean Commission.

[10] For details of this, see letter from Williams to Governor Muñoz Marin of Puerto Rico, November 8, 1951. In his letter to Dean Price requesting a sabbatical, Williams stated, "I am very tired, my doctor has recommended a reduction of schedule . . . and . . . a change of climate and environment." Williams to Dean Price, June 4, 1948. Eric Williams Memorial Collection, University of the West Indies, Trinidad. Microfilm 001–051 no. 25. For further details, see chapter 5.

[11] Reported by Leo Edwards, in interviews conducted in Washington on March 14 and June 11, 1999. Mr Edwards arrived in Washington from Jamaica in August 1948 to begin studies at Howard University. He assisted with the Williams family's move to Bryant Street and remained a very close friend and surrogate father to Alistair and Pamela. He has resided in Washington for over 50 years.

[12] Ibid.

[13] James Bain reported this conversation in an article in the *Trinidad Guardian*, Port of Spain, June 16, 1991. "Bill" in the quotation of course refers to Williams; "Bertie" was a popular name for Albert Gomes.

[14] Interview with Rolf Moyou, Port of Spain, Trinidad, December 4, 1997. Rolf, Soy's brother, was the only male and fifth child. Soy was the second.

[15] Data obtained from a Legal Opinion to the Executor for the estate of Eric Eustace Williams. The Opinion was prepared by Inskip Julien, Solicitor, July 31, 1981. Mr Julien was required to provide an opinion on whether the deceased died having a widow". Hereafter referred to as *Legal Opinion*. Archives, Library, *Trinidad Guardian*.

[16] Letter from James to Webb, August 18, 1948, in A. Grimshaw, ed., *Special Delivery: Letters of C. L. R. James to Constance Webb, 1939–1949*. Cambridge: Blackwell Publishers, 1996: 51.

[17] For this hypothesis, see A. M. Jones, *Eric Williams and his Publics*: 32. A pamphlet, n.d.

[18] Letter to Muñoz Marin, op. cit.: 1.

[19] A. Jones, op. cit.: 32.

[20] Letter to Muñoz Marin, op. cit.: 3.

[21] E. Williams, *Inward Hunger: The Education of a Prime Minister*. London: Andre Deutsch, 1969: 108.

[22] *Legal Opinion*, op. cit.: 3.

[23] Interview with Rolf Moyou, op. cit.

[24] The following three quotations from letters from Williams to Soy reveal a dimension of the man that the society did not know. These letters were written on June 20 and November 22, 1952, and are on display at the Eric Williams Memorial Collection, Library, University of the West Indies, Trinidad.

[25] E. Mahabir, "Oral Reminiscences", in R. Pemberton and B. Samaroo, eds., *A Journal of Caribbean Studies*. Special Edition, Vol. VIII, No. 11. St Augustine: March 1999: 159.

[26] K. Boodhoo, "My Father: Interviews with Erica Williams-Connell" in K. Boodhoo, ed., *Eric Williams. The Man and Leader*. New York: University Press of America, 1986: 6. This first-person account was written by the author after very extensive interviews with Mrs Williams-Connell during 1983–84. For more details concerning Williams's motivation for entering politics, see chapter 7.

[27] Interview with Dr Halsey McShine, Port of Spain, July 24, 1997.

[28] Interview with Rolf Moyou, op. cit.

[29] Interview with Ibbit Mosaheb, op. cit.

[30] Interview with Rolf Moyou, op. cit.

[31] Interview with sister of Williams, op. cit.

[32] Interview with Hugh Gittens, Port of Spain, December 2, 1997.

[33] Interview with Rolf Moyou, op. cit.

[34] Interview with Diane Dupres, San Fernando, September 20, 1998. Ms Dupres served as political secretary, and her family was very close to the Williams family. She contributed to Erica's upbringing.

[35] Interview with Celia de Freitas, Port of Spain, September 22, 1998. De Freitas first met Erica Williams in kindergarten at Bishop Anstey High School and has remained a close friend.

[36] Letters dated June 14, 1954 and April 4, 1954, on display at Eric Williams Memorial Collection, op. cit.

[37] Interview with Joan Massiah, Port of Spain, March 23, 1998.

[38] This description was confirmed by D. Dupres, op. cit.

[39] Interview with Celia de Freitas, op. cit.: 4.

[40] As reported in Dupres interview, op. cit.

[41] Williams's comment concerning marriage is recorded in E. Richardson, *Revolution or Evolution*. Port of Spain, Inprint Caribbean, 1984: 187.

[42] As reported in the *Trinidad Guardian*, December 7, 1958: 1.

[43] *Trinidad Guardian*, December 6, 1958: 1.

[44] Ibid.

[45] As reported in the *Trinidad Guardian*. December 20, 1984.

[46] This argument was proposed by James Bain in op. cit.: 11.

[47] Interview with Sir Ellis Clarke, Maraval, September 25, 1998. It was believed that by this time Williams owed his first wife approximately TT$36,000.

[48] This description was provided by Lady Erna Reece in an interview. Port of Spain, December 5, 1997.

[49] It is believed that a grant from a local businessman hastened a resolution of the problem.

[50] Leo Edwards, interview, op. cit.

[51] Rolf Moyou, interview, op. cit.

[52] Interview with Alfonso de Lima Jr., Port of Spain, September 21, 1998.

[53] Interview with Ivan Williams, Port of Spain, April 25, 1999.

[54] De Freitas interview, op. cit. The issue of Williams's resignation and return is discussed in detail in chapter 14.

[55] As recorded in Ken Boodhoo, op. cit.: 7.

[56] De Freitas interview, op. cit.

[57] Ibid.

[58] See chapters 14 and 15 for details.

CHAPTER TEN

[1] The entire note stated, "Dear Jimmy, Your Godchild! In appreciation, Bill". November 21, 1944. Reproduced in S. Cudjoe, ed., *Eric E. Williams Speaks*. Wellesley: Calaloux Publications, 1993: 327.

[2] A. Grimshaw, ed., *Special Delivery: Letters of C. L. R. James to Constance Webb 1939–48*. Cambridge: Blackwell Publishers, 1996: 51.

[3] I. Oxaal, *Black Intellectuals Come to Power*. Cambridge: Schenkman Publishing Company, 1968: 61.

[4] C. L. R. James, *Beyond A Boundary*. New York: Pantheon Books, 1983: 32. This text was originally published by Stanley Paul and Co. (London) in 1963.

[5] Ibid.: 37.

[6] Ibid.: 31.

[7] Ibid.: 43.

[8] Ibid.: 41.

[9] Ibid.

[10] A. Grimshaw, op. cit.: 5.

[11] Interview with N. Simonette, Diego Martin, Trinidad, September 22, 1998.

[12] James's recollection is recorded in his "A Convention Appraisal", S. Cudjoe, ed., op. cit.: 332.

[13] C. L. R. James, *Beyond a Boundary*, op. cit.:114.

[14] Ibid: 117

[15] Ibid.: 119.

[16] C. L. R. James, in S. Cudjoe, ed., op. cit.: 332.

[17] Ibid.: 333.

[18] E. Williams, "A Colonial at Oxford". *The Nation* Christmas Annual, Port of Spain, 1959: 89.

[19] E. Williams, "My Relations With the Caribbean Commission", in S. Cudjoe, ed., op. cit.: 146.

[20] C. L. R. James, *Party Politics in the West Indies*. Port of Spain: Vedic Enterprises, n.d.: 158.

[21] James was interviewed for *KAS-KAS. Interviews with Three Caribbean Writers in Texas*. Austin: Occasional Publication of the African and Afro-American Research Institute, University of Texas, 1972: 36.

[22] James in S. Cudjoe, ed., op. cit.: 333.

[23] James in *Beyond a Boundary*, op. cit.: 124.

[24] This is the first stage in the political transformation of James. Ibid.: 149.

[25] R. Hill, "In England, 1932–38", in P. Buhle, ed., *C. L. R. James: His Life and Work*. London: Alison and Busby, 1986: 68.

[26] Ibid.: 69.

[27] E. Williams, *Inward Hunger: The Education of a Prime Minister*. London: Andre Deutsch, 1969: 48.

[28] James in interview with *KAS-KAS*, op. cit.: 36.

[29] Ibid.

[30] For details, see footnote 21.

[31] James in interview with *KAS-KAS*, op. cit.: 36.

[32] James in S. Cudjoe, ed., op. cit.: 341.

[33] Letter from James to Webb, April 4, 1939, in A. Grimshaw, ed., op. cit.: 50–51.

[34] James to Webb, July 4, 1944. Ibid.: 163.

[35] James to Webb, June 14, 1944. Ibid.: 124.

[36] E. Williams, *Capitalism and Slavery*. London: Andre Deutsch, 1964: 268.

[37] W. Darrity, "Eric Williams and Slavery", in S. Pouchet Paquet, ed., *Callaloo*, Vol. 20, No. 4, Fall 1997: 807.

[38] Williams to Little John, June 3, 1994. Eric Williams Memorial Collection, University of the West Indies, Trinidad. Microfilm reel 051–100, no. 59.

[39] Little John to Williams, June 6, 1944. Ibid.

[40] James to Webb, Summer 1945, in A. Grimshaw, ed., op. cit.: 209.

[41] James to Webb, April 4, 1947. Ibid.: 283.

[42] James to Webb, August 18, 1948. Ibid.: 324.

[43]   C. L. R. James, *Party Politics*, op. cit.: 99.

[44]   This incident is reported by W. Mahabir, another Cabinet member, in W. Mahabir, *In and Out of Politics*. Port of Spain: Inprint Caribbean, 1978: 49.

[45]   Interview with President Arthur N. R. Robinson, the President's House, Port of Spain, Trinidad, September 22, 1998.

[46]   C. L. R. James, *Party Politics*, op. cit.:13.

[47]   W. Mahabir, op. cit.: 70. Mahabir observed that Williams treated James as though he was his father.

[48]   As reported by N. Simonette in an interview, July 23, 1997.

[49]   C. L. R. James, *Party Politics*, op. cit.: 14.

[50]   E. Williams, in S. Cudjoe, ed., op. cit.: 215 and 217.

[51]   For details, see James's letter to Williams in James, *Party Politics*, op. cit.: 15.

[52]   Ibid.: 14.

[53]   E. Williams, in S. Cudjoe, ed., op. cit.: 231.

[54]   Interview with N. Simonette, op. cit.

[55]   P. Sutton, P., ed., *Forged From the Love of Liberty: Selected Speeches of Dr Eric Williams*. Port of Spain: Longman Caribbean, 1981: 318. By a "nation of three million people" Williams was apparently referring to the Federation of the West Indies.

[56]   I. Oxaal, op. cit.:134.

[57]   C. L. R. James, op. cit.: 77.

[58]   Ibid.: 78 and 93.

[59]   Ibid.: 104.

[60]   As reported by James in ibid.: 109.

CHAPTER ELEVEN

[1]   W. Mahabir, *In and Out of Politics*. Port of Spain: Inprint Caribbean, 1978: 69. Mahabir, however, would probably not include himself among those who suffered that fate. He chose to resign, probably before an attempt was made to crucify him.

[2]   Ibid.: 70.

[3]   P. Solomon, *Solomon: An Autobiography*. Port of Spain: Inprint Caribbean, 1981: 137.

[4]   Ibid.: 234.

[5]   E. Williams-Connell, "Foreword", in H. Ghany, ed., *Kamal: A Lifetime of Politics, Religion and Culture*. St Augustine: Multimedia Production Centre, 1996: xii.

[6]   Interview with a medical consultant to Williams, Port of Spain, Trinidad, July 24, 1997.

[7]   Erica Williams, "Address to the PNM Women's League", in S. Cudjoe, ed., *Eric Williams Speaks*. Amherst: Calaloux Publications, 1993: 354.

[8]   A public speech by John S. Donaldson, "The Eric Williams That I Knew: A Tribute". March 31, 1996: mimeo.

[9]   Interview with Carlton Gomes, Trincity, Trinidad, September 22, 1998.

10   W. Mahabir, op. cit.: 67–92. By this time Mahabir had completed his training in psychiatry, lending credence to his analysis.

11   Ibid.: 80.

12   Interview with Max Awon, Port of Spain, December 5, 1997.

13   Interview with Ferdie Ferreira, Port of Spain, Trinidad, September 21, 1998.

14   Ibid.

15   Interview with Hamilton Holder, Port of Spain, Trinidad, July 22, 1997.

16   Interview with medical consultant, op. cit.

17   Interview with a junior member of the PNM government who served in parliament from 1971 to 1981. He tendered his resignation to Prime Minister Chambers on the day of Dr Williams's funeral, but stayed in office for the remainder of that term. Port of Spain, Trinidad, September 21, 1998.

18   Ibid. Lack of respect for the crude behaviour of his colleagues is clearly demonstrated in this comment.

19   P. Solomon, op. cit.: 151.

20   Interview with N. Simonette, Diego Martin, September 22, 1998.

21   This observation was provided anonymously, by an individual who had worked closely with Williams for about 20 years.

22   Interview with medical consultant, op. cit.

23   Erica Williams in S. Cudjoe, op. cit.: 354.

24   Interview with anonymous aide, op. cit.

25   Ibid.

26   Interview with Ibbit Mosaheb, Port of Spain, Trinidad, March 18, 1998.

27   Interview with aide, op. cit. Obviously Williams employed actions rather than words to convey his feelings toward particular individuals. According to this observer, was thus unable to "dog back", that is, to seek to make amends for a mistake.

28   Erica Williams in S. Cudjoe, op. cit.: 354.

29   Interview with medical consultant, op. cit.

30   Interview with anonymous aide, op. cit.

31   Interview with Ivan Williams, Port of Spain, Trinidad, April 23, 1999.

32   Interview with anonymous aide, op. cit.

33   N. Simonette, op. cit.

34   P. Solomon, op. cit.: 237.

CHAPTER TWELVE

[1]   Interview with Joan Massiah (née Dolly), Port of Spain, March 23, 1998.

[2]   Ibid.

[3]   Interview with Lucille Mair (née Best), Bayshore, Port of Spain, July 20, 1997.

[4]   Ibid.

[5]   Ibid.

[6]   Ibid. Also interview with Barbara McLachlan (née Best), Westmoorings, Port of Spain, March 20, 1998.

[7]   Ibid.

[8]   L. Mair, op. cit.

[9]   J. Massiah, op. cit.

[10] Interview with Lilia Jeremie, Port of Spain, March 21, 1998. Ms Jeremie served as one of the secretaries in the Prime Minister's office.

[11] Interview with Alfonso de Lima, Port of Spain, September 21, 1998.

[12] L. Jeremie, op. cit.

[13] Interview with Hamilton Holder, Port of Spain, July 22, 1997. The high school in question was a private school owned and administered by Holder. Thus Williams could pay students' fees without the knowledge of the public.

[14] Interview with unofficial adviser and medical consultant, Port of Spain, July 24, 1997. The relationship between Williams and this individual was marked by warm affection until it was broken about five years before Williams's death.

[15] Interview with family friend, Port of Spain, July 23, 1997. This daughter was quite upset by her mother's refusal to accept Williams's generous offer.

[16] This was reported in the *Trinidad Guardian*, April 1, 1981, shortly after the death of Williams.

[17] Interview with Peggy Gittens, Port of Spain, September 25, 1998. Peggy considered it a privilege to live at her uncle's home, and looked on him as a warm, loving relative.

[18] Interview with Carlton Gomes, Trincity, September 24, 1998.

[19] Ibid.

[20] For details see K. Boodhoo, "My Father: Interviews with Erica Williams-Connell", in K. Boodhoo, ed., *Eric Williams: The Man and the Leader*. Lanham: University Press of America, 1985: 5.

[21] Interview with Celia de Freitas, Port of Spain, September 22, 1998. Since childhood Ms de Freitas has been a close personal friend of Erica Williams-Connell.

[22] Information provided by Dr Halsey McShine in interview, Port of Spain, March 22, 1998.

[23] Interview with Ivan Williams, Port of Spain, April 27, 1999.

[24] This incident was reported by Carlton Gomes in op. cit.

[25] If this analysis of the "power of the will" to overcome illness is correct, then Williams's religious convictions appear somewhat similar to that of the Christian Science movement, which emphasizes spiritual healing.

[26] This unusual incident was related by C. Gomes in an interview, op. cit.

[27] Interviews with Dr C. Bartholomew and C. Gomes, op. cit.

[28] Letter from Eric Williams to Erica Williams, June 14, 1954, on display at the Eric Williams Memorial Collection, University of the West Indies Library, Trinidad.

[29] Interview with H. Sampson, Port of Spain, December 4, 1997.

[30] Interview with H. Stecher, Port of Spain, March 23, 1998.

[31] Interview with Mrs O. Sampson, Port of Spain, March 21, 1998.

[32] For an analysis of Williams's final years, see chapter 14.

CHAPTER THIRTEEN

[1] Interview with President Arthur N. R. Robinson, President's House, Port of Spain, September 22, 1998.

[2] R. Pantin, *Black Power Day: A Reporter's Story*. Santa Cruz: Hatuey Productions, 1990:25. This small book provides one of the very few detailed accounts of events leading up to the crisis, and of the crisis itself.

[3] Interview with President Robinson, op. cit. While Robinson had travelled with the negotiating team, he himself did not participate in negotiations with the US authorities.

[4] Ibid.

[5] The amazing story of Williams's apparently private negotiations with representatives from local business is carefully documented in R. Pantin, op. cit.: 25-28.

[6] Ibid.: 28

[7] A. N. R. Robinson, op. cit.

[8] G. Rohlehr, "The Culture of Williams: Context, Performance, Legacy", in S. Pouchet-Paquet, ed., *Callaloo: Eric Williams and the Post-Colonial Caribbean*. Vol. 20, No. 4. Baltimore: Johns Hopkins University Press, Fall 1997: 849–888.

[9] Ibid.: 869.

[10] Ibid.: 868.

[11] Ibid.

[12] J. Wong Sang, "The Prime Minister's Best Village Competition", in R. Pemberton and B. Samaroo, ed., *Caribbean Issues*. Special Edition, *Eric Williams: Images of His Life II*. Vol. VIII, No 1. Trinidad, March 1999: 17–30. Ms Wong Sang was Williams's sister-in-law — the sister of his second wife, Soy.

[13] Rohlehr, op. cit.: 868. Rohlehr argues that the gulf within Creole society was as profound as the gulf that separated Creole from Indo-Trinidadian.

[14] D. Walcott, quoted in ibid.

[15] R. Pantin, op. cit.: 55. I am indebted to Pantin for background information on Granger. He himself relied to some extent on a two-part series by R. Mitchell in the *Trinidad and Tobago Review*, September 1987, on the life of Granger.

[16] Ibid.: 56. Here Pantin is quoting from the R. Mitchell article.

[17] D. Granado, *An Autobiography*. Unpublished manuscript. Mimeo, n.d. West Indian Collection, University of the West Indies Library, Trinidad: 69–70.

[18] G. Granger, "Corruption" in *East Dry River Speaks*. Issue No. 3. Mimeo, n.d. (early

1970). Reproduced in I. Oxaal, *Race and Revolutionary Consciousness*. Cambridge: Schenkman Publishing Company, 1971: 64–67.

[19] D. Darbeau, "The Chains are Bursting", in ibid.: 64.

[20] Ibid.

[21] E. Williams, "Revolution and Dignity". Nationwide broadcast. In P. Sutton, ed., *Forged From the Love of Liberty: Selected Speeches of Eric Williams*. Trinidad: Longman Caribbean, 1981: 162–167.

[22] Granger's statement was reported in R. Pantin, op. cit.: 54–55.

[23] S. Stuempfle, *The Steelband Movement: Forging of a National Art in Trinidad and Tobago*. Philadelphia, University of Pennsylvania Press, 1995: 118. This publication arose from a Ph.D. thesis researched in Trinidad, 1987–89.

[24] George Yeates, quoted in ibid.: 119. Yeates believes that this was how the "crash" programme, continued under different names such as Special Works, DEWD, etc., was initiated.

[25] Bertie Marshall, quoted in ibid.: 120.

[26] E. Mahabir, "Reminiscences of Eric Williams", in R. Pemberton and B. Samaroo, ed., op. cit.: 162 and 160.

[27] This statement by Erica Williams is recorded in K. Boodhoo, "My Father: Interviews with Erica Williams-Connell", in K. Boodhoo, ed., *Eric Williams: The Man and the Leader*. Lanham: University Press of America, 1985: 7.

[28] This often-repeated caution by Williams is reported by E. Mahabir in R. Pemberton and B. Samaroo, ed., op. cit.: 162.

[29] This peculiar request is recorded in D. Granado, op. cit.: 76–78.

[30] As reported by R. Pantin, op. cit.: 61.

[31] Carlton Gomes worked closely with Williams as one of his Parliamentary Secretaries during this period. National Security reports were sent to Gomes. He also served as an adviser to Williams during the crisis. Interview with C. Gomes, Trincity, September 24, 1998.

[32] E. Williams in P. Sutton, ed., op. cit.: 162–163.

[33] Ibid.

[34] Ibid.: 163–164. Interestingly, Williams generalizes that the lack of awareness is "a world problem."

[35] Ibid.: 164.

[36] Ibid. Williams's prescription for a complicated problem was a financial handout, illustrating the chasm between the government and its former ardent supporters.

[37] "We Do Not Want Crumbs. We Want the Whole Bread". A pamphlet by the National Joint Action committee. Mimeo. Late March, 1970.

[38] Ibid.

[39] *Black Power and National Reconstruction*. Pamphlet. Tapia House, 1970.

[40] Interview with C. Gomes, op. cit. The additional fee paid to Ms Jackson was approximately TT$35,000.

[41] Ibid.

[42] R. Pantin, op. cit.: 79.

[43] Interview with President Robinson, op. cit.

[44] Robinson's resignation is reported in R. Pantin, op. cit.: 80.

[45] Information summarized from ibid.: 80–81.

[46] Interview with C. Gomes, op. cit. He was the only member of the government to remain at Williams's side for the next few months, together with a small group of loyal advisers.

[47] H. Ghany, *Kamal: A Lifetime of Politics, Religion and Culture.* Port of Spain: Cassims Concepts and Designs, 1996: 265. This claim is unsubstantiated.

[48] As reported by C. Gomes, op. cit.

[49] This information was provided anonymously by an aide to Williams.

[50] As told to K. Boodhoo in K. Boodhoo, ed., op. cit.: 9.

[51] Interview with Jack Williams, Port of Spain, September 23, 1998.

[52] E. Williams in P. Sutton, ed., op. cit.: 168.

[53] Ibid.

[54] Ibid.: 169. Williams, of course, did not elaborate on the "constructive aspect" of Black Power, other than the cited statement.

CHAPTER FOURTEEN

[1] People's National Movement, 15th Annual Convention: *Address by the Political Leader, Dr Eric Williams,* September 28, 1973.

[2] Ibid.: 2

[3] Ibid.: 9.

[4] Ibid.: 10. During the 1970s, tourism contributed less than 5% to Trinidad and Tobago's gross national product.

[5] Ibid.: 11.

[6] Ibid.: 13. Ironically, within two months, his daughter joined the migrating group.

[7] Ibid.: 17.

[8] Ibid.: 18.

[9] Ibid.: 23. It is revealing that Williams was willing to admit publicly that "my daughter and I have decided to proceed jointly to secure an appropriate home." He and Erica would thus have had extensive discussions concerning his decision and his future.

[10] Ibid.: 25. Williams emphasizes the involvement of his daughter in his decision to resign.

[11] Interview with Ivan Williams, Port of Spain, April 27, 1999. Another confidant, Ferdie Ferreira, concurs.

[12] Interview with Alfonso de Lima, Port of Spain, September 21, 1998.

[13] Eric Williams Memorial Collection (hereafter EWMC), University of the West Indies, Trinidad. Williams to Deutsch, March 1973. Microfilm no. 81 to 94.

[14] Deutsch to Williams, ibid.

[15] E. Mahabir, "Oral Reminiscences of Colleagues", in *Caribbean Issues,* Special Edition, *Eric Williams: Images of His Life.* Vol. VIII, No. 1, March 1999: 161.

[16] Ibid.: 142. Alleyne served as Permanent Secretary in three different ministries, but states: "always whichever ministry I was at, I worked very closely with him."

[17] EWMC. File no. 559–561.

[18] File no. 560, ibid.

[19] File no. 561, ibid.

[20] This information was obtained from an interview with D. Dupres, Palmiste, April 25, 1999. As his political secretary, Ms Dupres worked out of Williams's home during this period.

[21] See, for instance, H. Ghany, *Kamal: A Lifetime of Politics, Religion and Culture.* Port of Spain: Cassims Concepts and Designs, 1996: 302.

[22] Interview with Archbishop Anthony Pantin, Miami, Florida, September 27, 1999.

[23] H. Ghany, op. cit.: 302.

[24] Interview with Archbishop Pantin, op. cit.

[25] Conversation with Erica Williams, Miami, April 1998.

[26] Interviews with Ivan Williams and Ferdie Ferreira, op. cit.

[27] As reported in H. Ghany, op. cit.: 301.

[28] Ibid.: 302.

[29] E. Williams, "15th Annual Convention Resolution — Acceptance", in P. Sutton, ed., *Forged From the Love of Liberty: Selected Speeches of Dr Williams.* Port of Spain: Longman Caribbean, 1981: 179–180.

[30] Ibid.

[31] Interview with Carlton Gomes, Trincity, April 30, 1999.

[32] Interview with Marilyn Gordon, Trincity, December 12, 1997. See also M. Gordon, "Oral Reminiscences of Colleagues", in *Caribbean Issues,* op. cit.: 151–155.

[33] Interview with Nicholas Simonette, Diego Martin, September 22, 1998.

[34] Interview with John Babb, Port of Spain, March 14, 1998.

[35] Ibid.

[36] Interview with anonymous aide, December 7, 1997, and September 19, 1998.

[37] Interview with anonymous PNM parliamentarian, September 21, 1998.

[38] Interview with anonymous aide, op. cit.

[39] Interview with Overand Padmore, Port of Spain, July 24, 1997. In the final years with Williams, Padmore was Minister of National Reconstruction.

[40] Interview with anonymous parliamentarian, op. cit.

[41] EWMC, op. cit. Microfilm no. 81–94.

[42] Williams to Deutsch, April 19, 1978. Ibid.

[43] Ibid.

[44] Williams to Manley, January 18, 1955. Ibid., file no. 39. On this occasion Williams told Manley: "I am biding my time here, pushing off as best as I can all the work that de Vriendt tries to push on me."

45   Williams to Deutsch, October 13, 1978. Ibid.

46   Williams to Deutsch, April 20, 1979. Ibid.

47   Williams to Deutsch, n.d., October, 1979. Ibid.

48   Interview with E. Bynoe, Port of Spain, July 21, 1997. Bynoe was Manager of Longman's Trinidad office at that time and participated in meetings concerning the publication.

49   Ibid.

50   Ibid.

51   Deutsch to Williams, November 7, 1980. EWMC, op. cit.

52   Williams to Deutsch, December 1, 1980. Ibid.

53   Deutsch to Williams, December 31, 1980. Ibid.

54   Interview with Dr Halsey McShine, Port of Spain, December 3, 1997.

55   Ibid.

CHAPTER FIFTEEN

1   Interview with former President Sir Ellis Clarke, Maraval, Port of Spain, September 25, 1998.

2   Ibid.

3   H. Ghany, *Kamal: A Lifetime of Politics, Religion and Culture.* St Augustine: Multimedia Production Centre, 1996: 388.

4   Interview with Diane Dupres, Palmiste, September 1998. Ms Dupres was one of the secretaries who participated in the special Mass.

5   Polling results were reported in S. Ryan, *Revolution and Reaction.* Port of Spain: Institute of Social and Economic Research, 1989: 25.

6   Ibid.: 256.

7   Summarized from the *Trinidad Guardian*, March 27, 1981.

8   The data on Williams's last day in parliament are drawn from "The Last Days of Dr Williams", Express Special Writer. Reprinted in R. Deosaran, *Eric Williams: The Man, His Ideas and His Politics.* Port of Spain: Signum Publishing Company, 1981: 160–168. See also "The Last Time Kamal Saw Dr Eric Williams", in H. Ghany, op. cit.: 387–389.

9   Express Special Writer in R. Deosaran, ibid.: 163.

10   Interview with President Clarke, op. cit.

11   Interview with Dr Courtney Bartholomew, Port of Spain, July 24, 1997.

12   Interview with Dr Halsey McShine, Port of Spain, December 3, 1997. How Bartholomew learned of Williams's illness remains unknown.

13   Interview with President Clarke, op. cit.

14   Interview with Dr McShine, op. cit.

15   Ibid.

16   Ibid.

[17] "The Last Days of Dr Williams", op. cit.: 165.

[18] Ibid.: 166.

[19] Ibid.: 167.

[20] Interview with former President Clarke, op. cit.

[21] "The Last Days of Dr Williams", op. cit.: 168.

[22] It is possible that Williams had become upset with McShine because by this time he was apparently aware that he was a diabetic. He may have blamed McShine for not making this diagnosis earlier. In his defence, McShine said that diabetes was not evident when Williams's blood was last tested, and that this problem could appear quite suddenly. Interview with Dr Halsey McShine, March 22, 1998.

[23] Ibid.

[24] Statement by Dr Winston Ince to the *Trinidad Express*, April 19, 1981.

[25] "The Last Days of Dr. Williams", op. cit.: 168.

[26] Summarized from S. Ryan, op. cit.: 247.

[27] Interview with Dr McShine, op. cit. See also S. Ryan, op. cit.: 248. In retrospect, the demand for secrecy was unnecessary — even impractical, as events later that evening demonstrated. More than a few learned of Williams's death. Yet the agitated state of his aides was understandable.

[28] The details of the apparent intrigue that surrounded the selection of a new Prime Minister at the President's home that evening, though not directly relevant to this study, are well-documented in H. Ghany, op. cit.: 379–387. Included in that account are statements from participants.

[29] Interview with Peggy Gittens, Port of Spain, September 21, 1998. See also diary of Ms Gittens for March 29, rewritten on May 5, 1996, a copy of which was provided to the author. The same was reprinted in H. Ghany, op. cit.: 390–394.

[30] Ibid. See also interview with sisters of Williams, Port of Spain, July 25, 1997.

[31] Diary of Peggy Gittens, op. cit. See also ibid.

[32] For details of this controversy and statements by President Clarke and de Souza, see H. Ghany, op. cit.: 395–396.

[33] Interview with Marilyn Gordon, Trincity, December 6, 1997.

[34] T. Williams, "The Williams Clan Treated Like Dogs", *The Challenge*. Port of Spain: April 8, 1981 (no longer in circulation).

[35] *Trinidad Guardian*, Port of Spain, April 1, 1981: 1.

[36] "Last Will and Testament of Eric Eustace Williams". February 12, 1979. The Archives, *Trinidad Guardian*. A copy of the will was printed in *Trinidad Guardian*, Port of Spain, August 12, 1981.

[37] T. Williams, op. cit.

[38] *Trinidad Guardian*, April 3, 1981: 1–2.

[39] Statement from Erica Williams made on April 2, 1981, reprinted in *Trinidad Guardian*, April 5, 1981: 12.

[40] T. Williams, op. cit.

[41] One could assume that it was more convenient for Cabinet officials to announce a heart attack as the cause of death rather than a disease which would serve to diminish the elevated status of Williams.

42 Letter from Dr McShine to the *Trinidad Guardian*, May 27, 1984. This letter sought to end the controversy over the cause of Williams's death.

43 Interview with Dr H. McShine, op. cit.

44 President Clarke's formal statement was reprinted in the *Trinidad Guardian*, March 31, 1981: 3.

45 As quoted in R. Deosaran, op. cit. Italics have been added for emphasis.

46 Letter from Dr McShine, op. cit.

47 This information was summarized from the *Trinidad Guardian* and the *Express*, Monday, April 6, 1981.

48 As reported in the *Trinidad Guardian*, August 12, 1981.

49 "Last Will and Testament of Dr Eric Williams", op. cit.

50 Gomes, a disciple of Williams for about 20 years, was placed in "cold storage" while he served as Minister of Education. At the time of the 1976 election he opposed Williams's demand for an undated letter of resignation. The issue was taken to the High Court where he lost. Costs were assessed at TT$21,881.

51 "Last Will and Testament of Dr Eric Williams", paragraph ix, op. cit.

52 Ibid. For further details of Williams's marriage to Mayleen Mook Sang, see chapter 9.

53 For details of this announcement, see the *Sunday Guardian*, May 3, 1981.

54 Ibid.

55 The government's legal opinion was quoted in the *Trinidad Guardian*, September 13, 1981.

56 Ibid.

57 As reported in the *Trinidad Guardian*, September 30, 1981.

58 Legal Opinion to National Commercial Bank (the Executor) "whether the deceased died leaving a widow." By Inskip Julien, July 31, 1981.

59 Ibid.: 9–10.

60 Ibid.: 10.

61 Ibid.

62 The Executor's defence was summarized in the *Trinidad Guardian*, July 19, 1984.

63 Ibid.

64 As reported in the *Trinidad Guardian*, December 19, 1984. While Mook Sang's share of Williams's estate appeared substantial, after three years of legal wrangling, it is probable that legal fees were also substantial.

CHAPTER SIXTEEN

[1] E. Williams, *Inward Hunger.* London: Andre Deutsch, 1969: 30.

[2] Ibid.: 31.

[3] Ibid.: 30.

[4] Ibid.: 27.

[5] Ibid.: 43.

[6] E. Williams to N. Manley, June 17, 1954. Eric Williams Memorial Collection, University of the West Indies, Trinidad. File no. 039.

The publishers would like to thank the following for permission to use copyright photographs:

Mrs Flora Gittens: pages 2, 12, 24

The Trinidad Guardian: pages 14, 26, 42, 56, 100

Paria Publishing Co. Ltd.: pages 40, 54, 214

The Eric Williams Memorial Collection at the University
of the West Indies, Trinidad: pages 68, 84, 134, 136, 154, 172, 184, 252

Mark Lyndersay: page 82

The Ministry of Communications and Information Technology,
Trinidad and Tobago: pages 102, 118, 120, 134, 230, 232, 254, 259

Professor Ken Ramchand: page 152

The Main Library, University of the West Indies,
Trinidad: pages 170, 198, 216

Mrs Peggy Gittens: page 182

Trinidad Express Newspapers: page 196

Jeffers, Angela 138 *see also* Angela Williams
Jerningham Gold Medal 47
John, George 126, 128
Johnson, Gaston 26
Johnson, Mordecai 74
Joseph, Roy 5
Joseph, Winnie 241
Julien, Dr Kenneth 127, 189, 236f, 247
Julien, Inskip 249

K

Kent House, Maraval 82p
Kenyatta, Jomo 59
Kitchen Cabinet 190, 224

L

Lamont, Norman 27
Lassalle, Lieutenant Rex 212
Laswell, Harold 122f
Laurence, Stephen 18
Lawson, Warner 139
Leadership 256f
League of Women Voters 185
Lee, Ulric 114, 147
Legislative Council 15f
"Let Down my Bucket" speech 59f, 105, 162
Lewis, Arthur 158
Lewis, J. O'Neil 127
Limelight 142
Little John, Mary 161f
Locke, Alain 63, 69f, 72f, 79f, 160
      Bronze Booklet Series 77
Longman Caribbean 227

M

Macpherson, Sir John 88

N

National Commercial Bank 247, 249
National Joint Action Committee (NJAC) 202, 208f
National Steelband Association 208
Nelson, David 97, 110f
News-carrying 173f
NJAC *see* National Joint Action Committee
Nkrumah, Kwame 59
Nurse, Malcolm 63

O

O'Connor, P. E. T. 20f, 28
    Some Trinidad Yesterdays 20
O'Halloran, John 147, 170p, 173, 176, 178p, 189, 223, 247
Oil 19f, 220f
Oilfield Workers Trade Union
    Vanguard 210
ONR 234f
Organization for National Reconstruction *see* ONR
Oxford 56f, 255
    doctorate 159

P

Padmore, George 59, 63, 70, 77, 87, 92, 157f
Palmiste estate 27
Panday, Basdeo 235
Pantin, Archbishop Anthony 29, 221
Park's Nursing Home 38
Parris, Aldwyn 241
Pearce, Jenny 85
PEG *see* Political Education Group
Pegasus 205
    Project Independence 201
PEM *see* People's Education Movement
People's Education Movement 105, 111
People's National Movement *see* PNM
Perspectives for Our Party 164